LAST

*700 Final Quotes from the
Famous, the Infamous, and the
Inspiring Figures of History*

WORDS

OF SAINTS AND SINNERS

Herbert Lockyer

kregel
PUBLICATIONS

Grand Rapids, MI 49501

Last Words of Saints and Sinners: 700 Final Quotes from the Famous, the Infamous, and the Inspiring Figures of History

© 1969 by Kregel Publications, a division of Kregel Inc., 2450 Oak Industrial Dr. NE, Grand Rapids, MI 49505.

Library of Congress Catalog Number 78-85429

ISBN 978-0-8254-3157-9

To my kind friend, Hockey Smith, who knows he will see his Pilot face to face, when he has crossed the bar.

2018-12

CONTENTS

Introduction   9

1
The Cameos of Death   21

2
The Modes of Death   29

3
Farewell at Death   41
  Actors/Authors/Children/Earls/Evangelists
  Famous Women/Infidels/Kings/Lovers/Martyrs
  Orators/Painters/Patriots/Philosophers
  Physicians/Poets/Politicians/Preachers
  Prelates/Presidents/Queens/Rulers/Saints
  Sailors/Sculptors/Singers/Soldiers/Statesmen
  and Writers

4
The Company of Martyrs   137

5
Records of Dying Words   161

6
The Scottish Covenanters   183

7
The Fear of Death   209

8
The Art of Dying Well   217

9
The Death of the Saints   227

Index   233

INTRODUCTION

Death is the greatest fact in life!

"Thou, O Death
What is thy meaning? Some there are of men
Deny thee quite — 'There is no death' they say;
But ever with veil'd aspects com'st thou still."

As soon as we leave the cradle we commence our funeral march to the grave. Old Bishop Hall in *Epistles* says, "Death borders upon our birth, and our cradle stands in the grave." Another has reminded us, "There is no sure thing in life, but death." Quaint Francis Quarles, expressed it thus, "He that begins to live begins to die." A German proverb reads, "Man begins to die before he is born." Ovid, the philosopher, voiced the wish, "When I die, may I be taken in the midst of my work." Surely there is no better way to go.

Death is with us from our earliest consciousness. If, as the sage of old has reminded us, "The day of our death is better than the day of our birth," surely death is a matter of utmost consideration.

The mourning message of the late Sir Winston Churchill on King George the Sixth will never be forgotten. Long before death came, his late Majesty knew that his life hung upon a thread, and the Prime Minister said of him, "The King walked with Death as if death were a companion, an acquaintance whom he recognized and did not fear. In the end . . . he fell asleep as every man or woman who strives to fear God and nothing else in the world may hope to do." We have the immediate sentence of death in ourselves; may we be found walking with the One Who conquered death on the Cross and in His triumphant Resurrection. Walking thus, Death will come as a welcome friend to guide us into the sublimer realm where there is no death.

Through the centuries can be traced changing attitudes toward death. According to their light, men have approached the end of life in different ways. In early Bible days, with the twilight of revelation, the hope of immortality was not as clearly understood as it was after Jesus came. He it was who brought life and *immortality* to light through His Gospel. Having destroyed Satan who had the power of death, Christ is able to deliver us from the fear of death (Heb. 2:14, 15).

Job's question, "If a man die, shall he live again?" (Job 14:14) is answered by Christ's declaration, "Because I live, ye shall live also" (John 14:19). Solomon's meditations on death and the grave are destitute of the glorious certainty of Paul who said, "Absent from the body, present (at home) with the Lord" (2 Cor. 5:8).

With the development of traditional literature and the birth and expansion of Roman Catholicism, the presentation of death during medieval Christianity was full of dread anticipation of judgment and the hope of Divine mercy. Pagan aspects of death in classical literature were ironical and insolent. Death produced a state of gloom and emptiness in which life and hope were to be left behind. Death was looked upon as a bitter, inevitable separation, which must be faced with a manly spirit.

In medieval times, death was a favorite theme. Mystery plays, for example, nearly all ended in heaven or hell, and the influence of these plays colors the writings on death during such a period. The grave and thoughtful writings of men of weight and the popular plays of the fifteenth century were alike in their approach to death. The spiritual life of the soul was depicted as being contested for by the good and bad angels. At death, this struggle was at its fiercest.

"The deathbed was the great battlefield where man's enemy, the devil, staked his last throw and drew up all his strongest forces for one final and bitter assault," say Burrell and Lucas. "Every temptation to which the soul had been subjected in the long days of its pilgrimage on earth was now arranged against it; but against each diabolical temptation was set the Inspiration of the Good Angel, as we see in the pictures of the old black-book." How different is the Christian's conception of death!

The same vagueness of hope in ancient literature characterizes non-Christian writers today, although they seemed to have absorbed some of the sweetness of the Christian hope after death. Tagore, in his contemplation of death, expressed something of the melody of the Gospel's hope of a blissful after-life. Remembering his partial light, Tagore had some expressive sentiments to set forth —

"On the day when death will knock at thy door, what wilt thou offer him?

Oh, I will set before my guest the full vessel of my life –

I will never let him go with empty hands . . .

Ask not what I have with me to take there. I start on a journey with empty hands and expectant heart . . .

I shall put on the wedding garland. Mine is not the red-brown dress of the traveller, and though there are dangers in the way, I have no fear in my mind.

The evening star will come out when my voyage is done and the plaintive notes of the twilight melodies be struck up from the King's gateway."

Christianity gave men and women a new attitude towards death. The early saints and martyrs manifested a heroic cheerfulness and tranquil hope in the face of terrible suffering. Christians of every age, although expressing themselves in different ways as they approached their last hour, all knew what it was to share in the victory Christ secured when He died and rose again.

The records of the martyrs down the centuries, who overcame by the blood of the Lamb, the Word and their testimony and loved not their lives unto the death, need to be re-told for an age like ours when it is far too easy to be a Christian. Under the Roman Empire, Christians were exterminated because they would not swear by the life of Caesar nor adore his image. During the fearful Inquisitions of the Roman Catholic Church, thousands perished because they would not recognize the absolute authority of a pope. The Covenanters in Scotland suffered torture and death over the issue whether Christ alone or King Charles should be owned as head and lawgiver of the Church. One wonders whether the majority of professing Christians today have any deep convictions worth dying for.

Those worthy sufferers for Christ's sake were trained in His school, and had learned how to condemn the world, mortify the flesh, bear the cross, and cheerfully sacrifice riches, honors, pleasures, liberty and life itself because of their adherence to the truth and honor of the Lord they loved. It was because of their allegiance to Him that they were prepared to suffer whatever He permitted. Having made large discoveries of Christ's love and grace, especially through the Cross, their hardest trials were accounted light. From Stephen and Polycarp all down the ages, the martyred saints had such lively sights of Christ under their sharpest sufferings that they were enabled to die with the note of victory on their lips. Theirs was the resolute disposition of Victorianus who defied his persecutors to do their worst. The dying words of such saints form speech at its best, for on the borders of eternity, they were heavy with heavenly fragrance. To them it was easier to choose the greatest torture than the least sin. How shamed we are as we think of their sacrifice and compare it with our ease, self-satisfaction, pride and lifeless profession!

What about those who were responsible for the brutal treatment of God's children who were able to die both with magnanimity and meekness? Unless they were convicted of their wickedness and, by grace, turned to the Christ the martyrs gladly died for, they must have left this world with visible symptoms of God's wrath and judgment upon them and with hell in their souls. What a fearful place of torment hell must be for brutes like Nero, Claverhouse and Hitler who with an awakened conscience realize too late the terribleness of the crimes committed against God's dear children! For the martyrs, all is well for they are in heaven, in an unchangeable state of rest and blessedness, but for their persecutors and murderers there is nothing save blackness of darkness for ever and undying remorse for their crimes.

As this volume deals with the last words of both saints and sinners about to enter eternity, what they had to say before their stammering tongues lay silent in the grave demands our deepest attention and most earnest concern. If, when the soul is face to face with eternal realities, true character is almost invariably manifest, then we can expect the lips to express glorious certainty or terror concerning the future. We have endeavored to cite the dying words of Royalty, Martyrs, Saints, Infidels, Agnostics and Worldlings as a study of strange and vivid contrast. We are conscious of the fact that not every believer is privileged to bear witness in a dying hour to the reality of Christ and the glorious assurance of heaven. Saints, like sinners, are subject to delirious diseases, to sudden death or to death in a coma. God, who orders the steps of His people, in His own inscrutable wisdom and changeless goodness regulates all matters pertaining to their death. Whether it be an ecstatic dismissal or a dreary valley under afflictive and depressing circumstances, like the Saviour, who when expiring amidst the darkness of earth cried, "My God, My God, Why hast Thou forsaken Me?" the believer has the inner assurance that "to die is gain."

It has been said, "The man who is fit to live is the only one ready to die, and to die daily is the sure way to die with security and comfort." Shakespeare must have had some knowledge of the last words of some distinguished and worthy people to lead him to write:

> "The tongues of dying men
> Enforce attention like deep harmony;
> Where words are scarce they're seldom spent in vain,
> For they breathe truth that breathe their words in pain."

Dr. Andrew Bonar in his valuable contribution to literature on last words, *The Last Days Of Eminent Christians*, makes this observation:

> "Who can watch the vessel as she makes her way over the Waters, gradually diminishing to a speck, without thinking of her course? – who can watch a bird wing its flight and not desire to know its aim? – who can watch what seems a star dart from its bright place in the heavens into night and vacancy without an emotion of interest in its fate? And what is the ship, with chart and compass to guide it to other lands – what the bird, directed by instinct as it cuts the air – what the star, a thing of wonder and amazement though its fate be, but which has no claim on human sympathy – to a human soul on its way to the unseen world – on its way to eternal happiness or misery?"

Expressions of gratitude for past mercies and hopes of, and prayer for, support in life's last hour reveal the destiny that has been already chosen. When testimony is borne to Christ's saving grace and all-sufficiency, the frail vessel is bound for the right haven. The question we must put to our own heart is, "How will I act through the swellings of Jordan?" The dying testimonies we are to consider can animate us to renewed zeal and fresh activity in life and to say in humble trust, yet with holy boldness, "To depart and be with Christ, is better." It is He alone who can impart good hope in death. We, therefore, trust that the following selection of farewell words – not only from 'the noble army of martyrs' and heroic men and women who testified against papal superstition and religious bigotry and from saints in general, but also from those in different walks of life who were destitute of the sure and certain hope of eternal life – will prove to be both informative and inspirational.

During the Middle Ages, largely through the influence of Roman Catholicism, men were taught to approach death with a certain amount of fear. There were those, however, who knew how to die well and without fear. The story is told of the last days of Saint John of the Cross during the Middle Ages. We read that on December 7th, the surgeon in attendance told him that he had but a few days to live. The saint answered with a joyful face in the words of the Psalmist, "I was glad when they said unto me, we will go into the house of the Lord." Then after a momentary pause he added, "Since I have heard of these good tidings, I feel no pain whatever."

The joy of this saint and of all others who come to die in hope is not in the mere fact of dying, of dissolution, but in what is beyond the grave. In death itself there is nothing to desire.

> "No man ever truly longed for death;
> 'Tis life, not death, for which we pant,
> 'Tis life whereof our nerves are scant;
> More life and fuller life than we want."

Through the coming of Christ, then, Death is no longer that "incomprehensible enemy, that frightful phantom that the senses see in it." Death comes to the Christian as the benefactor, the deliverer, working his perfection, not his destruction. This is why he can meet it courageously and hopefully. The last words of the dying need not be "drowned in the mutter of black men mopping and mowing around the white pillows from which their faith can almost see the soul go fluttering on its way to the fires of pergatory or the redder flames of hell." This grotesque presentation of death is not a Christian hope.

It may be that the farewell sayings of men of all callings for the last century or so lack something of the romantic, eloquent, passionate style of those who died centuries ago; nevertheless, they are expressive. "The searcher of biographies gains the impression that the typical Victorian departed in a pompous stupor, while serried ranks of children and grandchildren sang, 'O God, our help in ages past', all round the bed." But the fact that they could sing such a song of hope must not be discounted.

The more modern Christian attitude towards death, is given by John Bunyan in his immortal *Pilgrim's Progress*, which for its poetry, feeling, thought and humor is incomparable. If you are acquainted with this spiritual classic, you will remember how Bunyan instructs Pilgrims to approach the river of death separating them from the heavenly city. It is a river without a bridge. The last words of *Mr. Despondency* were: "Farewell Night, Welcome Day." "His daughter went through the river singing, but none could understand what she said."

When the reader comes to peruse the following chapters, he will detect irony on the part of some as they came to die, and it would seem as if irony helped to soften the grim fact of death. "To strut is stupid – to preach is tiresome – to lament is weak. The best answer to life's irony is – irony." But irony is not fitting on the part of those who welcome Death as a friend introducing them to a world without tears.

In these days when Death rides the winds of the world so freely that there is scarcely a newspaper or radio report that does not bear some reference to it, one may find it profitable to meditate upon that which is as much an incident in life as our birth. While it may be true that the bulk of "mankind must get off the stage with what grace their own wits can find them," I have found this theme of dying well most fascinating.

M. de Montaigné (1712-1759), the French essayist, evidently found the last sayings of men so fascinating as to wish he might compile a register of the same:

> "Neither is there anything of which I am so inquisitive, and delight to inform myself, as the manner of men's deaths, their words, looks, and bearing; nor any places in history I am so intent upon; and it is manifest enough, by my crowding in examples of this kind, that I have a particular fancy for that subject. If I were a writer of books, I would compile a register, with a comment, of the various deaths of men: he who should teach men to die, would at the same time teach them to live."

In his search for material, the writer expresses his gratitude for help received from several unusual volumes. First, mention must be made of *The Book Of The Craft Of Dying*, and other early English tracts concerning death, by Frances Comper and George Congreve. "These short treatises on the never-worn-out subject of death," says the writer, "were rescued from the shelves of the British Museum and Bodleian libraries." In spite of its Roman Catholic flavor, this remarkable compilation, published in English over 50 years ago, teaches one how to die well.

For the chapter on "Farewells at Death", I had at my disposal not only a quantity of cuttings from papers and magazines filed away through the years, but the lists given by Bega in his *Last*

Words Of Famous Men; The Art of Dying by Francis Burrell and F. L. Lucas; *Dying Sayings* by Cobham Brewer in *Phrase and Fable;* Putnam's *Complete Book of Quotations And Proverbs; Death In Art and Epigram* by F. Parkes Webber, a truly monumental work, and other volumes mentioned in the study before you.

Tao-Chien, the Chinese philosopher, wrote —
> "When you must go, then go
> And make as little fuss as you can."

The following pages will reveal that men and women of all walks of life faced death in different ways. Some made a good deal of "fuss" in passing. Others made no "fuss", but simply, quietly and confidently slipped away into the unseen world. Do you not appreciate these unusual lines of D. C. Clausen? —

Let Me Die As The Leaves Die

Let me die
As the leaves die,
Gladly.

Clad in the golds and reds of triumph,
They make the mountains a miracle
And the valleys a fairyland of wonder.

Yet these leaves are dying.
They are about to flutter from the trees
Down to the waiting earth where in death
They will become soft mulch, brown mold,
And indistinguishable earth,
And then new leaves again.

So they die,
Refusing to remember with anguish
Other days long ago
When they were fresh little tendrils
Breaking from the buds in the lush warmth of spring,
Or the summer days when they were green luxuriant foliage
Swept by the threat of sudden storm.

Instead, they deck themselves in joy,
Because after the mulch and the mold and the earth
They will become new leaves again.
This must be the meaning of their reds and their golds.
They are happy as they die.

> God, let me die
> As the leaves die,
> Gladly.

Our end may be nearer than we realize. When it comes, let us not cringe before death as a tyrant. If He Who conquered death and all its powers is resident within the heart, then death is only a departing to be with the Lord, which is far better. No fear will be ours. "How strange this fear of death is!" George Macdonald once exclaimed to a friend, "Yet we are never frightened at a sunset." And what is death to the Christian, but a glorious sunset and the dawning of a more blessed day in a summerland where eyes are never wet with the tears of separation.

The Cameos of Death

I.

The Cameos of Death

Research in literature dealing with man's philosophy of dying and death reveals a remarkable diversity of opinion regarding his last enemy. The following selected quotations, gathered from various sources, are literary gems and clearly prove how one's approach to death is largely influenced by training, position or aspects of religious upbringing. For example, we would expect John Wesley to come to the last hour in a different frame of mind from Voltaire, who carried no hope beyond the grave.

> 'Tis sweet to grow old in the fear of the Lord,
>> As life's shadows longer creep.
> Till our step grows slow, and our sun swings low —
>> He gives His beloved sleep.

ROBERT BURNS, the famed Scottish bard, in his poem "Man was Made to Mourn," describes death as —

> "The poor man's dearest friend,
> The kindest and the best."

Another poet, the great JOHN DRYDEN, speaks of death as being welcome both as "Thief" and "Kind." In his "Indian Queen" we have the stanzas —

> "Welcome, Death!
> Thou best of thieves! who, with an easy key
> Dost open life, and, unperceived by us,
> Even steal us from ourselves.
>> Kind Death,
> To end with pleasure all my miseries,
> Shut up your image in my closing eyes."

SAMUEL COLERIDGE, in his *Complaints*, tell us of man's —
> "Three firm friends, more sure than day and night,
> Himself, his Maker, and *the angel Death*."

JOHN BRIGHT, in a speech delivered in The House of Commons in February, 1855, also referred to the angelic side of death —

"The Angel of Death has been abroad throughout the land,
You may almost hear the beating of his wings."

In "Evangeline," HENRY LONGFELLOW expresses another beautiful sentiment —

"As she looked around, she saw how *Death*, the *Consoler*,
Laying his hand upon many a heart, had healed it up forever."

In his "The Reaper and the Flowers", LONGFELLOW has the line —

"There is a *reaper*, whose name is Death."

His "Light of the Stars", has a similar description —

"Oh, not in cruelty, not in wrath,
The *Reaper* came that day:
'Twas an angel visited the green earth,
And took the flowers away."

JOHN MILTON, the blind poet, in *Paradise Lost* views Death in a somewhat different light —

"Death, the *grisly terror*"
"Grim Death."

"Death
Grinned, a horrible and ghastly smile, to hear
His famine shall be filled."

is another Miltonic phrase.

Man has long spoken of Death as, "The King of Terror." The child of God, through grace, however, can sing in life's latest hour —

"The fear of death has gone forever."

Such softened language is found in Milton's *Paradise Regained* —

"A deathlike sleep,
A gentle wafting to immortal life.
Truth shall retire
Bestruck with sland'rous darts, and works of faith
Rarely be found.
And to the faithful, Death the *gate of life*."

Turning to WILLIAM SHAKESPEARE's *Hamlet*, we find this expressive metaphor —

"This *fell sergeant* Death,
Is strict in his arrest."

To which agrees STIRLING's sentence in *Doomsday* —
"That fatal sergeant, Death, spares no degree."

An anonymous treatise from the seventeenth century, *The Lamentations Of The Dying Creature,* commences,

"Alas, that ever I sinned in my life. To me is come this day the dreadfullest tidings that I ever heard. Here hath been with me a *sergeant of arms* whose name is Cruelty, from the King of all Kings, the Lord of all Lords, and Judge of all Judges, laying on me the mace of His office, saying unto me: 'I arrest thee and warn thee to make ready, and that thou fail not to be ready in any hour when thou be called on, thou shalt not know when.'"

Among Dr. Edmond Young's *Thousand Nights,* we cull the following aspect of death —

"A deathbed's a detector of the heart,
Here tired dissimulation drops her mark."
"Death is the crown of life."
"Death but entombs the body: life the soul."
"Life is much flattered, Death is much traduced."
"Death gives us more than was in Eden lost,
The king of terrors is the prince of peace."

From *Greek Proverbs,* we gather these orchids of knowledge —

"Thou alone, O Death, are the *healer of deadly ills.*"
"But learn that to die is a *debt* we must all pay."
"Death takes no excuse."

Latin Quotations provide us with further descriptions —

"We are all bound hither."
"We are hastening to the same goal."
"Black Death calls all things under the sway of its laws."
"The gods conceal from those who are to live
How happy a thing it is to die,
So that they may continue to live."

From a collection of miscellaneous proverbs we pick these choice attributes of Death —

"Death and Marriage settle debts."
"Death and the sun are not to be looked on with a steady eye."
"Death devours lambs as well as sheep."

"Death is bitter to a man in prosperity or in much business."
"Death keeps no calendar."
"Death meets us anywhere."
"Death pays all debts."
"Dying is as natural as living."
"Every door may be shut but death's door."
"He hath not lived that lives not after death."
"One cannot die twice" (But see Revelation 2:11).
"There is remedy for all things except stark death."

LORD BYRON, in "Beppo", wrote —
"Oh God! it is a fearful thing
To see the human soul take wing
In any shape, in any mood —
I've seen it rushing forth in blood,
I've seen it on the breaking ocean,
Strive with a swoln, convulsive motion."

Yet in his "Two Foscari," BYRON asks and answers the question —
"Yet what is
Death, so it be glorious? 'Tis a sunset."

In *The Woman Hater,* by FLETCHER and BEAUMONT, we have this unusual cameo —
"This world's a city, full of straying streets,
And Death's the market place, where each one meets."

SAMUEL GARTH, in his *Claremont* has many interesting sidelights on death. Here is a sample —
"When honor's lost, 'tis a relief to die;
Death's but a sure retreat from infamy."

GEORGE ELIOT, in "Scenes of Clerical Life," approaches the theme thus —
"In every parting, there is an image of death."

Old SAMUEL FOOTE would have us remember that —
"Death and dice level all distinction."

The *sleep* aspect of death is touched upon by many poets and writers. PHINEAS FLETCHER, for example, says —
"Sleep's but a short death;
Death's a longer sleep."

SHAKESPEARE, in *Hamlet,* has a similar approach —
"To die — to sleep —

To sleep! perchance to dream; aye, there's the rub,
For in that sleep of death what dreams may come."

As CHEVALIER DE BOUFFLES died he said to those around —
"My friends, believe that I am sleeping."

ALFRED DE MUSSET, the French poet, left the world saying —
"To sleep . . . at last, I am going to sleep."

FELICIA HEMANS, in *The Hour of Death,* views death from
another angle —
"Leaves have their time to fall,
And flowers to wither at the north-wind's breath,
And stars to set — but all,
Thou hast *all* seasons for thine own, O Death."

SIR WALTER RALEIGH's tribute to Death in his *History of The
World* must be included in our cameos —
"O eloquent, just and mighty Death!
Whom none could advise, thou hast persuaded;
What none hath dared, thou hast done;
And whom all the world flattered thou only hast cast out of
the world and despised.
Thou hast drawn together all the far-stretched greatness,
All the pride, cruelty, and ambition of man,
And covered it all over with these two narrow
Words: *Hic jacet* (here lies)."

ALEXANDER POPE in, "Elegy to the Memory of an Unfortunate
Lady," wrote —
"Tell me, my soul, can this be death?
Lend, lend your wings! I mount! I fly!
O grave! where is thy victory?
O death, where is thy sting?"

ROBERT SOUTHEY in his, "Poet's Pilgrimage to Waterloo," has
the couplet —
"Death is the only mercy that I crave,
Death soon and short, death and forgetfulness."

JOHN GREENLEAF WHITTIER has the suggestive line —
"Death moulded into calm completeness the status of his life."

The Modes of Death

II.

The Modes of Death

"The mode of death is sadder than death itself."
— Latin Proverb

Modes of exit from this world are many and varied. PHILIP MASSINGER, in *The Roman Actor* reminds us that —
"There are a thousand doors to let out life."

To which agrees the saying of SENECA —
"A thousand approaches lie open to death."

CICERO quotes the saying —
"From all sides there is equally a way to the lower world."

Might we add, to the upper world as well?

Perhaps the majority die in a coma, and it may be possible for medical science ultimately to make such a painless end universal. Others die in full possession of their faculties, clear and conscious until the last breath is taken. Some are semiconscious or delirious, with the ruling passions of life playing their part to the end, like Josephine who, as she died, repeated the long-loved name — "Napoleon."

For some death is tragic, violent, sudden —
"Oh sunderings short of body and breath,
Oh battle, and murder and sudden death."

VIRGIL wrote —
"The heavens thundered and the air shone with frequent fire;
And all things threatened men with instant death."

How common this style of death is in these days of wars, murders, tornados, floods, earthquakes and transportation fatalities! The number of sudden deaths from various causes is colossal.

29

THOMAS DE QUINCEY writes interestingly on the subject of "sudden death" —

> "Caesar the Dictator at his last dinner party, on the very evening before his assassination, when the minutes of his earthly career were numbered, being asked what death in his judgment might be pronounced most eligible, replied, 'That which should be most sudden.'"

Thereupon De Quincey remarks how the English Litany, by naming sudden death last in a series of dreaded calamities, agrees with Caesar —

> "From the lightning and tempest; from plagues, pestilence, and famine; from battle and murder, and from sudden death — Good Lord, deliver us."

And naturally De Quincey adds the opinion of Marcus Aurelius who ranked sudden death as the first of blessings.

The night before De Quincey died he said to his daughter, "I cannot bear the weight of clothes on my feet." She pulled off the heavy blankets.

> "Yes, my love," he said, "that is much better; I am better in every way. You know these were the feet that Jesus washed."

The Bible abounds with illustrations of those who died suddenly and tragically. Abel, slain by Cain; Eglon, king of Moab, whose fat belly received the dagger of Ehud most unexpectedly; Judas, who made a covenant with death and hanged himself; Stephen, who was stoned to death; Ananias and Sapphira, who dropped down dead.

If, as the Bible says, God has numbered our days, does He not also in His infinite wisdom appoint the means to convey us out of the world? As Drelincourt stated it over three hundred years ago —

> "If one dies in peace, another is killed war; if one departs in his bed, another is hanged on a gibbet; if one perishes with famine, another is stifled with the plague; if one is struck with thunder, the other is torn in pieces by wild beasts; if one is choked in the waters, the other perishes in the flames: in short, if the separation of the soul from the body happens in a different manner, it is not without the express leave and orders of our Heavenly Father. Therefore, when we see the strangest accidents come to pass, and the most unexpected tragic deaths before our eyes, we must remember the saying of the prophet Jeremiah when he saw the burning and plunder

of Jerusalem: 'Who is he that saith, and it cometh to pass when the Lord commandeth it not?'" (Lam. 3; See Amos 3).

When Abimelech assaulted the tower of Thebez with a resolution to win it quickly, a woman cast from the top of the tower a piece of a mill-stone that fell upon his head and broke his skull (Judges 9). If we look only upon second causes, this action may appear to be strange and unexpected. We must lift up our eyes to the Almighty Hand of an all-seeing power and wisdom, however, for the same relation declares that God by this means brought to pass Jotham's prophecy and rendered the wickedness of Abimelech, which he did unto his father in slaying his seventy brethren with his unmerciful hand, upon his own guilty head.

We can look upon the anguish and passion of our Lord Jesus Christ in a twofold way. First, the causes of His death were the Pharisees' envy, Judas's treason, the mutiny of the rude rabble, Pilate's injustice, Herod's jests and the cruelty of the Roman soldiers. The other view is that of the Apostles to whom the Saviour had revealed the rarest secrets of His wisdom: namely, the outward agents of Calvary were but the instruments to bring God's great design — man's redemption — to pass. So we have the pronouncement, "Against thine holy child Jesus, whom thou has anointed, both Herod and Pontius Pilate, with the Gentiles and the people of Israel, were gathered together, to do whatsoever Thine hand and Thy counsel determined to be done" (Acts 4).

What matter is it if our lamp goes out of its own accord or if it be blown out by some envious blast, just so it be lighted again by the immortal beam of the Sun of Righteousness and continue forever glorious in the highest heavens? If we die in the Lord, then it does not matter how death assaults us. Socrates, one of the most famous men of the first ages, drank poison in obedience to the decree of the Athenian judges. When he felt the venom benumbing his senses and death creeping into his veins, he declared with a pleasant countenance, "I have never swallowed anything more sweet and comfortable." If a pagan philosopher can so face death, surely there is nothing more pleasant than the death of a saint as he leaves time for eternity! When Jacob had ended the instructions to his sons we read, "He gathered up his feet into the bed, and yielded up the ghost" (Gen. 49). What a lovely way to end one's pilgrimage!

It is said that Philip of Macedon commanded his valet to rouse him out of his sleep every morning with the greeting —

"O King! remember thou art a mortal man."

By this oft-repeated lesson Philip sought to humble his lofty mind and teach his frail nature not to glory so much in the splendor of his crown and sceptre nor to abuse the power committed to his trust. A similar reminder of the certainty of death was adopted by Emperor Meruan who caused this motto to be engraved on his seal, "Remember that thou must die." Such a phrase reminded the Emperor of that which his courtiers were afraid to mention.

In past ages the noblemen of China were wont to have their coffins ready-made in their chambers so that at every moment they might look death in the face. The Egyptians were accustomed, in their most sumptuous feasts, to place a dead man's skull in an eminent corner of the room that by such a spectacle, the guests might not only moderate their pleasures and restrain their unruly lusts, but also accustom themselves to behold death amongst all their delights.

When Alexander the Great was preparing to leave Macedonia for the conquest of Persia, he gave all his goods to his faithful friends and servants. Peridiccas, one of his favorites, asked the King what he had reserved for himself, and he answered that he had reserved *HOPE.* If ours is the hope, as a sure and unmoveable anchor within the veil, then we shall die well.

It is said that Caesar could not endure to see his pilot tremble in a furious storm at sea, because he was in the boat and it made him afraid of shipwreck. We carry in our hearts the Master of ocean and earth and sky and a greater Emperor and Monarch than Caesar, and He has all the winds at His command. He can still the most disturbed sea and at the end of life's voyage can pilot our frail bark into the safe haven of eternal rest.

The modes of death the Scottish Covenanters faced were as varied as they were hellish. Legs and feet were squeezed to pieces in the *Boot;* fingers and hands were crushed in the *Thumbkin;* torture by firebrands often resulted in a terrible death. They were treacherously and bloodily murdered on the moors, quartered alive, their ears cropped, their hands cut off; they were hung and then their bodies were cut in pieces with the pieces fixed on steeples and poles as a warning to others.

When that excellent gentleman, David Hackston, was yet alive on the gallows, the brutal executioner cut out his heart and exposing it to the crowd said, "Here is the heart of a traitor," and then threw it into a fire.

"Cut up in parts, they hung them up in chains;
Heads, legs and arms they placed on every port
Of burghs, or other places of resort,
As standing trophies of their victory
O'er Divine truth and human liberty."

Going back for a moment to the cruel instrument of torture, the *Thumbkins,* William Carstairs, the first upon whom this new mode of torture was used, said of them that they were of a size so large that the whole hand could be used in turning the screw to crush the fingers. Carstairs himself bore such torture for an hour and a half. After the Revolution, when the once-tortured man was Principal Carstairs, he came into possession of the instrument that had caused him so much pain and explained its use to King William who put his thumb in it and asked Carstairs to turn the screw. This he did until the King cried out, "Hold, hold! Principal Carstairs, another turn, and I would confess anything!"

Deaths can also come from strange causes. The mighty giant Goliath died by a stone out of David's sling. Samson, the strongest man who ever lived, killed himself and many of his foes by his last feat of strength. Death by drowning is mentioned by SHAKESPEARE in his *Sonnets* —

" 'Tis double death to drown in ken of shore."

A most interesting list of strange deaths is given by Dr. E. Cobham Brewer in his *Dictionary of Phrase and Fable.* Possibly the readers can add other examples from their own reading and observation.

THOMAS A BECKET, Archbishop of Canterbury, was murdered while at Vespers and died saying:

"I charge you in the name of the Almighty not to hurt any other person here."

AGOPETUS (164 B.C.), was the boy-martyr, 15 years of age, who refused to sacrifice to idols. Antiochus, King of Syria — a most inveterate persecutor of the Jewish Church — ordered the boy to be severely scourged, hung up by the feet, scalding water poured over him and then thrown to the wild beasts.

During this fearful scene, Antiochus, who witnessed it, suddenly fell from his judicial seat and died crying out,

> "My bowels burn with the fire of hell."

MARCUS PORCIUS CATO (149 B.C.), a renowned Roman patriot, committed suicide by stabbing himself. His last words were,

> "Have my friends yet embarked? Does anything yet remain that could be done to serve them?"

GIANGER (1552 A.D.), was the son of the brutal Turkish ruler, Solyman, who murdered his other son and then offered Gianger the house and possessions of his murdered brother. Griefstricken, Gianger refused and, thrusting a dagger through his own body, cried,

> "Dog, traitor, murderer! I cannot call thee father."

BENNY HAWKINS was a small boy bitten by a dog who, as he died of hydrophobia, said to his father,

> "Sit down, papa. I'm going to die soon. I know I've been a naughty boy, but forgive Benny and pray Jesus to take care of your little son."

Major D'ARCY TODD had his head shot off at the battle of Terogshahur. The day before he died in such a fashion he wrote to a friend:

> "'Be ye also ready,' sounds in my ears, and I only wish to live that the grace of God and the love of Christ may prepare me to leave a world in which there can be no joy for me. Oh, my brother, pray for me!"

GUSTAVUS ADOLPHUS (1632 A.D.), the King of Sweden, was struck by a cannon ball at the battle of Lutzen and fell from his horse and died. As the Croatians gathered around him he said, "I am a dead man; leave me and try to save your own lives." Expiring, he said,

> "I am the King of Sweden and seal with my blood the Protestant religion and the liberties of Germany! Alas! my poor Queen! My God! My God!"

AESCHYLUS was killed by the fall of a tortoise on his bald head — dropped from the claws of an eagle in the air.

AGATHOCLES, tyrant of Sicily, was killed by a toothpick at the age of ninety-five.

ANAEREON, Pliny tells us, was choked by a grapestone.

BASSUS died from the prick of a needle in his left thumb.

CHALCHAS, the soothsayer, died of laughter at the thought of having outpredicted the hour of his death. Other recorded deaths from laughter include:

MARGUTTE, who died of laughter on seeing a monkey try to pull on a pair of boots.

PHILOMENES also died in this way at seeing an ass eating the figs provided for his own dessert.

ZEUXIS, the celebrated painter, died of laughter at the sight of a hag which he had just depicted. (It would be interesting to know the origin of the oft-repeated phrase, "I could have died laughing").

CHARLES VIII of France, conducting his queen into a tennis court, struck his head against the lintel, and it caused his death.

FABIUS, the Roman praetor, was choked to death by a single goat hair in the milk he was drinking.

FREDERICK LEWS, Prince of Wales, died from the blow of a cricket ball.

LA BELLE GABRIELLE, mistress of Henry IV, died from eating an orange.

CORNELIUS GALLUS, the Praetor, and TITUS HATERIUS, a Knight, each died while kissing the hand of his wife.

ITADACH died of thirst in the harvest field because (in observance of the rule of St. Patrick) he refused to drink a drop of anything.

QUINTUS LEPIDUS, going out of his house, struck his great toe against the threshold and expired.

LOUIS VI met his death from a pig running under his horse, causing the animal to stumble.

OTWAY, the poet, in a starving condition, had a guinea (about three dollars) given him, with which he bought a loaf of bread, and died while swallowing the first mouthful.

PAMPHILIUS, a man of praetorian rank, died while asking a boy what time it was.

PHILLIPOT PLACUT, a Norman physician of Montpellier, died from a slight wound made in his hand in extracting a splinter.

APPIUS SANFEIUS was choked to death supping off the white of an under-boiled egg.

LUCIUS VALLA, the physician, died in the act of taking a draught of medicine.

WILLIAM III died from his horse stumbling over a molehill.

MATTHEW ARNOLD wrote —
> "The man who to untimely death is doomed
> Vainly would hedge him in from the assault of harm;
> He bears the seed of ruin in himself."

Many of the foregoing instances are supplied by Pliny, the great historian. In more modern times people have died from causes just as strange.

Our search has produced some beautiful thoughts regarding premature deaths.

EDGAR ALLAN POE, in "Lenore," wrote:
> "A dirge for her, the doubly-dead,
> In that she died so young."

HORACE, in his *Odes* has the couplet:
> "An early death took away the renowned Achilles;
> A long old age reduced Tithonus to insignificance."

From *Greek Proverbs* we have the saying:
> "He whom the gods love dies young."

Another *Proverb* reads:
> "Of young men die many,
> Of old men escape not any."

SHAKESPEARE gave us the lines —
> "Sweet rose, fair flower, untimely plucked, soon faded,
> Plucked in the bed, and faded in the spring."

FELICIA HEMANS in her *Death of Princess Charlotte* wrote:
> "Checked in the glory of her mid career."

ALEXANDER POPE who, in *Homer's "Odyssey"* has the arresting phrase:
> "The rest were *vulgar* deaths, unknown to fame."

also wrote,

> "Who dies in youth and vigour, dies the best,
> Struck through with wounds, all honest on the breast."

How true it is that in the midst of life we are in death! The Bible tells us that there is only a step between us and death. From an anonymous source we have the question —

> "One step to the deathbed, and one to the bier,
> And one to the charnel, and one — O where?"

It matters not whether we die young or old, naturally or tragically, unexpectedly or otherwise, if ours is the glorious hope that death is but the opening of a gate into a larger life. To all such, death has no terrors. It comes as a welcome friend, bidding us enter the eternal home of peace and bliss. Gerhardt has taught us to sing —

> "Let us in life, in death
> Thy stedfast truth declare,
> And publish with our latest breath
> Thy love and guardian care."

Farewells at Death

III.

Farewells at Death

Sɪʀ Hᴀʀʀʏ Vᴀɴᴇ is credited with saying:
>"It is a bad cause which cannot bear the words of a dying man."

For years the writer has filed away literature dealing with the last words of men and women, more or less famous, in the hope that some day he might classify them for the profit of others, and the selection before you represents his endeavour to give a cross section of *Last Words*.

It will be found that these farewell messages prove, not only the varied experiences of the dying themselves, but the opposite ways in which they faced their final hour. All kinds have been noted, whether pleasant or poignant, hopeful or hopeless, comic or tragic, inspiring or ironic. Our meditation will also show that through the centuries changes have taken place in human life, even under the shadow of death.

In his recent volume, *Death, Grief and Mourning In Contemporary Britain*, Geoffrey Gorer writes of a questionnaire about funerals and cremations sent out to "a carefully selected sample of 1,628 people of both sexes, of all ages over sixteen, coming from every social class and every region of Britain." Of those who answered, over 300 were then selected to receive thirty-three further questions about mourning, religious beliefs, deathbed scenes and so forth. Results convinced Gorer that, "A major change in customs over the last fifty years has taken place." For instance, about one quarter who responded rejected any belief in an afterlife; another quarter were uncertain, and just under one half believe; but of these only some fifteen per cent held orthodox beliefs. About one half of the men and one-eighth of the women never prayed. Funerals without religious rites were exceptional. Over half the women wore no mourning at a funeral. It was also found that the Anglican Church provides

41

the funeral service most widely used in which those assembled thank God for delivering the deceased out of the miseries of this sinful world. One religious woman, who had been bereft, spoke of the change she had observed in the reaction of people to death.

> "I think people do accept death far easier now than they did when I was a child. If anybody passed on when I was a child everything was hush-hush and everybody looked sorrowful and mournful and you were hardly allowed to whisper; well, I think all that has died out. It's the acceptance that one doesn't have to be miserable to mourn. . . . You must sort of hide your feelings for those around you; when you're on your own and think about those you've lost you do your mourning quietly, alone. The same as you might do praying."

BURRELL and LUCAS, in their volume, *The Art Of Dying*, state:

> "Dying has its fashions, and, at rare periods, may even become an art, and though ten times the number of quotations might not be enough, considered alone; to justify one in generalizing, yet when they are taken side by side with what we know from other sources, these utterances are often surprisingly characteristic. Pericles and Socrates, Theramenes and Diogenes remain true with their last breath to the grace and irony of the nation that produced the grave-reliefs of the Ceremanicus and the epigrams of the Palatine Anthology; the tongues of Rome keep to the end the sharper, stabbing brevity of that short sword of the legions with which 'the Roman fool' so often avenged on himself the conquest of the world . . .

> "With Margaret of Scotland, indeed, and that curt shudder of disgust at life, as at some draught too nauseous to be swallowed — 'Fi de la vie' (Shame on life) — we are approaching the time when human beings once more become aware that there can be a style and an art, a saving grace not of God but of humanity, in life and death also."

It is now our purpose to show how men and women, from all walks of life, came to say "Good-bye" to earth. It is but fitting to say that our selection is simply representative and is not given in any perfect chronological order.

How have the mighty and famous died? They were men and women of like passions as ourselves. Did royalty or nobility cause them to approach death differently from commoners?

I. New Testament Saints

The seven last sayings of the King of Kings as He died upon a cross are unparalleled for their trust and triumph, power and pathos. These final cries prove that Christ died, not merely as a *Victim*, but as a *Victor*. Through the centuries, multitudes have been inspired by His example to manifest calm resignation in the presence of death and to greet it with a triumphant smile.

To God above He prayed — "Father, forgive them for they know not what they do."

To the Thief He said — "Today thou shalt be with me in Paradise."

To His dear mother He called — "Woman, behold thy Son."

To John, His disciple, He exclaimed — "Behold thy Mother!"

To a closed Heaven He cried — "My God, My God, why hast Thou forsaken me?"

To His crucifiers He said — "I thirst."

To heaven and earth He shouted — "It is finished!"

To His Father He whispered — "Father, into Thy hands I commend my spirit."

Jesus was born to die. He took upon Himself the likeness of our sinful flesh that, through His death and resurrection, He might become the ransom for our sins. Entering His brief and dynamic public ministry of some three-and-one-half years after His hidden life of thirty years, He gathered around Him those He sought to train as His apostles. He tried to impress upon them the fact of His death, but they found it hard to believe that such a blessed and beneficial life as He lived among them could possibly end in the brutal manner He Himself predicted. But the dark day came when they saw their Master slain and hanged upon a tree. They saw Him die and were overawed at the way He did die — calm, sympathetic, forgiving, resigned and triumphant. So much so, that when their end came, remembering how the One they loved and faithfully served died victoriously as well as voluntarily, grace was theirs to end their pilgrimage in a God-glorifying way.

STEPHEN was the first martyr on the Church's illustrious roll to seal his witness for the Saviour with his life's blood. While not named among the Twelve, Stephen was nevertheless "the Prophet of the Gospel dawn in its western course, the link between Christ and Paul, and the first martyr of the Christian faith." Throughout his brief career he maintained the reputation of being "a man full of faith and of the Holy Spirit," and when he came to suffer and die for Christ's sake, his enemies gazing at it saw his countenance as an angel face in repose. Under the shower of the death-dealing stones, the angel-smile could still be seen on that blood-bespattered face because he saw Jesus standing on the right hand of God. Stephen remembered the victory of the Cross and patiently accepted the martyr-crown from the pierced hand of his crucified, risen and now glorified Lord. He died upon his knees committing his spirit to Christ, even as Christ died committing His spirit to His Father. "Lord Jesus, receive my spirit." The last breath of his soul was in intercession for his murderers. He fell asleep praying for his enemies, re-echoing the spirit of the last words of Jesus — "Lord, lay not this sin to their charge."

It seemed as if the martyrdom of Stephen was a crushing blow to the faith and witness of the newly-born Church, but the blood of that first noble martyr became a seed producing a glorious harvest. Saul of Tarsus had watched Stephen die, and that battered angel-like face haunted him. Stephen's prayer was answered on the Damascus road when Saul saw the glorified Saviour and became the great Apostle to the Gentiles.

ANDREW was a courageous fisherman and an average middle-class Galilean Jew who gave up all for Jesus. His Greek name means "manly" or "courageous", and the fishing industry on the Lake of Galilee produced manly men. Hearing the call of Jesus, Andrew immediately followed Him and brought Peter his own brother and fellow fisherman to the Master. It was also Andrew who brought the boy with the loaves and fishes to Jesus, thereby making it possible for Him to feed the five thousand. Historians inform us that Andrew labored in the Black Sea area with great success. Tradition has it that Andrew died on an X-shaped cross. While hanging alive for two days, he preached to the people, exhorting them to be constant and faithful to the truth. Egeas, the Proconsul responsible for Andrew's crucifixion, over-powered by the cry of the people to release Andrew from the cross, sought to liberate him, but the dying saint would not allow Egeas to free him and prayed as he died:

> "O Jesus Christ, let not thine adversary loose him that is hung upon thy grace; O Father, let not this small one humble any more him that hath known thy greatness. But do thou, Jesus Christ whom I have seen, whom I hold, whom I love, in whom I am and shall be, receive me in peace into thine

everlasting tabernacles, that by my going out, there may be an entering in unto thee of many that are akin to me, and that they may rest in thy majesty."

Tradition goes on to relate that having so said, "Andrew yet more glorified the Lord, he gave up the ghost, while we all wept and lamented at our parting from him."

PETER, who is always named first in all the lists of Apostles, was the first to declare his faith in the supernatural mission of Jesus and the first to see the risen Christ on the first Easter. Like Jesus, Peter was from Galilee where he made his living as a fisherman. Forthright, outspoken and impetuous, Peter yet had an intuition enabling him to pierce instantly the heart of a situation and act promptly without hesitation. It would take a large canvas to paint a life-size portrait of Simon Peter. None of the Twelve bulk so largely in the New Testament as Peter who had "the virtues and vices of creative minds, the lights and shadows of sanguine temperaments and the inconsistencies of genius." Peter was a most devoted servant of the Lord and was martyred for His name's sake, even as Christ predicted he would be. Tradition says that while in Rome on missionary work, he was crucified by Emperor Nero, about 62 A.D. It is said that at his own request Peter was crucified head downwards because he felt unworthy to die in the same manner as his Lord did at Calvary. Tradition also has it that the Christians in Rome urged Peter to escape that he might serve the Church in the world at large, and that yielding to their entreaties, he somehow escaped but was arrested on the way by the One he knew and loved best.

"Lord, whither art Thou going?"

Christ replied:

"I am come to Rome to be crucified a second time."

Peter hurried back to martyrdom. It is said that his wife was killed first, and as she was led forth, Peter comforted her with the words:

"Remember the Lord."

We totally reject the whole structure of Romish romance regarding Peter, and what Peter's last word was we are not told, but we do know that he proved himself to be the Rock against whom all the forces of hell had dashed in vain and had not prevailed to engulf his immortal soul.

JAMES, THE SON OF ZEBEDEE, one of the select three in the company of Christ, was the proto-apostolic martyr who sealed his testimony in blood. Not much is recorded of this first apostolic martyr of the Christian faith. His appearance in the sacred record is rare until the gleam of the sword ends his career in a flash of eloquent silence. The New Testament gives us a portrait of him in silhouette rather than in photograph. While he stands in the triumvirate between Peter and John, the latter two have far more prominence. James and his brother John were as inseparable as twins. They were so vengeful that before they met Christ, they were known as "The Sons of The Thunderstorm." The sons of Zebedee, they lived at Capernaum on the northwest shore of the Lake of Galilee, not far from Bethsaida. James anticipated and elevated the saying of Islam, "Heaven is found beneath the shadow of the sword," for when he fell before the sword of Herod, he became the first victim of the early persecution of the Church. "The Sanhedrin stoned Stephen, the Court slew James; but persecution by Church or State never killed a living faith."

The Martyrdom of James marked an epoch of increased energy over an enlarged area of operation and over which *The Herods* ruled —

Herod I, resolved on "The Slaughter of the Innocents."

Herod II, reluctantly beheaded John the Baptist.

Herod III, executed James, but each attempt to crush the cause of God miserably failed. While we have no authentic record of the end of James and his dying words, tradition tells us that the accuser of James was so struck with his calm heroism that he became a Christian and was executed at the same block freshly stained with the blood of James. Of this much we can be certain, that because of his intimate fellowship with Christ while He was here in the flesh, the Cross was present before the Apostle's eyes and like other martyrs, he died in triumph. Faith in the crucified Saviour made James heroic in life and death —

"I will not fear what man shall do unto me."

JOHN, the youngest among the disciples of Christ and the longest lived Apostle of the Church, was the younger son of Zebedee and Salome and was evidently the most gifted son of the family, being endowed with spiritual and poetical instincts of a high order. Once he came to know Christ as "the Lamb of

God" his clinging love never lost its hold of the strong Son of God. As the disciple Jesus loved, John reciprocated such love, and the shadow of the Lord's Cross made a deep and lasting impression on his tender heart; the memories of His final agonies lingered with him to the close of his long life. While the Bible tells us nothing of John's last hours, we do know that his death occurred about the close of the First Century. He crowned the Apostolic Age and closed the divinely inspired Word of God with the echo of the Ascension promise, "Even so, come, Lord Jesus." His grave, like that of Moses, is known only to God. There were rumors abroad at that time that John never died but, like Enoch and Elijah, ascended from earth to heaven without ever tasting death.

Tertullian is responsible for the tradition that, during the reign of Nero, John was brought to Rome and cast into a cauldron of boiling oil, but that he was miraculously preserved from burning and after this ordeal was banished to Patmos. The Apostle certainly lived in an age of terrible barbarity and cruelty when so many brave Christians perished. A story is related that John was the means of bringing a most unusual young man to Christ, but he later fell from grace and became a leader of brigands in the mountains. John sought him out and ultimately found him. The young man instantly recognized the venerable Apostle and tried to escape from his dignified presence:

> "My son, why dost thou flee from thy father? I am feeble and far advanced in years; have pity on me, my son; fear not. There is yet hope of salvation for thee; I will stand for thee before the Lord Christ. If need be I will gladly die for thee, as He died for us. Stop, stay, believe; it is Christ who has sent me."

The story goes on to say that the young man flung away his weapons, knelt with the aged Apostle and returned to God. Although John laid away the garments of his mortality 1900 years ago, "he lives and will ever live by his writings, and the future belongs to him even more than the past."

PHILIP, though he bore a Gentile name, was yet thoroughly Hebrew in religious conviction. It was the custom in parts of the Roman Empire to name children after the reigning prince, and Philip the Tetrarch of Galilee attained such a compliment in Philip the Apostle, who is closely associated with Andrew.

Both were attracted to the scene of John the Baptist's preaching, and their characters have much in common. Sometimes this Philip of Bethsaida is identified with Philip the Evangelist who led the treasurer of Queen Candace of Ethiopia to Christ. We feel, however, that Philip the deacon and evangelist who was remarkably used of God both in Samaria and in the desert was another disciple. Tradition has much to say of the Apostle Philip's miraculous acts and how in Hierapolis he was terribly persecuted and suffered the same fate as his Master, uttering as he was martyred the words of Jesus:

"Father, into Thy hands I commend my spirit."

BARTHOLOMEW, Nathanael Bartholomew to give him his full name, was led to Christ by Philip. Christ surprised Nathanael by saying —

"Before that Philip called thee, I saw thee."

Jesus saw in him a "genuine son of the Covenant, a child of Jacob purged of his ancestor's youthful deceit, without simulation or dissimulation, without any religious mark, and the admiration of Christ for the ideal character of the man broke into honest praise."

Ecclesiastical tradition says that Bartholomew became a missionary to many countries, and that while in India, he left behind *The Gospel of Matthew* which was greatly used of God. It is likewise affirmed that he died a martyr as he sought to overthrow idolatry in far countries. While we have no record of his dying testimony, we can be sure that as "an Israelite indeed" and therefore well versed in Scripture, its precious promises were on his lips as he passed into glory.

THOMAS was born "a twin" and appears as a man of dual consciousness, a sort of Jacob and Esau struggle between feeling and faith, with faith ultimately triumphant. Arnold of Rugby found a life study in the character of Thomas, and as he died he quoted the words of the Apostle:

"Blessed are they that have not seen and yet have believed."

Thomas, a hardheaded man of action who insisted on evidence instead of hearsay, demanded a tangible proof of Christ's resurrection. The moment he saw the crucified, risen One he cried, "My Lord and my God!" It is said that Thomas travelled to India on missions, and that there were many "Christians of St. Thomas" whose liturgy and hymns were in Syriac. It is said that he was finally martyred and departed in peace with this prayer on his lips:

> "Behold, Lord, I have accomplished Thy work and perfected Thy commandment. I have become a bondman; therefore today do I receive freedom. Do Thou, therefore, give me this and perfect me, and this I say, not for that I doubt, but that they may hear from whom it is needful to hear."

MATTHEW, before he left all to follow Christ, was known as "Levi" and discipleship meant sacrifice and self-denial. LEVI rose from his tax seat MATTHEW — "God's free man." His shackles fell off and without regret he left all worldly prospects for a life of devotion to Christ. He had been a "publican" — a term indicating the close relation of the *Publicani* to the public purse. The publicans or tax-gatherers were recognized throughout the Roman Empire as the "middlemen" between the rulers and the people, whose approach was to offer as little to the state as possible and to exact as much from the taxpayer as they were able to enforce. The record of Zacchaeus shows how rich this clan became. This son of Alphaeus is credited with collecting the Old Testament prophecies of the coming of the Messiah or Christ and introducing them with the formula: "This came to pass in the fulfilment of what had been spoken by the Lord through the prophet." Matthew's great object in the Gospel at the beginning of the New Testament was to prove that Jesus was the Messiah of God. It is reckoned that after the Ascension, Matthew preached the Gospel in Judea for several years. Socrates, the ecclesiastical historian of the Fourth Century, speaks of him as preaching in Ethiopia and Arabia. Of his end and where he was buried there is no account. It is generally held that he died a natural death. If this once shrewd, grasping, pitiless tax collector, changed by Christ's power into an Apostle, left any last word, we can imagine it being something akin to the apostolic confession —

> "By the grace of God, I am what I am."

MARK, the Evangelist, is credited with the founding of the Church of Alexandria. As nicknames were prevalent in his days the one ascribed to John Mark was "Stumpfinger". Whether he accidentally cut part of his finger off or purposely mutilated it as a vow of discipleship is not known. Eusebius and Jerome both fixed the martyrdom of Mark in the eighth year of Nero's reign, 68-69 A.D. The Egyptian tradition is that at the feast of

Alexandria's idol, Serapis, on April 25, Mark was dragged round the city and suffered a cruel death. However he died, we can be certain that his final testimony would be of the Christ Mark exalts as The Servant.

James, the son of Alphaeus, is not to be confused with James Boanerges, the son of Zebedee. For the sake of distinction, we can distinguish them as James I and James II. James I, or "The Greater," was one of the inner circle of the Twelve, while James II, or "The Less," heads the last division of the apostolic lists. Although the identification of this James with James "the Lord's brother," whom Paul speaks of, was one of the most intricate problems in Apostolic history, the weight of evidence favors the assertion that "the son of Alphaeus" and "the Lord's brother" indicate the same James who came of a well-to-do and deeply religious family. This one-time tax collector lived to witness most effectively for Christ for nearly thirty years. Tradition has it that he was martyred between 61-62 A.D. Given the opportunity to renounce the Lord and escape with his life, the loyal witness lifted up his voice and said:

> "Why do you ask me respecting Jesus, the Son of Man? He is now sitting in heaven, on the right hand of great power, and is about to come on the clouds of heaven."

The Pharisees and Scribes in their rage rushed upon James, cast him down the Temple steps, and at the foot, bruised and battered as he was, James knelt and prayed for his enemies. While praying with his dying breath, a man in the crowd killed him with a stout stick.

Saul of Tarsus, the Jewish bigot, became Paul the great Apostle to the Gentiles as the result of a transforming vision on the road to Damascus which completely revolutionized his whole life. Paul's record of consecrated, sacrificial service is unmatched in the annals of Church history. His was a pure life rooted in Christ and fruited with the graces of the Gospel, a life full of "Works of faith, labor of love and patience of hope;" his was a devoted spirit in the service of the One to whom Paul owed so much. What sufferings were his for Christ's sake!

Although the New Testament does not tell us how the illustrious Apostle died, there is a strong feeling that during the dark days of persecution, Paul was taken out to "the Appian Way" where his noble head was severed from his frail body. His *Second Epistle to Timothy,* the last letter from his mighty pen, is referred to as his "swan song", in which we have those inspiring words so many saints have used as their dying testimony and which can be looked upon as Paul's final witness before he departed to be with Christ:

> "I am now ready to be offered, and the time of my departure is at hand. I have fought a good fight, I have finished my course, I have kept the faith. Henceforth there is laid up for me a crown of righteousness, which the Lord, the righteous Judge shall give me at that day: and not to me only, but unto all them also that love His appearing."

II. Religious Leaders And Preachers

Preachers, because of their knowledge of God and of what His Word declares concerning the hereafter, should have a triumphant exit from earth as well as an abundant entrance into heaven. Alas, some die in fear! They forget that the sky, not the grave, is their goal. In the main, however, some of the most heartening last words fell from the lips of men who taught others not only how to live — but die!

EDWARD R. AMES (1806-1879), the American Bishop of the Methodist Episcopal Church who became well-known for his remarkable executive ability and pulpit oratory and who was often consulted by President Abraham Lincoln, was elected Bishop in 1852. Having fought a good fight he came to his last hour saying:

> "When I can do no more work I care not how soon I die. All right."

ANSELM (1033-1109), Archbishop of Canterbury and one of the greatest of scholastic theologians and philosophers, labored hard to free the ecclesiastical power in England from the control of the throne. At the same time, however, he favored the dominance of the popes of Rome. As deathpangs laid hold on him, he died giving utterance to what was uppermost in his mind:

> "I shall gladly obey His call; yet I should also feel grateful if He would grant me a little longer time with you, and it could be permitted me to solve a question — the origin of the soul."

ANSGAR (801-865), the zealous monk of Scandinavia who was called "The Apostle of The North", was the one who introduced Christianity into Scandinavia. An earnest and courageous preacher of the Christian faith, he likewise tithed his income to help the poor. Ansgar was privileged to see the Christian faith gain a stronghold on the people and at his peaceful end prayed:

> "Into Thy hands do I commend my spirit, for Thou hast redeemed me, Oh, Lord!"

THOMAS ARNOLD (1795-1842), was not only the gifted and famous Headmaster of Rugby School but also renowned as a preacher and author. Intensely religious, his manifest scholarship held a subordinate place to his lofty estimate of duty towards God and those he taught. His was a "regal supremacy of the morals and the spiritual element over his whole being and powers." His last days brought him much pain, but grace was his to say at the end:

> "Thank God for giving me this pain! How thankful I am that my head is untouched."

JOSEPH BELLAMY (1719-1790), who received his theological training from Jonathan Edwards and who became lifelong pastor of the Congregational Church in Bethlehem, Pennsylvania, at the age of 21, was a man of commanding presence and remarkable preaching ability. When dying, he was somewhat depressed, and a friend visiting him said, "If God should send you to hell, what would you do there?" Bellamy replied:

> "I will tell them there forever Jesus is precious."

WILLIAM BEVERIDGE (1637-1708), was the learned and devout English bishop who wrote extensively on Church History and the Canon Law. Because of his godly life and zeal in the discharge of his ministerial duties, he was spoken of as "the great reviver and restorer of primitive piety." At his end, memory failed him, so much so that his dear wife and his most intimate friends were unrecognized. Yet when asked, "Do you know Jesus?" his final word was:

> "Oh yes, I have known Him these forty years. Precious Saviour! He is my only hope."

HENRY WARD BEECHER (1813-1887), had a fame as a pulpit orator that was universal. He was also foremost in the advancement of the philanthropic reforms of his generation. His sermons were regularly published for over a quarter of a century and exercised a tremendous influence wherever they went.

Knowing that death was but a door into heaven, Beecher's last word was:

> "Going out into life — that is dying."

THEODORE BEZA, or De Béze, (1519-1605), colleague and successor of John Calvin, possessed great executive ability and after Calvin's death controlled the affairs of The Reformed Church with consummate skill. When he came to die at the advanced age of 86, he uttered a most expressive farewell:

> "Cover, Lord, what has been; govern what shall be. Oh, perfect that which Thou hast begun, that I suffer not shipwreck in the haven."

CATHERINE BOOTH, wife of the founder of the Salvation Army and like her evangelist-husband, given over to the salvation of lost men and women, knew how to die well. For her there was no moaning at the bar, as her last word reveals:

> "The waters are rising, but so am I. I am not going under but over. Do not be concerned about dying; go on living well, the dying will be right."

ALEXANDER ARCHIBALD (1772-1851), was the distinguished Presbyterian divine of Scotch descent renowned for his facilitiy of extemporaneous speaking. He became the first professor in the newly established Presbyterian Theological Seminary at Princeton. As an author his *Treateses* had a large circulation. Having passed the fourscore years, his last word was most apt:

> "Truly our life of threescore-and-ten years appears like a dream when we wake from sleep. Many dear relatives, loved it may be as our own life, have slept the sleep of death. But though friends die, God liveth for ever. The Divine promise is to the Christian, 'I will never leave thee.' As an aged man I would say to my fellow-pilgrims, 'endeavor to be useful as long as you are continued on earth.'"

JOSEPH ALLEINE (1634-1668), was an English non-conformist preacher who knew what it was to suffer for the faith. With others, he was ejected from his church and cast into prison. Conspicuous for his pastoral devotion, he yet prosecuted his theological and scientific studies with much success. Released from prison he continued his itinerant preaching until great physical weakness resulted in his death at 34 years of age. His final utterance was full of hope:

> "This vile body shall be made like Christ's glorious body.

Oh, what a glorious day will be the day of the resurrection! My life is hid with Christ in God."

AUGUSTINE, Bishop of Hippo, was one of the early lights of the Church. His story has been told ten thousand times. Although his father was a pagan, his mother was a woman of the most devoted piety whose prayers for her husband and son were graciously answered. It was while reading Romans 13:13, 14, that Augustine heard and responded to God's call. As he passed away, August 28, 430 A.D., he was heard to say:

"Oh, Lord, shall I die at all? Shall I die at all? Yes! Why, then, oh Lord, if ever, why not now?"

Die he did, and dying left behind him a rich treasure of scriptural and theological exposition.

ADAM CLARKE (1762-1832), the British Methodist preacher and commentator, enriched the whole Church with his elaborate work, *Commentary on the Whole Bible*, to which he devoted forty years of labor. A profound scholar, proficient in Oriental languages, Clarke gained wide recognition. During the cholera plague in London, Clarke became a victim of the plague and died August 16, 1832. The record of his last day on earth was moving. In the morning, while at prayers with his family, he thanked God for the blessed hope of eternal bliss through Christ. Asked if he was trusting the Saviour, he died saying:

"I do! I do!"

JAMES DURHAM, a Scottish preacher and author who died in 1658, knew that it was well with his soul and left the world with the statement:

"For all I have preached or written, there is but one Scripture I can remember and dare grip to — 'Him that cometh to Me I will in no wise cast out.' "

JONATHAN EDWARDS (1703-1758), one of the most eminent among American preachers, had a remarkable influence over audiences which seems almost incredible. He was greatly used in revivals which spread through New England like a prairie fire. In 1757 he was called to the presidency of Princeton College but was not privileged to fulfil his tasks. A week after his inauguration he was inoculated for smallpox; a fever ensued, and he died on March 22, 1758. After settling his worldly affairs and bidding adieu to his family, he expired saying:

"Where is Jesus, my never-failing friend?"

JONATHAN EDWARDS, JR., who was so much like his father in many ways, carried on the torch. He died about 55 years of age, the same age as his father, soon after his inauguration as President of Union College. His last word was:

"Trust in God and you have nothing to fear."

JOHN ELLIOT (1604-1690), was extensively used in the winning of Indians for the Master. He became known as "The Apostle to the North American Indians." Elliot gave himself to the mastery of their language that he might preach to them. In 1661 he published the New Testament in the Indian tongue, and three years later the entire Bible which was the first Bible published in America. He died in 1690 at the age of 86, his final utterance expressing his concern for the Indians he dearly loved:

"There is a dark cloud upon the work of the Gospel among the poor Indians. The Lord revive and prosper that work and grant that it may live when I am dead. It is a work which I have been doing much and long about. But what was the Word I spake last? I recall the words 'my doings'. Alas! they have been poor and small and lean doings, and I'll be the man to throw the first stone at them. The Lord Jesus, whom I have served for eighty years, like Polycarp, forsakes me not . . . Oh, come in glory! I have waited long for Thy coming. Pray! Pray!"

CHRISTMAS EVANS (1766-1838), was the Baptist preacher of Wales famed for his eloquence. It was not until he was seventeen, when he was converted, that he learned to read. His power as an illustrative preacher won him the title of "The Welsh Bunyan." His sway over audiences was remarkable. On his deathbed, speaking to those around him, he said:

"I am about to leave you. I have labored in the sanctuary fifty-three years, and this is my comfort and confidence, that I have never labored without blood in the vessel. Good by! Drive on!"

GEORGE FOX (1624-1690), founder of the Society of Friends, or The Quakers, was the child of devout, Godly parents. In his earliest years he had religious experiences of peculiar intensity. For his bold denunciations of false doctrines, he suffered imprisonment in many towns. His *Journal* is one of the most extraordinary and instructive narratives in the world. His dying testimony was:

"All is well, and the seed of God reigns over all, and over death itself."

ELIZABETH FRY (1780-1845), the English Quakeress who became noted for her endeavor to relieve the miserable condition of female prisoners in Newgate, was also active in the abolition of slavery and in the provision of libraries for the use of British sailors. A saintly soul, she used her last breath to whisper:

"My dear Lord, help and keep Thy servant."

THOMAS GOODWIN (1600-1679), was the famous Puritan of the Seventeenth Century who became President of Magdalen College, London. His published works consist mainly of his sermons, so rich in their spiritual content. Reaching his last hour, all he could say was:

"Ah, is this dying? How I have dreaded as an enemy this smiling friend."

MATTHEW HENRY (1662-1714), was the eminent non-conformist theologian who gave the Church the devotional commentary which held a foremost place in its field. He died a week after his settlement in London as pastor of a church in Hackney, but his end was full of confidence in the Saviour's grace. Almost his last words were:

"A life spent in the service of God, and in communion with Him, is the most comfortable life that any one can lead in this present world."

JERRY MCAULEY, the once noted river thief and one of the worst characters along New York's waterfront, was converted to God while serving a term in Sing Sing prison. After his release he returned to New York and establishing the famous Water Street Mission, was wonderfully used in the transformation of the down-and-outs. When he died in 1884, his final word was:

"It's all right up there."

ROBERT MURRAY MCCHEYNE, was only 28 years of age when he died in 1843. He once wrote in his diary:

"Live so as to be missed when dead."

Such was his impact upon the religious life of Scotland, that with his early passing, the whole nation mourned the silencing of the voice which God had so wonderfully used for the ingathering of lost souls. When living in Dundee, Scotland, I often visited his grave and prayed that something of his passion to save men might possess my heart. His *Memoirs* by his close friend, Andrew Bonar, are a spiritual classic to be treasured. Scripture formed his parting word:

> "Be stedfast, unmoveable, always abounding in the work of the Lord, forasmuch as ye know that your labour is not in vain in the Lord."

PHILIP W. OTTERBEIN (1726-1813), was the great German evangelist so mightily blessed of God in a revival ministry. He came to America in 1752 and after a while became associated with Martin Boehm of the Mennonite Church. Meeting for the first time, these two warriors said, "We are brethren," which greeting gave rise to the designation, "United Brethren In Christ" – a cause they founded and developed. Wherever they labored together or separately, there were striking scenes, and multitudes were added to the Lord. After half a century of strenuous and successful evangelistic activity, Otterbein reached the end of his earthly ministry and died testifying:

> "The conflict is over and past. I begin to feel an unspeakable fulness of love and peace divine. Lay my head upon my pillow and be still."

JOHN OWEN (1616-1683), the renowned Puritan, was honored both for his personal piety and high literary attainments. Such was his fame as a preacher that he was ordered to preach before Parliament; his sermon was a powerful appeal for liberty of conscience. Cromwell heard him preach and became his friend. Among his conspicuous works are *Exposition of the Epistle To The Hebrews* and *The Holy Spirit*. He died peacefully having survived all his children. His last words were characteristic of his devotion to Christ:

> "I am going to Him whom my soul loveth, or rather who has loved me with an everlasting love, which is the sole ground of all my consolation."

JAMES SPURGEON, grandfather of the celebrated C. H. Spurgeon, was likewise a Puritan preacher of no mean order. During his last hours, a friend visiting him said, "Firm as the earth His promise stands." The dying man replied:

> "That would be but sorry comfort to me now; the *earth* is slipping away from me. No! Firm as His *throne* His promise stands."

GEORGE WHITEFIELD (1714-1770), whose name will live for ever in the annals of evangelism, was co-worker of the

Wesleys before he settled in America. His name still stands as a synonym for the most marvelous exhibitions of pulpit eloquence. It was given to William Cowper to appropriately delineate Whitefield's most prominent qualities:

"He loved the World that hated him; the tear
That dropped upon his Bible was sincere;
Assailed by scandal, and the tongue of strife,
His only answer was — a blameless life:
And that he forged, and he that threw the dart,
Had each a brother's interest in his heart.
Paul's love of Christ, and steadiness unbribed
Were copied close in him, and well transcribed.
He followed Paul — his zeal a kindred flame,
His apostolic charity the same.
Like him, crossed cheerfully tempestuous seas,
Forsaking country, kindred, friends and ease.
Like him, he laboured, and, like him content
To bear it, suffered shame wher'er he went."

Dying the death of a righteous man, Whitefield gave utterance to the prayer:

"Lord Jesus, I am weary *in* Thy work, but not *of* Thy work. If I have not yet finished my course, let me go and speak for Thee once more in the fields, seal the truth, and come home to die."

HOWARD CROSBY (1826-1891), who occupied the prominent pulpit of the Fourth Avenue Presbyterian Church of New York City and made valuable contributions to Biblical literature, was likewise conspicuous in philanthropic and educational reforms. His trust in the Saviour was of a simple nature, so much so, that as he finished his course he could say:

"My heart is resting sweetly with Jesus, and my hand is in His."

MATTHEW COTTON (1633-1728), was one of the famous Cottons of early American religious history. A descendant of John Cotton, the noted English Puritan who fled to America to escape the wrath of Archbishop Laud for not kneeling at the sacrament, Matthew Cotton was no less Puritan in life and witness. As he reached the swellings of Jordan, he remarked to his dear ones, sorrow-stricken over the departure of the one they loved:

"I am going where all tears will be wiped away."

DWIGHT L. MOODY (1837-1899), the shoe salesman God called to rock two continents, still lives in the institutions he founded, prominent among which is the Moody Bible Institute. The motto by which this renowned evangelist lived and laboured is found in the verse of Scripture adorning his grave at North-field, "He that doeth the will of God abideth for ever." His death, like his life, was one of triumph. With joy he exclaimed in his last moments:

"I see earth receding; heaven is opening. God is calling me."

JOSEPH BEAUMONT was an English minister who died while conducting a Sunday service in 1855. He was suddenly summoned to the courts above as he repeated the lines:

"The while the great archangel sings,
He hides His face behind His wings,
And ranks of shining hosts around
Fall worshipping and spread the ground."

JOCK TROUP, my very dear friend through many years, was a Scottish evangelist whom the Lord so wonderfully used. Along with his wife, he was touring America on a preaching mission, and on an Easter Sunday while preaching on John 3:16, he fell over the pulpit and slumped on the floor. His wife, who was present, rushed to his aid and took his head in her arms, but dear Jock simply rolled his eyes, looked at his beloved and said:

"Katie,"

and died. Jock often used to say that he wanted to die with his boots on — and he did! For him it was sudden death, sudden glory.

JOHN WOOLTON (1535-1594), who became Bishop of Exeter, insisted upon standing up to die:

"A Bishop ought to die on his legs."

DUNSTAN (925-988), became Archbishop of Canterbury. Scholar and administrator though he was, he yet had skill in various arts. He gave much time to prayer vigils, consoled orphans, pilgrims and strangers, and covered England with his holy doctrines. His last words on the Saturday before Ascension Day were:

"The merciful and gracious Lord hath so done His gracious works that they ought to be had in remembrance. He hath given meat to them that fear Him."

Almost immediately after uttering this tribute of praise, Dunstan rendered his spirit to his Creator and Redeemer.

FRANCIS OF ASSISI (1183-1225), founder of the Franciscan Order of monks, had a passionate love of nature and spoke of the birds as his little brothers and sisters.

> "God gives special grace to those who love their little brothers and sisters, the birds and beasts."

He was the author of many religious poems written in the Italian of that period. Of his life and labors it was said that they "fell like a stream of tender light across the darkness of the time." His last faint cry was:

> "Welcome, sister Death."

SAINT BEDE, or Beda (673-735), the English scholar, historian and theologian, was styled "The Venerable Bede." Known as "The Father Of English History", he wrote prolifically some forty treatises coming from his pen. Apart from his renowned scholarship, Bede was likewise a man of singular beauty of character, devout, humble and trustful. In his final days he suffered much from an inflammation of the lungs and found it difficult to breathe. Yet his time was taken up with prayer, thanksgiving and meditation upon the Bible. To those who were distressed over his approaching death Bede said:

> "I have not lived so as to be ashamed to live among you, nor am I afraid to die, because we have a gracious God."

Knowing that his departure was at hand, the dying saint, seated on the floor of his apartment, said to one of his brethren:

> "Hold my head that I may have the pleasure of looking towards my little oratory, where I used to pray, and that I may once more call upon my Heavenly Father."

Then repeating the Benediction, he immediately expired.

WILLIAM BEDELL (1570-1642), was an eminent and beloved Bishop of the Anglican Church. As Bishop of Kilmore and Ardagh, he exercised a tremendous religious influence throughout Ireland, and it was under his direction that the Old Testament was translated into Irish. During the 1641 rebellion, he was seized and imprisoned in the Castle of Cloughboughter. Afterwards he found refuge in the home of a Protestant minister until he died. After blessing his children and all those around his deathbed, he said, with a loud voice:

"God of His infinite mercies bless you all, and unreproveable in His sight, that we may meet together at the right hand of our blessed Saviour, Jesus Christ, with unspeakable joy and full of glory. I have finished my ministry and life together. I have kept the faith, and I am persuaded that He is able to keep that which I have committed to Him against that day."

JEAN CLAUDE (1619-1687), one of the most eminent of French Protestant divines, was among the Protestants driven out of France during the reign of Louis XIV. As leader of the French Protestants, he vigorously defended the tenets of the Protestant faith. Stricken with a fatal illness, Claude gathered all his family around the bed. To his wife, kneeling at the side he said:

"I have always tenderly loved you. Be not afflicted at my death. The death of the saints is precious in the sight of God. In you I perceive a sincere piety; I bless God for it. Be constant in serving Him with all your heart, and He will bless you."

Then, after blessing his son and an old servant who was also present, godly Claude uttered his last word on earth:

"I am so oppressed that I can attend only to two of the great truths of religion — the mercy of God, and the gracious aids of the Holy Spirit. . . . My whole resource is the mercy of God. I expect a better life than this; our Lord Jesus Christ is my only righteousness."

EDWARD PAYSON (1783-1827), the well-known American Congregational preacher who labored with remarkable success, was smitten in the midst of his years of tremendous usefulness. In the joy that God reigneth, his mind rose over bodily pain, and in the hope of a glorious eternity, he seemed almost to lose sense of his suffering. Just before his death, Payson wrote to his sister:

"Were I to adopt the figurative language of Bunyan, I might date this letter from "The Land of Beulah", of which I have been for some weeks a happy inhabitant. The celestial city is full in my view. Its glories beam upon me, its odours are wafted to me, its sounds strike upon my ears and its spirit is breathed into my heart. . . . Why should God deign thus to shine upon a sinful worm."

When his last agony commenced, he said of his racking pains:

"These are God's arrows, but they are all sharpened with love."

Within sight of the gates of paradise, he looked round on his dear ones and said:

"I am going, but God will surely be with you."

Sometime before his death, Dr. Payson had directed that a label be attached to his breast as soon as his happy spirit was set at liberty, bearing the words:

"Remember the words which I spake unto you while I was present with you."

The words were engraven on the plate of his coffin and were read by thousands on the day of his burial.

WILLIAM CAREY (1761-1834), known as "The Father and Founder of Modern Missions," developed remarkable gifts as a linguist. He became the first missionary to India sent out by the Baptist Missionary Society. His motto was:

"Expect great things from God.
Attempt great things for God."

In his will, Carey directed that the following words be cut on his tombstone:

"William Carey, born August 17, 1761: died
'A wretched, poor, and helpless worm,
On Thy kind arms I fall.'"

On his deathbed he said to a friend:

"When I am gone, say nothing about Dr. Carey; speak about Dr. Carey's Saviour."

DAVID LIVINGSTONE (1813-1873), the Scottish missionary who spent over thirty years in Africa, mostly in unexplored country, was the one who discovered the Victoria Falls. Shortly before he died, he said to his servants:

"Build me a hut to die in. I am going home."

He was found dead kneeling at his bedside. His heart was removed and buried in the Africa he gave his life for, and his body was preserved in salt and carried by affectionate natives to the coast over one thousand miles distant and ultimately buried with honors in Westminster Abbey.

JOHN HOWARD, the English philanthropist, became renowned for his great work in the relief of prisoners and the introduction of prison reform. Just before he died in 1790, he left this request:

"There is a spot near the village of Dauphiny; this would suit me nicely. You know it well, for I have often said that

I should like to be buried there. Let me beg of you not to suffer any pomp to be used at my funeral, nor any monument nor inscription to mark where I am laid. Place a sun dial over my grave, and let me be forgotten."

But God-inspired and noble hearted reformers like John Howard cannot be forgotten.

JOHN BUNYAN, the tinker of Bedford who became the immortal dreamer and gave to the world one of its greatest spiritual classics, *The Pilgrim's Progress*, died in the service of the Master he had suffered so much for. In 1628 a father and son became alienated, and Bunyan went to London on a mission of reconciliation. On the way home, he was caught in a violent storm and contracted a mysterious sickness which resulted in his death ten days later. His last words had a ring of triumph and certainty about them as he said to those at his deathbed:

"Weep not for me, but for yourselves. I go to the Father of our Lord Jesus Christ; Who will, no doubt, through the mediation of His Blessed Son, receive me, though a sinner: when I hope we shall ere long meet to sing the new song, and remain everlastingly happy, world without end, Amen!"

RICHARD BAXTER of Kidderminster, who preached as a dying man to dying men and women, wrote many of his most useful works between 1682 and his death in 1691. Notwithstanding his wasted, languishing body, Baxter continued preaching, and the last time he did so, he almost died in the pulpit. While upon his deathbed, the saintly Baxter gave utterance to some of the most precious truths ever to leave his anointed lips.

"I am the vilest dunghill worm that ever went to heaven. Lord! what is man; what am I, vile worm, to the great God!"

A friend who assured Baxter of the blessing his preaching and writings had been to him received the comment:

"I was but a pen in God's hands, and what praise is due to a pen?"

Baxter's last word was spoken to a fellow minister who had called to see him:

"The Lord teach you to die."

DAVID BRAINERD, whose intercessory prayer life and remarkable work among the American Indians still inspire the Lord's people, was not permitted to serve the Master for a great length of time. Once his frail tabernacle began to fail him, the thought of death filled his soul with rapture. The last sentence he wrote in his diary was a fitting conclusion to a life spent in fear of God and a labor of love:

> "Oh my dear God, I am speedily coming to Thee, I hope! Hasten the day, O Lord, if it be Thy blessed will. O come, Lord Jesus, come quickly, Amen."

Just before he died, Brainerd was heard to whisper:

> "He will come; and will not tarry. I shall soon be in glory; soon be with God and His angels."

JOHN COWPER was the infidel whom William Cowper, his brother, won for the Lord. John became a Fellow of Ben'et College, Cambridge, and an honored minister of the Gospel. Toward the end of his pilgrimage severe and continued pain was his; yet smiling he said to William:

> "Brother, I am as happy as a king."

On the morning of his death, William asked John what sort of a night he had had:

> "A sad night, not a wink of sleep. I endeavored to spend the hours in the thoughts of God and prayer; I have been much comforted, and all the comfort I got came to me in this way."

JOHN WESLEY, of whom it has been said that eternity alone will reveal what the world owes to his mighty ministry, was active up to the last. Until the end, he was full of praise, counsel and exhortations. In his last moments with what remaining strength he had, he cried out twice over, in holy triumph:

> "The best of all is, God is with us."

The very last word Wesley was heard to articulate was:

> "Farewell!"

Then, without a lingering groan, the evangelist of the highways and by-ways, beloved pastor of thousands, and father of the great Methodist Church entered into the joy of his Lord.

JOHN NEWTON (1725-1807), one of the most prominent men of his age, wore himself out in the service of Christ, but died at the advanced age of eighty-two. Two years before he entered into rest, he was so feeble that he could hardly stand in the pulpit. A male attendant used to stand behind him as he preached.

The last year of his pilgrimage, Newton was confined to his room, calmly awaiting his end. Pleasantly he said to a visitor:

"I am like a person going a journey in a stage coach, who expects its arrival every hour, and is frequently looking out of the window for it. . . . I am packed and sealed, and ready for the post."

Before he died, Newton said to a preacher-friend visiting him:

"The Lord has a sovereign right to do what He pleases with His own. I trust we are His, in the best sense, by purchase, by conquest, and by our own willing consent. As sinners, we have no right, and as believing sinners we have no reason, to complain; for all our concerns are in the hand and care of our best Friend, who has promised that all things shall work together for His glory and our final benefit. My trial is great, but I am supported, and have many causes for daily praise."

Dead, Newton still speaks in his printed works, especially in his hymn:

"Amazing Grace, how sweet the sound."

HENRY MARTYN, the renowned missionary to India and translator of the New Testament into the language of those he labored so faithfully among, surrendered his soul to his Redeemer, October 16, 1812. He succumbed to the plague which then raged at Tocat and was buried in a grave among men who were strangers both to him and his God. A day or two before he died, Martyn wrote the following words in his diary:

"I sat in the orchard and thought with sweet comfort and peace, of my God in solitude — my Companion, my Friend, and Comforter! O, when shall time give place to Eternity? When shall appear that new heaven and new earth wherein dwelleth righteousness? There — there shall in no wise enter in anything that defileth; none of that wickedness that has made men worse than wild beasts — none of those corruptions that add still more to the miseries of mortality shall be seen or heard any more."

CHARLES SIMEON (1759-1836), will ever be remembered as the man God used for the revival of a deeper attachment to the doctrines of the Reformation and as the spiritual father of countless numbers who came under the influence of his life and preaching. His chief literary work was the monumental commentary on the Bible as a whole. Simeon's last days were spent meditating upon the goodness and Word of God. Although harassed at times with the most acute pain, he bore it with uniform patience and unusual gentleness. Expressing surprise that he should be so long in dying, a visiting preacher quoted the verses:

> "I will wait all my appointed times."
> "He will make all thy bed in thy sickness."
> "Let patience have her perfect work, that ye may be perfect, and entire, lacking nothing."

The godly Simeon answered in a very affective way:

> "And that is quite sufficient for me."

Then the friend solemnly pronounced the benediction and Simeon faintly said:

> "Amen!"

and spoke no more.

ANDREW FULLER (1754-1815), friend of Dr. Ryland and cofounder of The Baptist Missionary Society, was greatly used of God as a pastor, author and missionary statesman. As a preacher his messages were practical exhortations based upon evangelical principles. As an author he manifested originality, simplicity and perspicuity. Much fame became his through his constant advocacy of foreign missions, and he played a large part in William Carey's going to India. Fuller's health began to decline, but his widespread labors were unabated. Gradually he came to feel that his days were numbered – "I am very ill – a dying man," he remarked to a friend. The eminent contemporary preacher, Toller, said of Andrew Fuller, "He died as a penitent sinner at the foot of the Cross," which was true for just before the end, hardly able to see or converse with any one, he said to one of his deacons:

> "I am a great sinner; and if I am saved, it can only be by great and sovereign grace."

repeating the words emphatically:

> "by great and sovereign grace."

JOHN WARBURTON was a remarkable witness to the saving truth of the Gospel. Along with William Gadsby and John Kershaw, he founded the denomination known as Strict Baptists. These three men pioneered a testimony for deep spiritual and vital godliness which helped to stem the tide of Modernism and false profession at a critical period in the history of the Church. Warburton's full story is told in *The Mercies Of A*

Covenant God, "Being an account of some of the Lord's wonderful dealings with John Warburton."

The chapter describing this great saint's last days is a most inspiring narrative. How fully occupied with the Lord he was! Before he died, he requested pen, ink and paper. Not being able to write, Warburton asked his daughter to write. "What must I write, Father? Is it about the church?" He shook his head and said, "No." "Is it about the family?" and again he said, "No." Then said the daughter, "Is it to tell us how good the Lord is to you in your last moments?" Lifting up his hands and waving them with peculiar delight, he said, "Yes, yes!" Then with great exertion he tried to articulate something, and at last said: "Hal —, Hal —!" Then followed with a firm voice, without a waver:

"Hallelujah!"

and he breathed his last.

WILLIAM GADSBY (1773-1844), who travelled sixty thousand miles and preached some twelve thousand sermons, was both holy and humane. So great was respect for him that thirty thousand people attended his funeral. His last words were:

"I shall soon be with Him. Victory, Victory, Victory (then raising his hand), for *ever.*"

JOHN KERSHAW (1792-1870), one of the founding fathers of the Strict Baptists, was brought to experience God's saving grace after a fling in sin. On January 2, 1870, he preached his last message from the words: "By them that have preached the gospel unto you with the Holy Ghost sent down from heaven" (1 Peter 1:12). On his deathbed and sinking fast he repeated the lines:

"Far from a world of grief and sin
With God eternally shut in,"

and added as he died:

"God is faithful! God is faithful."

WILLIAM TIPTAFT (1803-1864), was a brilliant star amongst the cluster of bright luminaries that adorned the Strict Baptist denomination of his day. He seceded from the Anglicans and at his own expense built a fine chapel where he preached without salary until he died. A pattern of godly living and self-sacrifice, his final testimony was:

"What a mercy, my last moments are my best. Thy love is better than wine, Praise God! Praise God! Grace shall have all the praise."

ARTHUR TRIGGS (1787-1859), another honored servant of God in Warburton's time, became deeply concerned about his soul at the age of nineteen. The word "eternity" struck him with overwhelming force and led to his conversion. As he lay dying he said:

"If any friends ask about me, tell them it is sweet to die in Jesus. Oh, I am longing to be with Him. He is my Redeemer."

His last utterance was:

"Come Lord Jesus!"

RICHARD HOOKER was only 46 years of age when he died after a long and painful illness brought on by his unceasing study. How his works have enriched the Church! The nearer he came to death, the more he grew in humility, in holy thoughts and resolutions. Toward the end of his sojourn, he told his doctor that he had been:

"Meditating on the number and nature of angels, and their blessed obedience and order, without which peace could not be in heaven; and oh! that it might be so on earth!"

His last few words were:

"God hath my daily petitions, for I am at peace with all men, and He is at peace with me; my conscience beareth me witness, and this witness makes the thoughts of death joyful. I could wish to do the Church more service, but cannot hope for it, for my days are past as a shadow that returns not."

SAMUEL RUTHERFORD (1600-1661), the saintly Scottish minister and writer of revered memory, was another of those faithful pastors evicted from their parishes because of their defence of Presbyterian doctrine against the Arminians. Cited to appear before Parliament on a charge of high treason, death prevented his appearance. As he was dying, Rutherford, whose *Letters* are permeated with the fragrance of Christ, sent this farewell message to all concerned:

"Tell the Parliament that I have received a summons to a higher bar. I must needs answer that first, and when the day you name shall come, I shall be where few of you shall enter. Oh, dear brethren, preach for Christ, feed the flock of God! Oh, beware of men-pleasing! Glory! Glory!"

JOHN SHEPPERD, of whom little is known apart from the fact that he was a godly pastor and most fruitful in his ministry, addressed his farewell message to a few fellow pastors gathered in the death-room:

> "The secret of my success is in these three things: the studying of my sermons frequently cost me tears; before I preached a sermon to others, I derived good from it; I have gone into the pulpit as if I were immediately after to render an account to my Master."

PAUL GERHARDT, was a notable German preacher and hymn-writer. During a season of great trial he sought to encourage his wife and wrote the hymn:

> "Hope, and be undismayed,
> Give to the winds thy fears."

When he died in 1676, he repeated the lines from another of his hymns:

> "Him no death has power to kill,
> But from many a dreaded ill
> Bears his spirit safe away."

ROWLAND HILL. (Not to be confused with Sir Rowland Hill, the British reformer who instituted the Penny Postage for letters.) The Rowland Hill we have in mind was the stirring revivalist preacher and author of such hymns as:

> "Let names and sects and parties fall,
> Let Jesus Christ be all in all."

He died in 1833 repeating the lines:

> "And when I'm to die,
>   Receive me, I'll cry;
> For Jesus hath loved me,
>   I cannot tell why."

LEIGH RICHMOND (1772-1827). An Anglican minister, he wrote several books, but his fame rests upon his two volumes, *The Annals Of The Poor*, which contain the well-known composition, "The Dairyman's Daughter." It is to one of his own daughters that we are indebted for an account of his last hours. Bidding farewell to all he said:

> "Behold, I die: but God be with you."

Then several times he repeated:
> "It will be all confusion."

His wife asked him what would be confusion.
> "The Church! There will be such confusion in the Church."

But for the soul taking its flight to heaven, there was no confusion. A holy calm settled upon his countenance in the silence of the death chamber.

GREGORY THE GREAT (540-604), reckoned by the Roman Catholic Church to be the first pope of that name, was without doubt an exemplary Christian. He believed that self-imposed asceticism was one way by which he could glorify God. Fond of sacred music, he was the originator of the system known as *Gregorian*. Excess of fastings and ceaseless labors produced much physical weakness and pain. Near his end, he said:
> "My body is dried up as if already in the coffin. Death is the only remedy for me."

ADONIRAM JUDSON (1788-1850), the missionary apostle to Burma, was privileged to see hundreds converted to Christ, and his name holds an exalted place in the history of modern missions. Broken in health, he died while making a voyage to the Isle of Bourbon. Before he breathed his last and his body was committed to the great deep, he said to those around him on board ship:
> "I go with the gladness of a boy bounding away from school, I feel so strong in Christ."

JOHN AND BETTY STAM, those two noble missionaries to China, were killed by bandits. All day long they had awaited their execution, locked up in the village post office. From this death house came the message written by John Stam:
> "So now also Christ shall be magnified in my body, whether by life, or by death" (Phil. 1:20).

As for the young wife, and mother of a three-month-old baby, she faced death without fear. As she left for China, she wrote the following poem:
> "And shall I fear
> That there is anything
> That men hold dear
> Thou would'st deprive me of,
> And nothing give in place?

"That is not so.
For I can see Thy face.
I hear Thee now:
'My child, I died for thee,
And if the gift
Of love and life you took from me,
Shall I one precious thing
Withhold to all eternity —
One beautiful and bright,
One pure and precious thing withhold —
It cannot be.' "

CARDINAL HENRY BEAUFORT (1377-1447), English statesman, is credited with saying:
"I pray you all, pray for me."

MOHAMMED (570-632), Arabian Prophet and Founder of Mohammedanism, said:
"O God, pardon my sins. Yes, I come."

BEAUMONT, a Roman Catholic prelate, asked:
"What! is there no escaping death?"

THOMAS A BECKET (1118-1170), Archbishop of Canterbury who was assassinated as he went to the altar in Canterbury Cathedral, said in addition to other statements:
"I confide my soul and the cause of the Church to God."

BISHOP BROUGHTON, of the Anglican Church, cried:
"Let the earth be filled with His glory."

MARTIN OF TOURS (315-399), French prelate and Patron Saint of France, addressed himself to Satan:
"What doest thou here, thou cruel beast?"

CARDINAL MARTINUZZI, referred to as "the Wolsey of Hungary," uttered the words as he was assassinated:
"Jesu, Maria!"

ARCHBISHOP SHARP, full of hope, whispered:
"I shall be happy."

SAINT FRANCIS, Italian monk, hailed death thus:
"Death, my sister, welcome be thou."

ISAAC CASAUBON (1559-1614), French theologian and scholar, lightly said:

"I am like Theophrastus, dying of a holiday."

CARDINAL DE ROHAN-CHABOT, conscious of his unworthiness, cried:

"I am nothing, nothing, less than nothing."

DEAN ARTHUR STANLEY (1815-1881), English prelate and author, Minister of Westminster Abbey, had his sphere on his heart as he died:

"I always wished that I could die at Westminster. The end has come in the way that I most desired that it should come. . . . I wish to send a message of respect to the Queen."

ARCHBISHOP TAIT died with this sigh of relief on his lips:

"And now it is all over. It isn't so very dreadful after all."

CARDINAL MANNING (1808-1892), author of repute, came to his end conscious he had done his best:

"I am glad to have been able to do everything in due order. . . . I have laid aside the yoke; my work is accomplished."

GENERAL WILLIAM BOOTH (1829-1912), founder of the Salvation Army, turned to his son Bramwell, his successor, saying:

"I'm leaving you a bonnie handful."

BISHOP THOMAS KEN (1637-1711), English prelate and hymnwriter, whose final sentence was:

"God's will be done."

JOHN BROWN, of Haddington, a godly preacher, had as his last words:

"My Christ."

CHARLES INWOOD, English Keswick evangelist who was a veritable flame of fire, whispered during an interval of consciousness:

"The Lord is good to all, and His tender mercies are over all His works."

JAMES C. DAWSON, gifted Bible teacher among the Plymouth Brethren, quietly passed away saying:

"I am going."

F. B. MEYER, famous Baptist preacher and author, dismissed the king of terrors with confident casualness. His last articulate word was:

"Read me something from the Bible, something brave and triumphant."

GEORGE H. MORRISON, gifted preacher of the Scottish Presbyterian Church, "Morrison of Wellington" as he was known, turned to his nurse and said:

"It's an ever-open door, never closed to anyone. It is wide open now, and I'm going through."

DINSDALE T. YOUNG, scholarly Methodist preacher who ministered for many years in Westminster, London, uttered this triumphant phrase as he entered the presence of the Master he faithfully served:

"I triumph!"

III. Reformers

MARTIN LUTHER, the monk God used to shake the world, was spared the agony of a torturous death. When he came to die, his lips were laden with Scripture. Thrice over he repeated the prayer:

"Into Thy hands I commend my spirit!
Thou hast redeemed me, O God of truth."

As he breathed his last Luther repeated John 3:16 and the verse from Psalm 68:

"Our God is the God of whom cometh salvation.
God is the Lord by whom we escape death."

With his hands clasped together, and without a finger or a feature being disturbed, this mighty man of God ended his pilgrimage.

PHILIP MELANCTHON, friend of Martin Luther, had to struggle with a very weak constitution all through his 64 years of life. Pain and uneasiness came to sharpen his visage, hollow his cheeks and completely wrinkle his once handsome face. He loved to think of heaven as a place in which there would be no more contention. It was with this hope that he exhorted Peucer to cultivate peace:

"Let them curse, but bless thou. My soul hath dwelt with Him that hateth not peace. I am for peace; but when I speak, they are for war."

After meditating upon his favorite portions of the Bible, Melancthon begged the friends around him not to disturb his repose, and while in sleep he fell asleep in Christ. His once pain-ridden body was buried by the side of Martin Luther's remains to await the Resurrection Morn.

ULRICH ZWINGLI (1484-1531), the notable Swiss Reformation leader, died on the battlefield of Kappel. The burning of a Protestant pastor of Zurich by the Catholics resulted in Zurich declaring war on the Roman Catholic cantons. The battle of Kappel was fought, and Zwingli, as Chaplain of the army of Zurich, was present. While in the act of giving comfort to a dying soldier, he was himself fatally wounded. With the words of the Master uppermost in his mind — "Fear not them which kill the body, but are not able to kill the soul" (Matt. 10:28), the last words of Zwingli were:

"They can kill the body, but not the soul."

ZUINGLE, another Swiss saint of renown, was deeply affected by the death of his friend, Zwingli. As he had been tenderly attached to his godly companion, the sad news was too much for Zuingle's infirm body, and a painful and fatal ulcer developed. On his deathbed, after committing his wife and three young children to God's care, he addressed himself to a few ministers who had gathered to pray with and for him. On the last day, with gasping breath, he repeated Psalm 51, and said:

"In a short time I shall be with Christ my Lord. Save me, O Christ Jesus."

As the sun rose on the little group kneeling at the bed, with a gentle sigh Zuingle resigned his spirit into the hands of his Redeemer.

JOHN CALVIN, whose stern theology exercised a tremendous influence for generations, spent his last days in constant prayer with relatives, ministers and senators. After his last repast with a few friends, he was carried back to his bedchamber and smilingly said:

"This intervening wall will not prevent me from being present with you in spirit, though absent in body."

Shortly after he died in so very tranquil a manner that he seemed to resemble one in a state of sleep rather than death.

JOHN KNOX (1503-1572), the renowned Scottish Reformer, was another who feared not the face of man. Educated in the popish faith, he broke with it and became the chief instrument under God in establishing Protestant ascendency in Scotland. After a life of unremitting labor and severe privation and suffering, he died bearing a firm testimony to the glorious truths he so firmly believed and so fruitfully propagated. As he died, he was full of scriptural exhortations for those around. On the day of his death he asked his wife to read to him 1 Corinthians 15, which he called "a comfortable chapter". A little later he said to his wife:

"Go read where I cast my first anchor,"

upon which she read John 17 and afterwards a part of Calvin's *Sermons on Ephesians*. His very last word was given with a deep sigh of relief:

"Now it is come."

Immediately, his secretary, seeing Knox was speechless, requested him to give a sign that he died in peace. Knox lifted up one of his hands and died without a struggle.

IV. Kings and Rulers

History provides us with the death scenes of those conspicuous in many realms, and their last words, whether traditional or true, make interesting reading as the following catalogue proves. If only all of these recorded personalities had followed the example of Him Who by "dying, death He slew", how different the exit from the world would have been.

JUGURTHA (104 B.C.), King of Numidia, as he was thrown into the dungeon of the Tullianum at Rome to starve, ironically exclaimed: "Hercules! How cold is your bath."

JULIUS CAESAR (44 B.C.), as Brutus stabbed him cried:

"You too, my son!"

AUGUSTUS CAESAR (14 A.D.), turned to his friends and as a farewell asked:

"Do you think I have played my part pretty well through the farce of life?"

NERO (68 A.D.), who wallowed in blood, hearing the horse-hoofs of his pursuers, quoted a line of Homer —

"In my ears resounds the gallop of fury-footed steeds."

Plunging a dagger in his throat he cried:

"What an artist dies in me! It is now too late."

GALBU (69 A.D.), Roman Emperor, motioned to his murderers and said:
> "Strike on, if it seems for the common weal of Rome."

VESPASIAN (79 A.D.) is credited with leaving these statements:
> "Alas! I suppose I am turning into a god."
> "An emperor should die standing" (and he stood).

HADRIAN (138 A.D.), quoted the lines —
> "Little soul, wandering one, gentle one,
> My body's long companion,
> What habitation waits for you
> My pallid, shivering, naked one,
> No more to jest as you used to do."

MARCUS AURELLIUS ANTONINUS (180 A.D.), Roman Emperor:
> "Think more of death than of me."

JULIAN (363 A.D.), the Roman Emperor known as *Julian the Apostate:*
> "Thou hast conquered, O Galilean!"

KING DARIUS II (404 B.C.), whose son Artaxerxes asked his father what had been the guide of his conduct that he might imitate him in the government of the Empire, replied:
> "The dictates of justice and religion."

SEVERUS (146-211 A.D.), said:
> "I have been everything, and everything is nothing. A little urn will contain all that remains of one for whom the whole world was too little."

WILLIAM OF NORMANDY (943 A.D.), ordered his body to be placed in a stone coffin and not buried but placed under the eaves outside the chapel, in order as he said in a farewell word:
> "That the drippings of the rain from the roof may wash my bones as I lie, and cleanse them from the impurity contracted in my sinful and neglected life."

It is to be hoped that his soul was made white by the blood of the Lamb ere he died.

YUSUF SALADIN (1193), Sultan of Egypt and Syria, commanded that his shroud should be fastened to a lance:
> "Go carry this lance, unfurl this banner, and while you lift up

this standard proclaim this! 'This is all that remains of Saladin the Great, the Conqueror and King of the Empire, of all his glory.' "

SULEYMAN (1010), King of Spain, was defeated by Hamad and appeared before the victor with his father and brother for whose lives he prayed to be spared:

"Strike me only; these are innocent."

PRINCE WILLIAM of Orange (1584), surnamed *The Silent*, was shot in his own house in Holland by one Gerard and prayed as he died:

"God pity me, I am sadly wounded! God have mercy on my soul, and this unfortunate nation."

CALIPH ABD-ER-RAHMAN III (961 A.D.), Sultan of Spain:

"Fifty years have passed since first I was Caliph. Riches, honors, pleasures — I have enjoyed all. In this long time of seeming happiness I have numbered the days on which I have been happy — *fourteen!*"

FERNANDO I (1383), King of Spain. As his end drew near his royal robe and crown were removed, and as he lay prostrate on the floor ashes were scattered on his head. As this great prince that swayed the sceptre in Spain died, he exclaimed:

"Thine, O Lord, is the power; Thine the dominion. Thou art the King of Kings, the Supreme alike in heaven and earth. I return unto Thee the crown which Thou hast given me, and which I have worn during Thy great pleasure; and now I only ask that when my soul leaves this body, Thou wilt receive me into Thy celestial mansion."

MOAHMMED I (1421), King of Spain. His dying words reflected the truth of Scripture:

"The path of kings is in appearance strewn with flowers, but thou seest not that roses have thorns. Is not the prince to leave the world as naked as the peasant?"

PHILLIP III, King of France, uttered this last word:

"What an account I shall have to give to God! How I should like to live otherwise than I have lived."

PHILLIP III (1621), King of Spain, left the world saying:

"Ah, how happy would it have been for me had I spent these twenty-three years that I have held the kingdom, in retirement!"

PETER I (1725), surnamed *The Great,* Czar of Russia, was filled with remorse as he came to die because of his cruelty to his son:

> "I believe, Lord, and confess, help my unbelief."

PETER III (1762), of Russia, was unpopular because of his friendship for the Prussians. Taking advantage of this, his wife crowned herself *Czarina.* After being forced to sign away his rights to the throne, he was strangled. Death facing him, he cried:

> "It was not enough to deprive me of the crown of Russia, but I must be put to death."

EMPEROR ZAHIR-DIN (1530), of Hindostan, on learning that his favorite son was ill, prayed that he might die instead. Shortly after, he fell sick and on his deathbed was heard to say:

> "I have borne it away. I have borne it away."

AGIS, King of Lacedaemonia, led out to execution said to his sorrowing followers:

> "Weep not for me."

EMPEROR NAPOLEON's (1821) last word revealed what thoughts were uppermost in his mind:

> "France — Army — Head of the Army — Josephine."

NAPOLEON III uttered as his dying word to Dr. Conneau,
> "Where you at Sedan?"

He was thinking of his great defeat.

CHARLES I (1649), of England, just before he laid down his life, bade Juxon, Archbishop of Canterbury, to tell Charles II to forgive his father's murderers and said:

> "I die before my time, and my body will be given back to the earth to become food for the worms. What an abyss between my deep misery and the eternal kingdom of Christ! Remember."

CHARLES II, referring to his mistress, Nell Gwyn, said:

> "Don't forget poor Nell. Open the curtains that I may once more see daylight."

CHARLES V, dying, thought of Christ:

> "Ah, Jesus!"

CHARLES VIII, of France, gave up the ghost with these words on his lips:

"I hope never again to commit mortal sin, nor even a venial one, if I can help it."

CHARLES II (1700), King of Spain:

"Now I am as one of the dead."

EDWARD VI (1553), King of England:

"Lord God, deliver me from this miserable, wretched life, and receive me among Thy chosen. Oh, Lord God, defend this realm and maintain Thy true religion. Lord, have mercy upon me and receive my spirit."

CHARLES IX, also of France, in whose reign occurred the Bartholomew slaughter, shrieked out:

"Nurse, nurse, what murder! What blood! Oh, I have done wrong. God pardon me!"

CHARLES OF BELA (1814):

"There is a Refuge."

FREDERICK WILLIAM I, father of Frederick the Great, said as he viewed his coffin:

"I shall sleep right well there."

FREDERICK V (1632), of Denmark, a timid man who shrank from the responsibilities of his position, could confess as he died:

"It is a great consolation to me in my last hour that there is not a drop of blood on my hands."

FREDERICK THE GREAT (1786), of Prussia, as he lay dying, saw one of his dogs shivering and said, "Put a quilt over it." His last words were:

"The finest day of life is that on which one quits it. The mountain is passed; we shall be better now."

FREDERICK IV (1888), Emperor of Germany, turned and said to his daughter as he died:

"Remain as noble and good as you have been in the past. This is the last wish of your dying father."

GEORGE IV (1830), turned to his page, Sir Walthen Waller, and asked:

"Walty, what is this? It is death, my boy. You have deceived me."

HENRY II (1154-1189), on learning that his favorite son John was one of those conspiring against him, said:

"Now let the world go as it will; I care for nothing more. . . . Shame, shame on a conquered king."

Shakespeare makes MACBETH say:

"I 'gin to be aweary of the sun,
And wish th' estate o' the world were now undone."

HENRY IV (1399-1413), who died suddenly, gave vent to adoration to the Father in heaven:

"I know I shall die in this chamber and depart this life for Jerusalem."

HENRY VII (1485), philosophically said:

"We heartily desire our executors to consider how behoofful it is to be prayed for."

HENRY VIII (1509-1547), plaintively cried:

"I trust in the merits of Christ. All is lost! Monks! Monks! Monks!"

PRINCE HENRY of Wales gave utterance to these lines:

"Tie a rope round my body, pull me out of bed, and lay me in ashes, that I may die with repentant prayers to an offended God. Oh! Tom! I in vain wish for that time I lost with thee and others in vain recreations."

LOUIS I is credited by Bouquet of turning his face to the wall, like King Hezekiah when he received divine announcement of his death, crying:

"Out! Out!"

Immediately he died.

LOUIS IX (1270), who was noted not only for his wisdom but piety, virtue, candor and justice, died saying to his daughter:

"I will enter now the house of the Lord. My dear daughter, I conjure you to love our Lord with all your might, for this is the foundation of all goodness. I wish you could comprehend what the Son of God has done for our redemption. Never be guilty of any deliberate sin, though it were to save your life. Shun too familiar discourse except with virtuous persons. Obey, my dear daughter, your husband. Aspire after a disposition to do the will of God, purely for His sake, independently of the hope of reward or fear of punishment."

Louis XI called to the Blessed Virgin of Embrun:

"My good mistress, help me."

Louis XII (1515), cried:

"I am dying. I recommend my subjects to you."

Louis XIII (1643), who, when his physician told him he had but two hours to live, said:

"Well, my God, I consent with all my heart."

Louis XIV (1715), as he lay dying, called the Dauphin to his bedside and said:

"My son, I might have lived a better life; profit by my errors; and remember this — kings die like other men."

His last word was:

"Why weep you? Did you think I should live for ever? I thought dying had been harder."

Louis XV. History speaks of this Louis as the most sensual and depraved of all French monarchs. Vice, in manifold forms, had entered into the depravity of his unlicensed pleasure, yet as this one died, he tried to varnish his sinful life:

"I have been a great sinner, doubtless, but I have ever observed Lent with a most scrupulous exactness. I have caused more than a hundred thousand masses to be said for the repose of unhappy souls, so that I flatter myself I have not been a very bad Christian."

What a hopeless way to end one's unworthy life!

Louis XVI, while on the scaffold, called to those around:

"Frenchmen, I die guiltless of the crime imputed to me. I forgive the authors of my death and pray God my blood fall not on France!"

Louis XVII (1795). This King of France left this last word:

"I have something to tell you."

Louis XVIII re-echoed the sentiment of Vespasian:

"A king should die standing."

To the priest beginning to read the prayers for the dying, Louis said:

"Is it as bad as that?" "Yes, sire."
"Well, never mind, go on with it."

LOUIS, DUKE OF ORLEANS (1752), is said to have been a model of self-denial, piety and virtue and to dislike the vanity of titles. He was kind to the needy and suffering, and much given to charitable works. His last words were:

"I have a son whom I am going to recommend to the All-Perfect Being. I entreat God that his natural virtues may become Christian graces, that his love for me may be the blossom of that immortal charity which the holy spirits and blessed angels enjoy."

What more beautiful dying request could a dying saint make for his offspring!

RICHARD I of England (1199), said to the archer, Bertrand de Gourdon, who shot him with an arrow:

"Young men, I forgive you my death. Let him go, but not empty handed; give him a hundred pieces and free him from these chains."

A monk bade him think of his three daughters:

"By God's legs, you lie, I have no daughters."

"Yes, you have, they are Pride, Avarice and Lust."

"Then I will marry them, the first to the Templars, the second to the Grey, and the third to the Black Monks."

RICHARD III, deserted by his best men, joined the army of Richmond, afterwards Henry VII. At Bosworth Field, as he rushed at Henry Tudor and was cut down, he cried:

"I will die King of England. I will not budge a foot. Treason, treason!"

WILLIAM I (1087), King of England, surnamed *The Conqueror*, Catholic-like prayed:

"To my Lady, the Holy Mary, I commend myself; that she, by her prayers, may reconcile me to her most dear Son, our Lord Jesus Christ."

OLIVER CROMWELL (1599-1658), Lord Protector of the Commonwealth, was one of the leaders of the Parliamentary Party in the struggle with King Charles I and was largely responsible for the King's downfall. Cromwell was a strong man and an able soldier, and when Charles was dethroned, established a practical dictatorship. Puritan in outlook, his soldiers fought with a psalm on their lips and sword in their hands. When he came to the end of his control of the country, his last words were:

"I would be willing to be further serviceable to God and His people, but my work is done! Yet God be with His people!"

Quietly he breathed his last, September 3, 1658. History records this conversation with his chaplain:

"Tell me, is it possible to fall from grace?"

The reply was, "No, it is not possible."

"Then I am safe," said Cromwell, "for I know that I was once in grace."

Being offered something to drink, he said:

"It is not my design to drink or to sleep, but my design is to make what haste I can to be gone."

ALEXANDER I of Russia said to his wife Elizabeth:

"I am dying of fatigue."

ALEXANDER II, full of divine faith, exclaimed:

"I am sweeping through the gates, washed in the blood of the Lamb."

CHARLEMAGNE repeated what scores of others have said:

"Lord, into Thy hands I commend my spirit."

LEOPOLD I, the Kaiser, said:

"Let me die to the sound of sweet music."

MASANIELLO, to his assassins, said:

"Ungrateful traitors."

WILLIAM II (1087-1100), shouted to Walter Tyrell:

"Shoot, Walter, in the Devil's name,"

and he did, killing the king.

WILLIAM III (1702), who suffered a broken collar-bone, uttered to his physician:

"Can this last long?"

and then died.

WILLIAM OF NASSAU, just before he was shot by Balt-Lazar Berard, prayed:

"O God, have mercy upon me and upon this poor nation."

MURAT, King of Naples, as he faced the men appointed to shoot him, pled:

"Soldiers, save my face; aim at my heart. Farewell!"

PRINCE ALBERT (1861), Husband of Queen Victoria, exclaimed as he died:

"I have such sweet thoughts."

EDWARD VII (1910):

"No, I shall not give in! I shall go on! I shall work to the end."

V. Queens

MARGARET OF SCOTLAND (1445), wife of Louis XI, left this world with a curt shudder of disgust at life, as at some draught too nauseous to be swallowed. Of this period Burrell and Lucas continue to remark, "We are approaching the time when human beings once more became aware that there can be a style and an art, a saving grace, not of God but of humanity, in life and in death also." So Margaret died saying:

"Shame on life."

MARGARET OF AUSTRIA (1497), who was on her way to marry the Spanish Infant, after being deserted by Charles VIII of France, bore on her arm the epitaph:

"Here lies Margaret, the gentle young lady,
Who had two husbands, and yet died a virgin."

Although almost drowned at sea, her ship happily escaped.

ANNE BOLEYN (1536), second wife of Henry VIII of England, said:

"Commend me to the King, and tell him he is constant in his course of advancing me. From a private gentlewoman he made me a Marchioness; and from a Marchioness a Queen. Now he hath left no higher degree of earthly honor; he hath made me a martyr."

As she came to her execution, she put her hands round her neck and laughing merrily said:

"I have heard say that the executioner was very good and I have a little neck."

On the block she prayed,

"O God, have pity on my soul: O God, have pity on my soul: O God, have pity — !"

CATHERINE OF ARAGON, first wife of Henry VIII, left a touching letter to her "dear lord, king and husband," part of which reads:

> "The hour of my death is now approaching. I cannot choose but out of the love I bear you advise you of your soul's health, which you ought to prefer before all consideration of the world or flesh whatsoever. For which yet you have cast me into many calamities, and yourself into many troubles. But I forgive you all; and pray God to do so likewise."

CATHERINE HOWARD, another of Henry VIII's wives, who died on the scaffold, turned to the headsman saying:

> "Pray hasten thy office . . . I die a Queen, but I would rather die the wife of Culpeper (previous lover). God have mercy on my soul. Good people, I beg of you pray for me."

LADY JANE GREY (1554), Queen of England for ten days. Owing to the uneasiness of Queen Mary, Lady Jane and her husband were beheaded the same day. From the block she addressed the bystanders and then committed herself to God. Her beautiful neck was bared, and after tying a handkerchief over her eyes and feeling for the block, she laid her head upon it, and as the axe was about to fall she prayed:

> "Lord, into Thy hands I commend my spirit."

MARY II (1689-1694), while Archbishop Tillotson was reading to her and paused to look at her:

> "My lord, why do you not go on. I am not afraid to die."

QUEEN JANE OF NAVARRE (1572), sometimes referred to as Jeanne D'Albrets, died saying:

> "Weep not for me, I pray you. God by this sickness calls me hence to enjoy a better life; and now I shall enter into the desired haven toward which this frail vessel of mine has been a long time steering."

QUEEN MARY OF ORANGE (1695), left this last word:

> "I thank God I have always carried this in my mind, that nothing was left to the last hour."

QUEEN MARY OF SCOTS (1587), prayed fervently for peace in the world, constancy to all suffering persecution, and for grace and the Holy Spirit in her last hour. Fervently she prayed for cruel Queen Elizabeth. Before the death stroke beheaded her, she exclaimed:

"Like as Thy arms, Lord Jesus Christ, were stretched out upon the Cross, even so receive me with the outstretched arms of Thy mercy."

QUEEN ELIZABETH OF ENGLAND (1603), sometimes called "The lion-hearted Elizabeth". It is said that she embodied the traits of a haughty temper, strong self-will, love of pomp and magnificence, combined with caution, prudence and suspicion. At her death she had about two thousand costly dresses in her wardrobe. Just before her death she uttered the words:

"All my possessions for one moment of time."

JANE D'ALBRETS (1562), Daughter of the Queen of Navarre:
"As I have lived, so am I resolved to die."

ANNE OF AUSTRIA (1666), on looking at her hands, celebrated for their beauty, said:

"Observe how they are swelled; time to depart."

ANNE HYDE, DUCHESS OF YORK (1671), who had secretly become Roman Catholic, turned to Bishop Blandford saying:

"I hope you continue still in truth? What is truth?"

As her agony increased, she repeated the word:

"Truth, truth, truth."

PRINCESS AMELIA, Daughter of George III:
"I could not wish for a better trust than in the merits of the Redeemer."

QUEEN ANNE (1714), repeated as she died:
"My poor brother — my dear brother, what will become of you?"

(She referred to The Old Pretender).

QUEEN CAROLINE (1737), addressing the distressed George II, said:

"Do not weep, you know you can marry again."

MADAME LOUISE (1787), daughter of Louis XV, died crying:
"To Paradise quickly, quickly, at full speed."

MARIE ANTOINETTE (1793), Queen of France, at her execution addressed her children:

"Farewell, my children, I go to your father."

Then accidentally she trod on the foot of Sanson, the executioner, and had, as her last word:

> "I beg your pardon, Sir."

EMPRESS JOSEPHINE (1814), wife of Napoleon I of France, by her farewell saying revealed what was close to her heart:

> "I can say with truth to all at my last moments that the first wife of Napoleon never caused a tear to flow."
> "Napoleon . . . Elba . . . Marie-Louise!"

JANE SEYMOUR. The last word attributed to this third consort of Henry VIII reads:

> "No, my head never committed any treason: but, if you want it, you can take it."

(As Jane died within two weeks of the birth of her son, Edward, the cause of unbounded delight to the King, it is doubtful whether this farewell saying is correct.)

LOUISE, QUEEN OF PRUSSIA (1810), died saying:

> "I am a Queen, but have not power to move my arms."

QUEEN AMELIA ELIZABETH CAROLINE (1821), wife of George IV of England:

> "Open the window! — pray!"

ELISABETH, sister of Louis XVI on her way to the guillotine, when her scarf fell from her neck, said:

> "I pray you, gentlemen, in the name of modesty, suffer me to cover my bosom."

PRINCESS CHARLOTTE (1817), requested that her husband at death might be laid by her side, expiring, said:

> "Is there any danger? I understand the meaning of that answer."

VI. Statesmen, Politicians, Patriots

Some of the most outstanding statesmen the world has known, whose government proved most beneficial for the world as a whole, were men who were not ashamed of their Christian faith and who in death left a clear witness that they were Christ's. Others there were, noble and just, who were not so pronounced in their interest in things spiritual.

FRANCIS BACON (1561-1626), was the English philosopher and statesman who worked consistently for the advancement of learning and contended that the only correct way to interpret Nature was by the induction of facts. In government circles he rose to be Lord Chancellor. A long line of thinkers have drawn inspiration from this great man who never substituted reason for faith. Bacon's genius was one of the glories of the Elizabethan age. Being a Christian, he had a peculiar affection for the *Psalms,* and dedicated his volume on *Certaine Psalmes* to George Herbert. Bacon's last word was an eloquent testimony to the Bible:

> "Thy creatures, O Lord, have been my books, but Thy Holy Scripture much more."

He left this word:

> "My name and memory I leave to men's charitable speeches, to foreign nations, and to the next age."

JAN VAN OLDEN BARNEVELDT, who died in 1619, was the Dutch statesman who earned the distinction of "The Father of Dutch Freedom and Religious Liberty." Because of jealousy on the part of Prince Maurice, Barneveldt was beheaded at the Hague in his 71st year and met his fate without regret or a sign of fear. As he bent his head to the executioner's sword, he exclaimed:

> "Oh, God, what then is man!"

THOMAS CROMWELL (1540), who became Earl of Essex, was the noted English statesman who was next to the King in power and influence. He was responsible for the digging up of the bones of Thomas à Becket and their burning as those of a traitor. Overambitious, Cromwell lost his influence and also his head, for he was executed. Historians tell us that as he died he said in a speech:

> "The Devil is ready to seduce us, and I have been seduced, but bear me witness that I die in the Catholic faith."

He uttered these words on the way to the scaffold:

> "Oh gentle Wyatt, good-by and pray to God for me. . . . Oh Wyatt, do not weep, for if I were not more guilty than thou wert, when they took me, I should not be in this pass."

His dying prayer was:

> "Oh, God, I prostrate myself to my deserved punishment; Lord, be merciful to Thy prostrate servant."

BENJAMIN FRANKLIN (1706-1790), was a man of many parts — printer, journalist, diplomat, philosopher and scientist. As a statesman, he had a share in the drafting of the American Declaration of Independence. Appearing before the Convention called to frame a Constitution for the United States, Franklin in a convincing manner declared that God governed in the affairs of men and quoted Psalm 127:1, "Except the Lord build the house, they labour in vain that build it," as he advocated political building under Divine guidance. When he came to the end of his fascinating career, all he could say as he expired was:

"A dying man can do nothing easy."

WILLIAM WILBERFORCE, who fought hard and long for the abolition of Negro slavery, was also a most sincere evangelical believer. One of his sons, describing his father's last days, said that in spite of distressing weakness, he seemed "like a person in the actual enjoyment of heaven within." He was constantly expressing gratitude to God and to those caring for him. On his last day, alluding to his bodily condition, Wilberforce said:

"I am in a very distressed state."

Consoling him, a friend nearby answered: "Yes, but you have your feet on the Rock." Wilberforce replied:

"I do not venture to speak so positively; but I hope I have."

STEPHEN GARDINER, although the Bishop of Winchester, was a cruel, bloodthirsty man who became a tool in the hands of Catholic rulers in the days of English martyrs. Becoming Lord Chancellor of England, Gardiner exercised tremendous power. On the day that Ridley and Latimer were burned at the stake, Gardiner was smitten with a fearful fatal disease and died in 1555 in terrible torments with curses on his lips. The last words to leave his blasphemous mouth were:

"I have sinned like Peter, but have not wept like him."

JOHN HAMPDEN (1594-1643), was the English statesman who with four other members of Parliament was arrested by Charles I, and who, in the Civil War that followed, took an active part and died from wounds received in action. Dying, he prayed:

"O Lord, save my bleeding country! Have these realms in Thy special keeping. Confound and level in the dust those who would rob the people of their liberty and lawful prerogatives. Let the King see his error, and turn the hearts of his wicked counsellors from the malice of their designs."

It is to such patriots like Hampden who were actuated by Christian principles that we owe our religious and civil liberty.

LORD GEORGE LYTTLETON, who died in 1773, was another British statesman who was not ashamed to own his Saviour's name and define His cause. Influenced by William Law's *Serious Call,* Lyttleton said of it that it was, "one of the finest books that ever was written." In his last testimony he affirmed that:

> "The evidence of Christianity, studied with attention, made me a firm believer of the Christian religion. I have erred and sinned, but have repented."

JULES MAZARIN (1602-1661), was the French statesman who succeeded Richelieu as First Minister of the Crown and whose foreign policy was conspicuously successful. The heavy taxation he imposed, however, led to the Civil War of the Fronde. Ambition proved the ruin of Mazarin who as he died lamented:

> "O! my poor soul! what will become of thee? Whither wilt thou go? Oh, were I permitted to live again, I would sooner be the humblest wretch in the ranks of mendicants than a courtier."

GABRIEL MIRABEAU (1749-1791), was the great French statesman during the Pre-Revolution period in France who could have prevented the terror of the Revolution. His unexpected death at 42 years of age with an unaccomplished task was a national calamity. He was likewise one of the greatest orators of his time. Alas, his farewell words lack that Christian fortitude enabling one to die in peace:

> "Give me more laudanum, that I may not think of eternity and of what is to come. I have an age of strength, but not a moment of courage."

PHILIP DE MORNAY (1549-1623), Lord of Plessia Marley, Councillor of State to Henry IV, was another French statesman and Huguenot who had his window opened toward Jerusalem. That he had a true appreciation of God's free grace is evident from his last word as he died in 1623:

> "Alas! What was there of mine in that work? Say not that it was I, but God by me. I laboured — yet not I, but the grace of God which was in me. Away with all merit, either in me or any other man whatsoever. I call for nothing but mercy — free mercy."

What better witness could one wish for as a believer comes to pass through the valley of the shadow of death?

AXEL OXENSTIERN (1583-1654), was the Swedish statesman who as Chancellor of Sweden exercised a tremendous influence both spiritually and politically in his country. As he died, he enjoined upon those at this deathbed this practical advice:

> "Make the study and practice of the Word of God your chief contentment and delight, as, indeed, it will be to every soul who savours the truth of God."

WILLIAM PITT (1759-1806), was the British statesman who became Prime Minister at the early age of 24. Renowned as an orator, he rallied the country during the war years of 1793-1806, and shouldered a heavy task with unshaken courage. Pitt was the bosom friend of William Wilberforce, another remarkable statesman who feared God. When Pitt, who became the Earl of Chatham, came to die at the comparatively young age of 47, his last word was a clear expression of his Christian faith:

> "I have, like other men, neglected too much to have any ground of hope that can be efficacious on a deathbed, but I throw myself on the mercy of God through the merits of Christ."

JOHN RANDOLPH (1773-1833), was an American statesman, well-known for his oratorical powers and most influential at a critical period in American history. Having neglected the interests of his own eternal welfare, his deathbed was not as peaceful as it might have been:

> "Remorse, remorse, remorse! Let me see the Word. Show me it in a dictionary. Write it then. Ah! remorse — you don't know what it means. I cast myself on the Lord Jesus Christ for mercy."

EDWARD SEYMOUR, who became Duke of Somerset, was another English statesman whose high principles cost him his life. In 1552 he was beheaded, and ere the axe fell he bravely said:

> "I desire you all to bear me witness that I die here in the faith of Jesus Christ, desiring you to help me with your prayers. Lord Jesus, save me!"

PHILIP SIDNEY was both a poet and statesman and master alike of the older learning and of the new discoveries of astronomy. J. R. Green says of him that he was "fair as he was brave, quick of wit as of affection, noble and generous in temper . . . his learning and his genius made him the center of the literary world which was springing to birth on English soil." Yet he flung away his life to save the English army in Flanders, and as he lay dying from a bulletwound a cup of water was pressed to his fevered lips. Seeing a soldier stretched out beside him Sidney said: "Give the water to him; his sufferings are greater than mine." Dying he exclaimed:

> "In me behold the end of this world. I would change my joy for the empire of the world."

SIR THOMAS SMITH, Secretary of State to Queen Elizabeth I who functioned as an Ambassador, was held in high repute for his sagacity as a statesman. When he died in 1577 he uttered a farewell message which multitudes who live only for this life should heed:

> "It is a matter of lamentation that men know not for what end they were born into the world until they are ready to go out of it."

HENRY VANE, the honorable English statesman who became Governor of Massachusetts, was arrested on his return to England and charged with influencing the Quakers to resist the government, and for this he was beheaded in 1662. His death was as noble as his life for he spoke thus before his head was severed from his body:

> "Blessed be the Lord that I have kept a conscience void of offence till this day. I bless the Lord that I have not deserted the righteous cause for which I suffer."

DANIEL WEBSTER of Massachusetts was the American orator and politician who represented the industrial and financial interests of the northeastern states in 1840. A leader of the Whig party, he was a firm nationalist. In 1852, knowing that death was not far distant, he dictated the following epitaph for his tombstone:

> "Lord, I believe; help Thou my unbelief."

THOMAS WENTWORTH, who became Earl of Strafford, was one who embodied "the very genius of tyranny". Ultimately the tide turned against him. The discovery of an Army plot sealed his fate. Tried for treason, he was found guilty and condemned to death. Great crowds gathered at the Tower, London, to witness his execution in 1641. Before the axe fell Wentworth said:

> "I know how to look death in the face and the people too. I thank God I am no more afraid of death, but as cheerfully put off my doublet at this time as ever I did when I went to bed."

The great multitudes were jubilant over his death and cried, "His head is off! His head is off!" Alas, life was cheap in those days!

BULSTRODE WHITELOCKE was active in state affairs during "The Long Parliament" in England, 1640-1644. He was also one of the trusted historians of Puritan England. That his heart was fixed, trusting in the Lord, is evident from what he said before he died in 1676:

> "I have ever thought there has been one true religion in the world; and that is the work of the Spirit of God in the hearts and souls of men. Since my retirement from the greatness and hurries of the world I have felt something of the work and comfort of it."

SIR EDWARD COKE (1553-1634), Lord Chief Justice of England, prosecutor of Essex and Rayleigh, said when dying:

> "Thy kingdom come, Thy will be done."

PATRICK HENRY (1736-1799), the renowned American statesman and orator, just before his death, remarked to a friend who found him reading the Bible:

> "Here is a Book worth more than all the other books which were ever printed; yet it is my misfortune never to have, till lately, found time to read it with proper attention and feeling."

THOMAS WOLSEY (1475-1530), Cardinal of the Roman Catholic Church and one of the most eminent statesman during the reign of Henry VIII, is worthy of mention if only for the confession he made on his deathbed. As he lay dying, he is reported to have said:

> "If I had served God as diligently as I have done the king, He would not have given me over in my grey hairs. But this is the just reward that I must receive for my diligent pains and studies that I have had to do him service, and not regarding my services to God, but only to satisfy his pleasure."

Had he served his God as diligently as he had his unworthy king, Wolsey would have left a more inspiring record behind him.

SIR THOMAS MOORE (1535), author of *Utopia,* was brought to the scaffold for his opposition to Henry VIII's divorce of Catherine in favor of Anne Boleyn. Noticing that the scaffold shook, he said to his executioner:

> "See me safe up. For my coming down I can shift for myself."

Then when the executioner asked his forgiveness, Moore with perfect composure replied: "Thou art to me the greatest benefit I can receive."

ROBERT CECIL (1612), who became Earl of Salisbury, said to his friend, Sir William Cope:
> "Ease and pleasure quake to hear of death; but my life full of cares and miseries, desireth to be dissolved."

A DUKE OF BUCKINGHAM, professed atheist, confessed as he died:
> "I sported with the holy name of heaven. Now I am haunted by remorse, and, I fear, forsaken by God."

RICHELIEU (1585-1642), French statesman and Cardinal, was asked by the priest, "Do you pardon all your enemies?" He replied:
> "I have none save those of the State."

To his niece Richelieu said:
> "I beg you to retire. Do not allow yourself to suffer the pain of seeing me die."

JOHN GRAHAM of Clavert House (1689), referring to the battle at Killiecrankie, said, "How goes the day?" A friend standing by said, "Well for the King; but I'm sorry for your Lordship." To which Graham replied:
> " 'Tis the less matter for me, seeing the day goes well for my master."

CHARLOTTE CORDAY (1793), French patriot, asked of her executioner, "Did you find it a long journey?" Then he tried to intercept her view of the guillotine, and she bent forward, saying:
> "I have reason to be curious, I have never seen one before."

GEORGES DANTON (1794), French revolutionist, said to himself, "Let us go, Danton, no weakness." To his executioner he said:
> "You will show my head to the people. It will be worth the trouble."

JOHN WILKES (1797), renowned English politician, asked his daughter for something to drink and murmured as he died:
> "I drink to the health of my beloved and excellent daughter."

WILLIAM PITT (Junior) (1708-1778), famous statesman, is credited with two farewell messages:

> "Oh my country! How I leave my country!"
> "I think I could eat one of Bellamy's pork pies."

CHARLES TALLEYRAND (1838), French statesman. As Louis Philippe left his bedside Talleyrand said:

> "It is beautiful to die in this house, where the king has paid a visit."

ROBERT OWEN (1858), English politician, uttered one brief sentence:

> "Relief has come."

RAMON NARVAEZ (1868), Spanish politician and patriot, on being exhorted by a priest to forgive his enemies, replied:

> "I have no enemies. I have shot them all."

GEORGE MAZZINI (1872), Italian patriot, died saying:

> "Yes, yes, I believe in God."

BENJAMIN DISRAELI (1881), famed British politician, who was told the Queen wanted to visit his deathbed, said:

> "Why should I see her? She will only want to give a message to Albert."

CHARLES PARNELL (1891), Irish politician, spoke of the "sunny land" where he and his wife would go as soon as he was better:

> "We will be so happy, Queenie; there are so many things happier than politics."

In his sleep he murmured:

> "The Conservative Party . . . Kiss me, sweet wife, and I will try to sleep a little."

CECIL RHODES (1902), British administrator, whose life was so full of dreams and deeds and who wrote his name across a continent, voiced the lament:

> "So little done, so much to do."

EARL OF LEICESTER:

> "By the arm of St. James, it is time to die."

ROBESPIERRE (1758-1794), another French revolutionist, who was taunted with the death of Danton, cried:

> "Cowards! Why did you not defend him?"

HUMBOLDT (1767-1835), German statesman, traveler and naturalist:

"How grand these rays! They seem to beckon earth to heaven."

CATESBY (1573-1605), English politician and one of the conspirators in the Gunpowder Plot, died saying:

"Stand by me, Tom, and we will die together."

When the DUKE OF HAMILTON was dying, his old tutor came to see him. They were talking about astronomy, and the Duke said:

"Within a little while, sir, I will know more about the stars than all of you put together."

Then, looking at his brother, he said:

"Within a few hours, perhaps, you will be a duke and I will be a king."

JOHN BROOKS (1825), Governor of Massachusetts, affirmed on his deathbed:

"I see nothing terrible in death. I'm looking to the future; I have no fears. I know in whom I have believed. I look back upon my past life with humility. I am sensible of many imperfections that cleave to me. I now rest my soul on the mercy of my Creator, through the only Mediator, His Son, our Lord. Oh, what a ground of hope there is in that saying of Paul that God is in Christ reconciling the guilty world to Himself, not imputing their trespasses unto them."

VII. American Presidents

After the discovery of the New World with its vast expanse and undreamed of potentialities, thousands of pilgrims, exiles and immigrants braved the perils of the deep to become the foundation of the now great American Republic. As the majority of those who crossed the ocean from Britain and Europe were forced to leave because of deep religious convictions, a new nation developed with freedom to worship and serve God unshackled by autocratic church or state laws. Thus, into the New World there poured a stream of spiritual life which, as America expanded, gathered momentum until today it is as a torrent surging through the nation. Because the founding fathers of the American Constitution were men with a strong religious bent, it is not surprising to find Scriptural truth woven into the Constitution. Many of the succeeding presidents were

God-fearing men who recognized that righteousness was able to exalt their nation. Adhering to the main purpose of this volume, dealing with the last words of distinguished people, let us see what is recorded of the dying testimony of some American presidents.

GEORGE WASHINGTON (1732-1799), the first President of the United States, had an ancestry going back through six centuries of English history. George Washington was born February 22, 1732. It was true in his case that "the boy is father to the man" for, brought up to observe the lessons of religion and virtue, George became a man of high force of character. His outlook upon his service as a soldier and administrator were summed up in a letter he wrote to Governor Trumbull of Connecticut:

> "The cause of our common country calls us both to an active and dangerous duty; Divine Providence, which wisely orders the affairs of men, will enable us to discharge it with fidelity and success."

The earthly life of George Washington, "Father of his country", closed somewhat unexpectedly on December 14, 1799, in the 68th year of his age. He died from the effects of a severe cold. Jefferson, a later U.S. President, said of Washington when he heard of his death:

> "His integrity was most pure: his justice the most flexible, I have ever known — no motives of interest or consanguinity, of friendship or hatred, being able to bias his decision. He was in every sense of the word, a wise, a good and a great man."

Having lived as under the Great Taskmaster's eye, Washington was well prepared for his exit from earth. At the end he said to his physician:

> "Doctor, I have been dying a long time; my breath cannot last long — but I am not afraid to die."

On the tablet over the door of his tomb at Mount Vernon, are the words of the Saviour Washington trusted in —

> "I am the resurrection and the life, He that believeth in Me, though he were dead, yet shall he live."

JOHN ADAMS (1735-1826), who succeeded Washington as President, came from a hardy Puritan stock. At 16, he entered Harvard College and graduated at 20. While at college he was esteemed for his integrity, energy and ability. After teaching for a while he entered Law, and his remarkable legal talent was in constant demand. Entering public life he served in several offices until the nation called him to the Presidency. At the age of 83 Adams lost his wife, and her death cast a deep shadow over his life, for his beloved Abigail and he had lived in great peace and had been mutual helpers to one another. In his declining years Adams grew more and more tranquil. He was so gratified to watch the rising recognition of his son's worth and lived to see him elected president of the government he had done so much to found. He died on July 4, 1826, just fifty years after the Declaration of Independence. Having a great admiration for his compatriot, Thomas Jefferson, the last words of Adams were:

"Thomas Jefferson still survives."

But unknown to Adams, Jefferson had died an hour before Adams was called Home.

THOMAS JEFFERSON (1743-1826), the third President, had ancestors on his father's side of good, religious Welsh stock. Jefferson was soon recognized as one of the outstanding scholars of his time. Successful as a lawyer, he became a legislator. On February 8, 1797, he was elected Vice-President under John Adams, and on March 4, 1801, became President of the United States.

Jefferson had a deep reverence for the Bible of which he wrote:

"I have always said, and always will say, that the studious perusal of the Sacred Volume will make us better citizens, better fathers and better husbands."

He left behind him a proof of his diligent study of the teachings of our Lord in the form of a scrap book, the title of which is: *The Life and Morals Of Jesus Of Nazareth, Extracted Textually from the Gospels in Greek, Latin, French and English.*

In a letter to John Adams in 1813, Jefferson sums up the Gospels as being "the most sublime and benevolent code of morals which has ever been offered to man." Thus, when he came to die, Thomas Jefferson, author of the Declaration of Independence, was fully prepared to meet the Christ he had sought to follow. His death came July 4, 1826, and after taking affectionate farewells of members of his family, his last audible words were:

"I resign my soul to God, my daughter to my Country. Lord, now lettest Thou Thy servant depart in peace."

Congressman Manning said of Jefferson after he had passed away:

> "Heaven, that lent him genius, was repaid."

JOHN QUINCY ADAMS, son of John Adams, America's second President, was born on July 11, 1767. After practicing law for a while, Quincy turned to writing, and his papers revealed great political and literary ability, moral character of a high order, a knowledge of foreign countries and knowledge of the language and etiquette of courts and diplomacy. Thus, at the age of 27, he was chosen as Foreign Minister by George Washington. Thereafter, he held several high offices and on March 4, 1825, was elected sixth President of the United States in succession to James Monroe. John Quincy Adams was a genuine Puritan, deeply and consistently religious, and a close student of the Bible. He once wrote:

> "So great is my veneration for the Bible that the earlier my children begin to read it the more confident will be my hopes that they will prove useful citizens to their country, and respectable members of society."

Although somewhat Unitarian in his outlook, he yet had broad sympathies for all Christians and could confess that he believed:

> "The Christian religion to be . . . the religion of wisdom, virtue, equity and humanity, let the blackguard Paine say what he will: . . . I have examined all, as well as my narrow sphere, my straitened means, and my busy life would allow me, and the result is that the Bible is the best Book in the World. It contains more of my philosophy than all the libraries I have seen."

One of America's grandest products and honored all over the world as one of the greatest and best of men, John Quincy Adams was stricken with paralysis. After this attack on November 20, 1846, another followed February, 21, 1848. Unconscious for two hours, he regained consciousness and was heard to say:

> "This is the end of earth, I am content."

Thus, at the age of 81, this unique man closed a life which will ever be worthy of the profoundest study and emulation by would-be politicians. A tablet over his tomb reads:

> "A Son worthy of his Father, a Citizen shedding glory on his Country, A Scholar ambitious to advance Mankind, this Christian sought to walk humbly in the sight of God."

ANDREW JACKSON, born March 15, 1767, died June 8, 1845, was of Scotch-Irish descent. "To all human appearance nothing was more improbable than that this babe of sorrow, poverty and extreme humility would ever rise to greatness and honour among men." As a youth he learned city ways of dissipation. He entered a law office and later became a lawyer, and in 1796 he was elected a member of the U.S. House of Representatives. In 1842, when war with England broke out, he became General Jackson and because of his military genius and triumphs became the hero of the American people. When he became the seventh President of America, he failed to exhibit the sterling qualities of leadership his predecessors had manifested. In his later years he became a devout Christian, and the evening of his life was a benediction. He loved to read the Bible, and heaven was near and dear to him. Just before he died, he was heard to murmur:

> "My sufferings, though great, are nothing in comparison with those of my Saviour, through whose death I look for everlasting life."

Andrew Jackson was one of those rebels Christ transformed into a priest and a king through His redemptive Gospel.

WILLIAM HENRY HARRISON is the next President whose last saying is preserved for posterity. Born in Virginia, February 9, 1773, the ninth President was the son of a signer of the Declaration of Independence. An ardent friend of human liberty, Harrison became prominent in the abolition of slavery. After a conspicuous military career, he entered politics and became governor of "The Indian Territory". In 1816 he was elected to the House of Representatives, and on March 4, 1841, was inaugurated President of the United States of America. Alas, however, his term of office only lasted a month. He caught a severe cold which developed into pleurisy, and on April 4, 1841, William Henry Harrison's life terminated. His unexpected death shocked the nation for he held the hearts and hopes of the people. The condition of the country called for a man with his excellence of character, devoted patriotism, talents and success, but Providence willed it otherwise. As the darkling shadows crept around him Harrison was heard to say:

> "I wish you to understand the true principles of government. I wish them carried out, and ask for nothing more."

ZACHARY TAYLOR, twelfth President, was born November 24, 1784, in Orange County, Virginia, and grew up in the wilderness. After a most conspicuous military career during which his genius was revealed, General Taylor became the nation's choice as President in succession to James Knox Polk. His inauguration took place March 4, 1849, but his term of office did not last long. On July 4, 1850, he attended the laying of the corner-stone of the Washington Monument. The heat of the day brought on a fatal sickness, and on July 9 the old soldier who had a host of friends and left behind him not an enemy in the world died saying:

> "I am not afraid to die: I am ready: I have endeavored to do my duty."

FRANKLIN PIERCE, the fourteenth President, who was born November 23, 1804, and died October 8, 1869, was not a success in office. His extreme sympathy for slavery made him most unpopular. At his funeral his favorite hymn was sung:

> "While Thee I seek, Protecting Power,
> Be my vain wishes stilled,
> And may this consecrated hour
> With better hope be filled."

JAMES BUCHANAN, son of a poor Irish immigrant, was born April 22, 1791. After a college education he was admitted to the bar and soon attained a lucrative practice. In 1820 he was elected to the lower house of Congress, in 1833 became a Senator, and in 1860 became the fifteenth President of the United States. Although he rose from obscurity to the highest office of his nation, Buchanan was destitute of those qualities making for a great president. One wrote of him, "He was a body of political rottenness in the chair of state — a pitiable shame to American manhood." Retiring from office, he lived in quiet obscurity until his death, June 1, 1868. His last words were:

> "O Lord Almighty, as Thou wilt."

ABRAHAM LINCOLN was a man of unique and providential character and has a niche all his own in American history. Born February 2, 1809, in Kentucky, Lincoln had a godly mother whose memory he held in profoundest respect. Speaking to a close friend one day about his early life, tears filled his eyes as he said:

"All that I am or hope to be I owe to my angel mother — blessings on her memory."

Soldier, surveyor, legislator, lawyer, congressman — all of these spheres prepared him for the office of president, and on March 4, 1861, he became America's sixteenth President and dedicated himself to the emancipation of the slaves. To a body of clergymen who sought his help he said:

"Whatever shall appear to be God's will, I will do."

On April 15, 1865, seeking release for an hour from his burdening cares, he went to a theatre where he was shot in the back and side of his head by John Wilkes Booth. Lincoln lived in a state of unconsciousness till seven the next morning, breathed his last, and dying left a nation in tears. Although there is no record of the last words he uttered before he was shot, we know that he was a deeply religious man. A short while before he died he asked an old friend, Joshua F. Speed, to spend the night with him. Arriving he found Lincoln reading a book. It was the Bible. Speed said, "I am pleased to see you are so profitably engaged." Looking up with that serious face of his, Lincoln replied:

"Yes, I am profitably engaged. Take all of this book on reason that you can, and the rest on faith, and you will, I am sure, live and die a happier and better man."

Among other presidents whose dying words have been preserved, we have

JAMES MADISON (1751-1836), sometimes called "The Father Of The Constitution" and who was the one who had the White House painted white after the British burned it. Madison met death somewhat humorously saying:

"I always talk better lying down."

WILLIAM McKINLEY (1843-1901), the twenty-fifth President of America, who earned the title "Liberator of Cuba", had a blissful yet tragic end. Six months after his inauguration he was shot by an anarchist at an Exposition in Buffalo, New York, and lingered for eight days, dying September 14, 1901. His farewell word was:

"Nearer, my God to Thee, Nearer to Thee. It is the Lord's way. Good-bye all!"

THOMAS HENDRICKS (1819-1885), Vice-President, died saying:

"At rest at last. Now I am free from pain."

VIII. Famous Women

MADAME DE FONTAINE — Martel, friend of Voltaire, died saying:

> "My consolation at this hour, I am sure that somewhere in the world, someone is making love . . . what is the time?"

"Two o'clock."

> "God be praised, whatever time it is, somewhere lovers keep their tryst."

MADAME DU DEFFUND, French noblewoman, confessed:

> "Priest, I accuse myself of having violated the ten commandments of God and of having committed the seven mortal sins."

Another French lady of high society, whose confessor remarked that her lover's coach still stood at the door, uttered as her last word:

> "Ah, my father, how happy you have made me. I thought I had forgotten it."

VICOMTESSE D'HOUDETOT, daughter-in-law of Rousseau's Madame D'Houdetot, left the sad lament:

> "I regret my life."

OLYMPIA FULVIA MORATA, an Italian lady illustrious for her godliness and culture, was born in 1526. She married a physician and retired to Germany where she died at 29 years of age after suffering severe calamities with Christian fortitude. Her husband wrote of her cheerfulness of mind and the inexpressibly sweet smile on her features. It was to be expected that a woman who had manifested the beauty of holiness in her short but troubled life should die in triumph. The last words leaving her lips made a profound impression upon her husband, who recorded them for posterity:

> "For the last seven years Satan has not ceased to use every means to induce me to relinquish my faith, but now it would appear that he has lost his darts, for I have no other sensation in this hour of my departure than of undisturbed repose and tranquility of soul in Jesus Christ."

SAINT MONICA sweetly murmured:

> "In peace I will sleep with Him and take my rest."

MARIA THERESA, celebrated nun of 1780, said:
"Your Majesty rests uncomfortably.
I am comfortable enough to die."

IX. Famous Authors

CHARLOTTE BRONTE (1816-1855), was one of the famous
Bronté sisters, all of whom were writers and poets. A few
months before her death, after a youth full of trial and sorrow,
she married, and her sorrows seemed to be over. But her cup of
earthly happiness was not to last. She became very ill and
heard her husband praying that her life might be spared. She
whispered:
"I am not going to die, am I? God will not separate us, we
have been so happy."

ELIZABETH BROWNING (1806-1861), a poet in her own right,
was the wife of Robert Browning. It was Elizabeth who wrote,
"We want the touch of Christ's hand upon our literature." The
Brownings certainly knew what it was to write under such a
Divine touch. Full of assurance that glory was ahead, she refused to contemplate death.
"I cannot look on the earthside of death. When I look death-
wards, I look over death and upwards, or I can't look that way
at all."

Elizabeth exclaimed as she died:
"It is beautiful."

ROBERT BURNS (1759-1796), the Scottish poet, ranks as one of
the two greatest figures in Scottish literature, the other being
Sir Walter Scott. That he appreciated, but failed to experience,
the power of the Christian faith, appears now and again in his
works. When he died at the age of 37, he said to his wife,
hourly expecting her sixth child:
"I have but a moment to speak to you, my dear."

To James Maclure, his attendant, who gave Burns his medicine
and saw the poet spread out his hands and die, he said:
"'Be a good man; be virtuous, be religious; nothing else will
give you any comfort when you come to be here."

GEORGE GORDON LORD BYRON (1788-1824), another outstanding figure in the long train of English poets, gained a love and
knowledge of the Bible which he never lost. He was only 36

years of age — a year younger than Burns — when he died and uttered as his last word:

> "Come, come, no weakness; let's be a man to the last. Shall I sue for mercy?"

then, in *Greek*, he said:

> "Now I must sleep."

THOMAS CARLYLE (1795-1881), British historian and one of the greatest of Victorian writers, acknowledged the unrivaled charm of the Psalms and was the one who translated Luther's German version of Psalm 46 into the English we love to sing: "A Mighty Fortress is our God." Although he could write feelingly of Christianity, Carlyle lacked the assurance of that eternal life Christ offers mankind. Thus, as he came to die, he left the world this note of despair:

> "I am as good without hope and without fear; a sad old man gazing into the final chasm."

JOHN MILTON (1608-1674), the English poet who ranks with Shakespeare and Wordsworth as one of the three greatest poets of England, had a sonorous grandeur suiting the theme of God's dealing with the world and with mankind. His famous *Paradise Lost* enshrines in stately verse the general scheme of Puritan theology. Because of the Godward aspect of his life, we can appreciate his farewell saying:

> "Death is the great key that opens the palace of Eternity."

HENRY WADSWORTH LONGFELLOW (1807-1882), the most famous of American Puritan poets, has an unchallengeable position among American writers. Having the Christian outlook on life both here and hereafter, Longfellow left us this testimony on the continuity of life beyond the grave:

> "There is no death;
> What seems so is transition."

CHARLES CHURCHILL, who died in 1764, was the English poet and satirist given to every kind of loose living, and whose literary productions were rough, ironical and insolent in tone. In his last hours, conscience-stricken, he regretted his lost life and the prostitution of his craft and died saying:

> "What a fool I have been."

JOHN CLARE, the Northamptonshire peasant and uneducated

poet who was one of England's sweetest singers of Nature, died in 1864 saying:

"I want to go Home."

WILLIAM COWPER (1731-1800), the English poet whose life was clouded by melancholia which resulted at times in fits of insanity, gave the world such superb literary compositions as "John Gilpin" and "The Task." It was Cowper who translated into English those spiritual songs from the gifted pen of Madam Guyon. As a hymn-writer, Cowper wrote many expressive hymns including "There Is a Fountain Filled with Blood." In his dying moments he rejected a refreshing cordial and died murmuring:

"What can it signify."

WENTWORTH DILLON, who became Earl of Roscommon, was another poet whose anchor was fixed within the veil. When he died in 1684, his last words were the language from one of his own hymns:

"My God, my Father, and my Friend
Do not forsake me in the end."

CHRISTIAN F. GELLERT (1715-1769), the German philosopher and versatile writer wrote many hymns including, "Jesus Lives, and I with Him." His *Fables* was one of the most popular books in Germany during the Seventeenth Century. Triumph in Christ was his when he died at Leipzig, where he had been Professor of Theology at the University. In his last moments Gellert requested:

"Only repeat to me the name of Jesus. Whenever I hear it or pronounce it myself I feel myself refreshed with fresh joy. God be praised, only one hour more."

JOHANN W. VON GOETHE (1749-1832), the renowned German man of letters of whom it was said, "To that man was given . . . a life in the Divine idea of the World." Cast in the Shakespearian mold, Goethe was the real founder of German literature. Among his great works we have "Faust," "Maxims And Reflections," and "Truth And Fiction." When he came to breathe his last he uttered one last request:

"Open the shutter and let in more light."

GOLDING, an English poet who died about 1590, whose history is buried in obscurity, welcomed the next world in the words:

"This is Heaven! I not only feel the climate, but I breathe the fine ambrosial air of Heaven, and soon shall enjoy the company."

MADAM JEANNE GUYON, who suffered much persecution from the leaders of the Roman Catholic reaction group, wrote many of her spiritual songs in her prison cell at Vincennes. Through many trials she came to the attitude of entire dependence upon God. "O my Lord," she prayed, "Thou didst continually defend my heart against all kinds of enemies." When she died, her heart leaped at the thought of seeing her beloved Master face to face:

"If my work is done, I think I am ready to go. I have already one foot in the stirrup, and am ready to mount as my Heavenly Father pleases."

GEORGE HERBERT (1593-1633), the quaint English divine and poet, was in temperament and character more typical of the Elizabethan age in which he was born. When he died he repeated the verse:

"Forsake me not when my strength faileth" (Ps. 71:8),

and committed his soul to God in the familiar words:

"Into Thy hands I commend my spirit."

To friends around his bed, George Herbert said:

"I shall be free from sin and all the temptations and anxieties that attend it: and this being fact, I shall dwell with men made perfect — dwell where these eyes shall see my Master and Saviour."

THOMAS HOOD (1799-1845), the British poet remembered as one of the great technical experts in English verse, is best remembered for his "Bridge of Sighs". His last word was:

"Lord, say, 'Arise, take up thy cross and follow Me.' "

JOHN KEATS (1795-1821), the English poet, was one of the supreme singers of all time. He left no clear witness as to his Christian faith but simply said as he died:

"I feel the daisies growing over me."

JOHN KITTO (1804-1854), the renowned English Biblical writer, met with an accident when but 13 years old which caused total deafness for the rest of his life. He gave himself to Biblical works, such as "Hours With My Bible," that have immortalized his name. As his decrease drew near, he longed to be taken and asked friends near to:

> "Pray God to take me soon."

EDGAR ALLEN POE (1809-1849), is the American author and poet credited with having pioneered the detective story. It is recorded that he uttered as he died the brief word:

> "Rest, shore, no more."

FRANCES QUARLES (1592-1644), became a servant to Queen Elizabeth of Bohemia and secretary to Archbishop Usher. He espoused the cause of Charles I, but lost all in the fall of that monarch. He is best remembered as a sacred poet, whose lines are often quaint yet noble. As the heavenly gates were about to open to receive the poet, he prayed:

> "O, sweet Saviour of the World, let Thy last words upon the Cross be my last words in this world — 'Into Thy hands I commend my spirit.' What I cannot utter with my mouth, accept from my heart and soul."

CLAUDIUS SALMASIUS, the distinguished French classical scholar, made this confession at the end:

> "I have lost a world of time! Had I one year more, it should be spent in perusing David's *Psalms* and Paul's *Epistles*. Mind the world less, and God more."

TORQUATO TASSO (1544-1595), a noted Italian poet, certainly entertained the hope of eternal life through Christ as his last word indicates:

> "This is the crown with which I hope to be crowned — the glory of the blessed in Heaven."

JAMES USHER (1581-1656), was the Irish Archbishop who became famous as a Biblical chronologist and gave the dates found in earlier Bible translations. A man of remarkable gifts, Usher authored many profitable works. During his life he said that he hoped to die with the language of the publican on his lips, and his wish was fulfilled:

> "O, Lord, forgive me, especially my sins of omission. 'God be merciful to me a sinner!' "

WILLIAM WORDSWORTH (1770-1850), was the British poet who was made Poet Laureate in 1843. It was from the valleys and rolling hills of Westmorland that he drew the healing power to

be found in his poems of solitude, one of which ends with the lines —
> "Shall in the grave Thy love be known,
> In death Thy faithfulness."

Wordsworth's last word was:
> "Is that Dora?"

CHARLES REEDE (1814-1884), was the English novelist and journalist who, persuaded to read the Bible through by Matthew Arnold, did so, and through reading became a Christian. When dying, Reede said:
> "Amazing, amazing glory! I am having Paul's understanding."

Reede wrote his own tombstone epitaph in which he cited a most logical and scriptural argument for eternal life and future happiness based upon John 6:37 and 1 John 2:1.

HORACE GREELEY, journalist and founder of *The New York Tribune,* uttered these words when dying:
> "I know that my Redeemer liveth."

WALTER SCOTT (1771-1832), the Scottish poet and novelist, rose to fame with his *Waverley Novels.* Just before his death he asked to be taken into his library and placed by the window, that he might look upon his much-loved river — The Tweed. Then he asked Lockhart, his son-in-law, to read to him.
> "What book shall I read?" asked Lockhart.

"What book?" replied the dying man, "there is but one, the Bible."

Lockhart read to the renowned writer from the incomparable 14th chapter of John. Scott listened with mild devotion, and at the end of the reading said:
> "Well, this is a great comfort. I have followed you distinctly, and I feel as if I was to be myself again."

LEW WALLACE (1827-1905), author of that remarkable book *Ben Hur,* had the sentence from "The Lord's Prayer" on his lips as he died:
> "Thy will be done."

LORENZO DE MEDICI, the famous Poet-Prince of Florence, died in 1492, saying:
> "Pursue the line of conduct marked out by the strictest integ-

rity, as regards the interests of the whole, nor the wishes of a part of the community."

ROBERT LOUIS STEVENSON (1850-1894), the British author, was one of the greatest story-tellers of his day and a master of beautiful language. Stevenson died at his beloved Samoa at 44 years of age from his lifelong disease of consumption. Just before he breathed his last, he gathered his household together and prayed:

> "Behold with favor, O Lord, the weak men and women gathered together in the peace of this roof. When the day returns God would call them with morning faces and morning hearts, eager to labor, eager to be happy if happiness should be their portion."

JAMES MATTHEW BARRIE (1860-1937), the Scottish novelist and dramatist, stands out as one of the most conspicuous writers of a past century. In his works, so full of pathos, he never journeyed far from his religious upbringing and inner convictions. While his own last words are not known, the way a person should die is described in *Margaret Ogilvy*, of whose end Barrie wrote:

> "They knew now that she was dying. She told them to fold up the christening robe, and almost sharply watched them put it away, and then for some time she talked of the long, lovely life that had been hers, and of Him to Whom she owed it. She said 'Good-by' to them all and at last turned her face to the side where her best beloved had lain, and for over an hour she prayed. They only caught the words now and again, and the last they heard were *God* and *Love*. I think God was smiling when He took her to Him, as He had so often smiled at her during those seventy-six years."

WILLIAM SHAKESPEARE (1564-1616), the world's outstanding figure in literature, of whose life, times and works a whole library of books has been written, lived near his Bible as the numerous quotations from it in his plays and dramas prove. His end came when he was but 52 years of age. His last will and testament prepared and signed in March, 1616, revealed his faith in God, as the first paragraph proves:

> "I commend my soul into the hands of God my Creator, hoping and assuredly believing, through the only merits of Jesus Christ my Saviour, to be made partaker of life everlasting; and my body to the earth, whereof it is made."

SAND (1803-1876), a French author:

"Leave the plot green, and do not cover the grave with bricks or stone."

MADAME ROLLAND (1866-1944), French authoress;

"O liberty! What crimes are committed in thy name!"

FRANCOIS RABELIAS (1494-1553), the French humorist writer:

"Let down the curtain, the farce is over."

BLAISE PASCALL (1623-1662), the French mathematician and philosopher:

"My God, forsake me not."

HEINE (1797-1856), German poet and critic and man of letters, uttered this cry of completion:

"My book! My book!"

DR. SAMUEL JOHNSON (1709-1784), the lexicographer author, said to his doctor, who hoped he was better:

"No, sir, you cannot conceive with what acceleration I advance towards death . . . Give me a direct answer. Tell me plainly, can I recover?"

Replied the doctor, "By nothing short of a miracle."

"Then I will take no more physic — not even opiates,"

said Johnson.

"I have prayed that I may render up my soul to God unclouded."

WILLIAM HAZLITT (1778-1830), renowned English author and essayist:

"Well, I've had a happy life."

CHARLES LAMB (1775-1834), English critic and essayist, murmured as he sank into death as placidly as into sleep, the names of his friends:

"Moxon, Proctor,"

and others.

MME. MAURICE DUFIN, mother of George Sand, and well-known French writer of 1837, said:

"Please tidy my hair."

HAYDON, another writer, committing suicide, left his last thoughts on paper, part of which we cite:

"No man should use certain evil for probable good, however good the object. Evil is the prerogative of the Deity . . . Wellington never used evil if the good was not certain."

MAX MULLER (1823-1900), British (German born) writer and philologist:

"I am *so* tired."

OSCAR WILDE (1856-1900), Irish author:

"I am dying, as I have lived, beyond my means."

JOEL CHANDLER HARRIS (1848-1908), American writer, on being asked how he felt, said:

"I am about the extent of a tenth of a gnat's eyebrow better."

COUNT TOLSTOY (1828-1910), Russian novelist, philosopher and mystic:

"But the peasants, how do peasants die?"

ALICE MEYNELL (1847-1922), English poet and essayist, wife of Wilfred Meynell, English journalist and biographer;

"This is not tragic. I am happy."

BOILEAU (1636-1711), French critic and poet who pursued his poetic calling to the end, had this to say:

"It is a great consolation to a poet on the point of death that he has never written a line injurious to good morals."

ANDREW MARVELL (1621-1678), father of the poet of the same name, was drowned in crossing the River Humber by ferry, with a pair of lovers on their way to be wed. As the boat left the land, with a sudden premonition, he cried:

"Ho, Heaven!"

and flung his stick ashore.

VINCENT HUNT (1784-1859), son of poet Leigh Hunt, after taking a cup of cold water, uttered, as he died:

"I drink to the morning."

JOSEPH ADDISON (1672-1719), English poet and essayist, said to his stepson, Warwick:

"See in what peace a Christian can die."

ALEXANDER POPE (1688-1744), another well-known English poet, left this nugget of truth:

"There is nothing that is meritorious but friendship, virtue, and indeed, friendship is only a part of everything."

JOHANN SCHILLER (1759-1805), German poet and dramatist, was asked how he felt.

"Calmer and calmer."

After a short sleep he opened his eyes for a moment and said:
"Many things are growing plain and clear to me,"
and then fell into the sleep of death.

DANTE ROSSETTI (1830-1894), English poet and artist, murmured:
"I believe I shall die tonight. Yesterday I wished to die, but today I must confess that I do not."

WILLIAM BLAKE (1757-1827), the British poet, artist and mystic, whose love for drawing was fostered by his parents who recognized his gift, near his death said:
"My beloved, they are not mine — no, they are not mine."
"I cannot think of death as more than the going out of one room into another."

As he was sinking, the artist in him came to life and he cried suddenly to his wife:
"Stay as you are! You have ever been an angel to me, I will draw you."

Seizing his pencil he started to sketch his beloved Catherine to whom he had been married exactly 45 years, but the sketch remained unfinished. Blake lay back in bed, sang a hymn and praising like a saint, entered heaven.

GEORGE CRABBE (1754-1832), another English poet, left us with a very brief but confident farewell:
"All is well."

THOMAS L. BEDDOES (1803-1849), English poet and dramatist who poisoned himself while at Zurich, was found with this note in his bosom:
"My dear Phillip, I am food for what I am good for — worms."

After instructions about his will, he commissioned a friend to look at a manuscript, then finished his farewell message by saying:
"I ought to have been among other good things a poet. Life was too great a bore on one peg (leg) and that a bad one."

CHARLES DICKENS (1812-1870), English novelist whose name and works will never be forgotten, declared in his will:

> "I commit my soul to the mercy of God, through our Lord and Saviour Jesus Christ, and I exhort my dear children humbly to try and guide themselves by the teaching of the New Testament."

To his sister-in-law, who urged him to lie down, he said:

> "Yes, on the ground."

EMILY DICKINSON (1830-1886), American poetess, simply said:

> "I must go in, the fog is rising."

JOHN G. WHITTIER (1807-1892), was the American poet whose pen was used to arouse the conscience of the North against slavery. "Icabod" was among the best of his poems. It is said that his last message consisted of six words:

> "Give my love to the world."

OLIVER GOLDSMITH (1728-1774), the English author whose doctor, surprised at the rate of his fever, asked:

> "Is your mind at ease?"
> "No, it is not," he replied and died.

BENJAMIN JOWETT (1817-1893), English and Greek scholar:

> "Mine has been a happy life. I thank God for my life . . . Bid farewell to the college."

SIR ISAAC PITMAN (1813-1897), phonographer and inventor of shorthand, said:

> "To those who ask how Isaac Pitman passed away, say, 'Peacefully, and with no more concern than passing from one room to another to take up some further employment.'"

X. Philosophers

ANAXAGORAS (502-428 B.C.), the Greek Philosopher who maintained himself by keeping a school, being asked if he wished anything as he died, replied:

> "Give the boys a holiday."

ARCHIMEDES (287-212 B.C.), Greek mathematician and inventor, being ordered by a Roman soldier to follow him, said:

> "Wait until I have finished my problem."

CICERO (106-43 B.C.), Roman orator and author, to his assassin:

"Strike."

DEMONAX:

"You may go home, the show is over."

PAULUS (250 A.D.), Roman Jurist, said:

"There is another life . . . though my life be gone, I pray God that my students might find the truth."

JOHN LOCKE (1632-1709), English philosopher, being read to out of the Psalms by Lady Masham, exclaimed:

"Oh, the depth of the riches of the goodness and knowledge of God. Cease now."

PERICLES of Athens:

"I have never caused any citizen to put on mourning on my account."

PLATO (427-347 B.C.), Greek Philosopher, is reported to have left this last word:

"I thank the guiding providence and fortune of my life, first, that I was born a man and a Greek, not a barbarian or a brute; and next, that I happened to live in the age of Socrates."

SOCRATES (470-309 B.C.), Greek Philosopher of whom Plato was so proud, lamented to his wife that he died innocent. To Crito, one of his disciples, he said:

"Crito, we owe a cock to Asclepois; pay it and do not forget."

(This bird was the usual thank offering for recovery from disease. Here it meant, the disease of life.)

DIOGENES (412-323 B.C.), Greek cynic and philosopher, was asked by his master Xeniades how he wished to be buried.

"Face downwards."

"Why?" asked Xeniades.

"Because everything will shortly be turned upside down." (Referring to national upheavals.)

SENECA (4 B.C.-54 A.D.), Roman statesman and philosopher, killing himself at Nero's order, sprinkled his slaves with water from his bath, saying:

"A libation to Jupiter, the Liberator."

ABELARD (1079-1142), French Philosopher and theologian:
"I do not know."

JACOB BOEHME (1575-1624), German philosopher and mystic:
"Now I go hence to paradise."

DESCARTES (1596-1650), French philosopher and mathematician:
"My soul, thou hast long been held captive; the hour has now come for thee to quit thy prison, to leave the trammels of this body; suffer, then, this separation with joy and courage."

LA MOTHE LE VAYER, the French philosopher, was passionately fond of traveling. As Bernier, the famous Indian traveler, drew his curtain, Vayer said:
"Well, my friend, what news from the Great Mogul?"

PERE BOUHOURS, French grammarian:
"Tis or I am going to die; one of these expressions is used."

DAVID HUME (1711-1776), Scottish philosopher and historian, who on being told by his doctor that he was a little better, said:
"Doctor, as I believe you would not choose to tell anything but the truth, you had better say that I am dying as fast as my enemies, if I have any, could wish, and as easily and cheerfully as my best friends could desire."

IMMANUEL KANT (1724-1804), German philosopher declining a refreshing draught as he died, said:
"It is well."

JOHANN FICHTE (1762-1814), German philosopher, died saying:
"Leave it alone; I need no more medicine; I feel that I am well."

GEORGE HEGEL (1770-1831), German philosopher, had this to say:
"Only one man ever understood me."

Then, dejectedly he said:
"And he didn't understand me."

AUGUSTE COMTE (1798-1857), French philosopher and mathematician:
"What an irreparable loss."

FREDERICK H. A. HUMBOLDT (1769-1859), the German philosopher, as the sun shone brilliantly into his death chamber exclaimed:

> "How grand those rays: they seem to beckon me to heaven!"

CONFUCIUS, or Kong-Fu-Tse (551-449 B.C.), whose pearls of wisdom are still greatly treasured, was the Chinese philosopher who, as he came to die, could say:

> "I have taught men how to live."

DEMOSTHENES (385-322 B.C.), Athenian orator and statesman, after taking poison to avoid being captured by Macedonian soldiers, said to their commander:

> "Now, as soon as you please, may commence the part of Creon in the tragedy, and expose this body of mine unburied. But, O Gracious Poseidon, I will first rise up, while I still have life, and depart from this holy place though Antipater and the Macedonians have not left so much as thy temple unprofaned."

MIRABEAU (1749-1791), French orator and revolutionist, looking at the sun shining into his death chamber, said:

> "If that is not God himself there, it is his cousin at least.
> . . . Let me fall asleep to the sound of delicious music."

XI. Musicians and Hymn Writers

Many of those who had the gift to touch the heart of man with their lyrics and literature spoke eloquently, gallantly and, at times, charmingly of death. From some of their last sayings we can learn the art of graceful exist from this world of sobs and sorrows.

LUDWIG VON BEETHOVEN (1770-1827), was the great German genius whose musical compositions covered a wide field. Although unable to hear his own productions because of his deafness, we can appreciate his dying word:

> "I shall hear in heaven. Clap now, my friends, the comedy is done."

JEAN BAPTISTE LULLI, (c.1687), was the noted Italian musical composer and the special favorite of Louis XIV of France. At the close of his life, conscious of the ungodliness of the past, he died with a halter around his neck as a sign of repentance for his sins and singing with tears of remorse and agony:

> "Sinner, thou must die."

WOLFGANG AMADEUS MOZART (1756-1791), the famous Austrian composer, is best remembered for his great operas, *The Marriage of Figaro* and *Don Giovanni*. At the end, his dear partner was at his side offering him refreshment for his parched lips. His last words were:

"You spoke of refreshment, my Emilie. Take my last notes, sit down to my piano here and sing them to the hymn of your sainted mother. Did I not tell you that it was for myself — I composed this death chant."

RAMEAU, famous musician of 1764, said to his confessor:

"What the devil do you mean to sing to me, priest? You are out of tune."

FRANZ SCHUBERT (1797-1828), Austrian musician, in his delirium cried:

"This is not Beethoven lying here."

FREDERIC CHOPIN (1810-1849), Polish pianist and composer, said to Princess Marceline and Mlle. Gavard:

"When you play music together think of me, and I shall hear you."

To Franchomme, his last word was:

"Play Mozart in memory of me."

HAYDN (1732-1809), Austrian composer, died singing;

"God save the Emperor."

FRANZ LISZT (1811-1886), Hungarian pianist and composer, after struggling through the last performance of *Tristan und Isolde* at Bayreuth a week before his death, had this last word to leave the world:

"Tristan!"

BERLIOZ (1803-1869), dramatist and composer, used Shakespearean language as he died:

"Life's but a walking shadow, a poor player,
That struts and frets his hour upon the stage,
And then is heard no more; it is a tale
Told by an idiot, full of sound and fury,
Signifying nothing."

Then came this last word:

"That is my signal."

Isaac Watts (1674-1748), was the English theologian and hymn-writer. Known as "The Evangelical Poet," it was Watts who gave the Church one of its most precious Calvary hymns, "When I Survey the Wondrous Cross." His version of Psalm 90, "O God, Our Help in Ages Past," is perhaps the finest hymn in the English language. How triumphant was his last hour as he died in the Lord! Listen to his dying testimony:

> "It is a great mercy that I have no manner of fear or dread of death. I could, if God please, lay my head back and die without terror this afternoon" —

which he did!

Bernard of Clairvaux was the active promoter of the disastrous Crusade of 1146 and author of many fine hymns, among them —

> "Jesus, the very thought of Thee
> With sweetness fills my breast."

He died with the words upon his lips:

> "May God's will be done."

Edward Bickersteth (1786-1850), leader of the Evangelistic Party in the Anglican Church and co-founder of The Evangelistic Alliance, was likewise a gifted composer of hymns. He it was who gave the Church such well-known compositions as "Peace, Perfect Peace," "Till He Come!" and "Come Ye Yourselves Apart and Rest Awhile." As Bickersteth was about to finish his earthly life he confessed:

> "I have no other ground of confidence than the blood of Jesus. Christ first, Christ all in all."

Charles Wesley (1619-1696), brother of John Wesley, the most famous poet and hymn-writer of all time, died in his 77th year. A few days before his death he dictated the following lines to his dear wife who wrote them down as they came from the lips of her slowly dying husband:

> "In age and feebleness extreme
> Who shall a sinful worm redeem?
> Jesus, my only hope Thou art,
> Strength of my failing flesh and heart;
> O, could I catch a smile from Thee
> And drop into Eternity."

Before he dropped into eternity he said:

> "Come my dearest Jesus, the nearer the more precious, the

more welcome. I cannot contain it! What manner of love is this to a poor worm? I cannot express the thousandth part of what praise is due to Thee. It is but little I can give Thee, but Lord, help me to give Thee my all. I will die praising Thee, and rejoice that others can praise Thee better. I shall be satisfie with Thy likeness! satisfied! satisfied! O my dearest Jesus, I come."

REGINALD HEBER, well known as Bishop Heber of Calcutta, was the notable hymnist who gave the Church some of her finest hymns including "Holy, Holy, Holy! Lord God Almighty!" Willingly he sacrificed the prospects of advancement and emoluments of his church that he might become "the chief missionary of the East." It was while he was on a visit to Madras in March, 1826, that Heber was suddenly summoned to appear before the Master of the vineyard. Archdeacon Robinson, who accompanied Bishop Heber, wrote of one of the last conversations they had together when they spoke "chiefly of the blessedness of heaven, and the best means of preparing for its enjoyment." On April 3, 1826, after a day devoted to the ecclesiastical affairs of the mission station, the Bishop went to the house, prepared for a bath and undressing, entered the water. Some time later, his servant, feeling that his master was unusually long, ventured to open the door and found the Bishop lifeless below the surface of the water in the outside spring-fed bath. Every possible means were immediately used to restore animation, but in vain. The devoted Christian missionary left no parting testimony. He did leave behind him, however, a thousand hearts in India who had trusted him as the bulwark of the Christian faith. "Hemans" is a poem to the memory of Bishop Heber and speaks of him thus in the closing verse:

"Praise! for yet one more name with power
To cheer and guide us onward endowed, as we press!
Yet one more image, on the heart bestow'd,
To dwell there, beautiful in holiness!
Thine, *Heber*, thine! whose memory for the dead,
Shines as the star that to the Saviour led."

JOHN KENT (1766-1843), was another remarkable hymn-writer of that period, whose first hymnbook appeared in 1803. Cultivating his gift for spiritual verse, Kent sought to manifest in his hymns the depth and reality of his conversion. It was Kent who wrote —

"O Blessed God! How Kind,"

the last verse of which reads:

> "A monument of grace,
>   A sinner saved by blood,
> The streams of love I trace
>   Up to the fountain, God.
> And in His sovereign counsels see
> Eternal thoughts of love to me."

When about fifty years of age, he became totally blind, but some of his sweetest hymns with their depth of spiritual beauty were taken down by his small grandson to whom he dictated the words. As he fell asleep in Jesus at the age of 77, he exclaimed:

> "I rejoice in hope, I am accepted — *accepted!*"

SAMUEL MEDLEY (1738-1799), who among his many hymns gave us that Christ-exalting one —

> "On Christ salvation rests secure" —

was born in Hertfordshire. After his conversion he devoted himself to exaltation of the grace of God in His salvation and to the promotion of real holiness in heart and life. He died at 61 years of age. Dying without a struggle or groan he was able to say as he died:

> "Dying is sweet work! sweet work! My heavenly Father, I am looking up to my dear Jesus, my God, my portion, my all in all. Glory, Glory, Home, Home!"

AUGUSTUS MONTAGUE TOPLADY (1710-1778), will ever be famous as the author of one of the most evangelical hymns of the Eighteenth Century, "Rock of Ages," which was first published in 1776. During the final illness, Toplady was greatly supported by the consolations of the Gospel:

> "The consolations of God, to so unworthy a wretch are so abundant; that He leaves me nothing to pray for but their continuance."

Near his last, awaking from a sleep, he said:

> "Oh, what delights! Who can fathom the joy of the third heaven? The sky is clear, there is no cloud; come, Lord Jesus, come quickly!"

He died saying:

> "No mortal man can live after the glories which God has manifested to my soul."

XII. Scientists

GEORGE CAVIER, French writer and naturalist:
"Oh, my poor head!"

LIEUTAND, physician to the King of France, was asked by his confessor: "Do you believe? Do you believe?" To which he replied:
"O sir, let me die in peace. I believe in everything except in medicines."

CHARLES DARWIN (1809-1882), English naturalist and father of the "Evolutionary Theory":
"I am not the least afraid to die."

SIR ISAAC NEWTON (1642-1727), the British scientist, mathematician and natural philosopher, gave us his "Law of Gravitation." Newton felt that he was able to think God's thoughts after Him. Among his last words we have this eager, expectation of the future:
"I do not know what I may appear to the world, but to myself I seem to have been only like a boy playing on the seashore, and diverting himself in now and then finding a smoother pebble, or a prettier shell than ordinary, while the great ocean of truth liest all undiscovered before him."

WILLIAM ALLEN (1843), a renowned chemist of his time, was a sincere believer and on his deathbed said:
"How often I think of those precious words of the Saviour, 'That they may be with me where I am.' "

SIR DAVID BREWSTER (1781-1868), the Scottish physicist distinguished in the science of optics and who invented the "kaleidoscope", was one of the founders of the British Association. This famous Scot humbly followed the God of his fathers and as he died left this testimony:
"I shall see Jesus, and that will be grand. I shall see Him who made the worlds."

THOMAS BATEMAN, a well-known English physician of his time who died in 1819, had no doubt whatever of the paradise awaiting him. He left behind this testimony:
"I surely must be going now, my strength sinks so fast. What glory! The angels are waiting for me! Lord Jesus, receive my soul. Farewell."

WILLIAM HENRY, the English physician who authored several works on chemistry, was a sincere Christian who ministered to the souls of his patients as well as their bodies. When he died in 1836, he peacefully passed away, saying:

"A sweet falling of the soul on Jesus."

WILLIAM BLAIR was a well-known English surgeon and medical author who said to a friend near his bed as he died:

"Reach me that blessed Book, that I may lay my hand on it once more. I rest in Christ."

HERMAN BOEHAAVE, a European physician of note, died in 1738 with these words on his lips:

"He that loves God ought to think nothing desirable but what is pleasing to the Supreme Goodness."

T. E. BOND was not only a physician but minister and editor. He died in 1856, leaving the world this farewell message:

"What is victory over death? Is it not the victory over the dread of death? Is it not the victory of patience under the sufferings which precede death? Is it not the victory of resignation in the prospect of death? Is it not the victory of faith, which looks beyond death, and trusts all to Christ?"

CURAENS was a German physician who was upheld and sustained by the hope of a glorious resurrection:

"My breast burns at the sight of eternal life, the beginning of which I do really feel within me. I desire to be dissolved. I groan for that dwelling above which Thou hast revealed to me. I see the Heavens now open. Thou, Jesus Christ, art my Resurrection and my life."

WILLIAM CEILLER was the eminent British physician and medical lecturer who said as he died:

"I wish I had the power of writing; I would describe how pleasant it is to die."

EDWARD JENNER was the discoverer of the benefits of vaccination who, shortly before he died in 1823, said:

"I do not wonder that men are grateful to me, but I am surprised that they do not feel gratitude to God for thus making me a medium of good."

DAVID M. MOIR, Scottish physician and poet who died in 1851, was likewise a sincere believer and on his deathbed said:

"May the Lord my God not separate between my soul and body

until He has made a final separation between my soul and sin, for the sake of my Redeemer."

ZUNIGER was a Professor of Medicine at Basel who, although renowned for his skill, was a simple-hearted believer who lived in the light of eternity. His last words were:

"I rejoice, yea, my spirit leaps within me for joy, that now the time at last is come when I shall see the glorious God face to face; whom I have by faith longed after, and after whom my soul has panted."

EDITH LOUISA CAVELL (1865-1915), was the British nurse who was martyred by the Germans on a charge of harboring British refugees. Miss Cavell loved all mankind, even her enemies. Her religious upbringing and personal experience of God enabled her to face the firing squad triumphantly. About to die, she said:

"Standing, as I do, in view of God and eternity . . . I realize that patriotism is not enough. I must have no hatred or bitterness against anyone."

EDWARD TURNER was a professor of chemistry in the University of London during the latter part of the Eighteenth Century. Although in possession of well deserved scientific fame, yet, like all true believers, he humbled himself and became even as a little child that he might enter the kingdom of heaven. Up until a few days of his death, he was at the University discoursing on his favorite scientific themes and in his unique way weaving into his lectures the spiritual truths he dearly loved. As the shadows deepened and sympathizing friends recognized that this noble man was nearing the border of eternity, they sought to console and relieve him in every possible way. Edward Turner said to them:

"O happy I am! How kind everyone is to me! It is worthwhile being sick to see how kind everyone is to me. My whole trust is in Christ. I should have no comfort without Him."

When the death struggle came, he turned and uttered his last word:

"I am content, content to die. Christ is the Resurrection and the Life. Whoever believeth in Him, though he were dead, yet shall he live. And whosoever liveth and believeth in Him shall never die. Let all be present, it may do them good. Pray for me, that my struggle will not be long. Pray that I may have peace."

All present *did* pray, and gathering what strength he could, Turner added:

> "I could not have believed that I could be happy on my death-bed. I am content my career to close."

HALLER, famous philosopher, anatomist and physician, feeling his own pulse to the last, said to a fellow doctor on hand:

> "My friend, the artery ceases to beat."

XIII. Artists and Sculptors

JOHN BACON, the British sculptor of great ability who died in 1799, left the following self-composed inscription for his tombstone:

> "What I was as an artist seemed to me of some importance while I lived, but what I really was as a believer in Christ Jesus is the thing of importance to me now."

MICHAELANGELO (1475-1564), the Italian artist and sculptor, was probably one of the greatest sculptors the world has ever known. His remarkable paintings in the Sistine Chapel at Rome made him justly famous. God-fearing, his brief will contained the paragraph:

> "I commit my soul to God, my body to the earth, my possessions to my nearest relatives. I die in the faith of Jesus Christ and in the firm hope of a better life."

His last word was in the form of an exhortation to those at his bedside:

> "Through life remember the sufferings of Jesus."

WILLIAM ETTY, the British painter who died in 1849, was another who believed that death was not an end but an episode in one's experience. Full of confidence of what was on the other side, he died saying:

> "Wonderful, wonderful, this death!"

THOMAS GAINSBOROUGH (1727-1788), the outstanding portrait painter of the Eighteenth Century, was known for his lightest and airiest touch. Dying, he said to those in the room:

> "Going to heaven, and Van Dyke is of the party."

JOSHUA REYNOLDS (1723-1792), was another British artist who achieved great fame for his portrait painting. He was one of the founders and first president of the Royal Academy. The last word he was heard to say was:

"I know that all things must have an end."

ANNA M. SHURMAN, who passed away in 1678, was the German artist and scholar whose works were of high repute. She was likewise a humble believer and as she died bore this testimony:

"I have proceeded one step farther toward eternity, and if the Lord shall be pleased to increase my pains, it will be no cause of sorrow to me."

WILLIAM J. TURNER (1775-1851), English artist, left this last word:

"The sun, my dear, the sun is God."

DR. WILLIAM HUNTER, English painter, remarked:

"If I had strength to hold a pen, I would write down how easy and pleasant a thing it is to die."

PERUGINO (1446-1523), Italian painter, being urged to see a priest, said:

"No, I am curious to see what happens in the next world to those who die unshriven."

JEAN COROT (1796-1875), French painter, artist-like, uttered the hope:

"I hope with all my heart there will be painting in heaven."
— a sentiment the late Sir Winston Churchill likewise expressed.

XIV. Actors and Actresses

DAVID GARRICK (1717-1779), English actor after whom a London theatre is named, simply said:

"My dear!"

VAUGHN MOODY (1869-1910), American dramatist and poet, repeated the lines also credited to Peterson, another actor:

"Reason thus with life,
If I do lose thee, I do lose a thing
that none but fools would keep."

PALMER (1842-1933), American scholar, as he came to die quoted a line used on the stage while performing in *The Strangers*:

"This is another and a better world."

LUPE DE VEGA (1562-1635), Spanish actor and dramatist, left this good word:
> "True glory is in virtue. Ah, I would willingly give all the applause I have received to have performed one good action more."

WILLIAM WYCHERLEY, English actor of 1716, made his young wife promise to consent to his last wish. "What is it?" she asked:
> "My dear, it is only this, that you will never be an old man again."

TOMMASO SALVINI (1829-1916), Italian actor, said:
> "I do not will to die — absolutely."

TCHEKHOV, Russian actor and dramatist, said to his doctor:
> "I am dying."

To his wife who gave him the champagne he ordered, he said:
> "I have not drunk champagne for a long time."

SIR HENRY JONES (1851-1929), English actor, was asked by his niece whether she or the nurse should sit up with him. "The prettier," he said, "now fight for it." His last word was:
> "The Lord reigneth, let the earth rejoice."

ELEONORA DUSE (1859-1924), Italian actress, uttered the lines:
> "We must start off again! Work again!
> Cover me up."

ISADORA DUNCAN (1878-1927), American actress and dancer, at her automobile accident:
> "Goodby, my friends, I am going to glory."

XV. Soldiers and Sailors

HENRY HAVELOCK, the eminent British General, in the last moments of his earthly pilgrimage said to his son:
> "Come, my son, and see how a Christian can die."

HORATIO NELSON (1758-1805), forever renowned as the British sailor who destroyed Napoleon's fleet in Aboukir Bay, was mortally wounded at Trafalgar. He died saying to a seafaring friend:
> "Send out the challenge — 'England expects every man this day to do his duty.'"

Then he added:

> "Don't throw me overboard, Hardy; take care of my poor Lady Hamilton. Kiss me, Hardy. Now I am satisfied. Thank God I have done my duty."

WALTER RALEIGH (1552-1618), the British soldier and courtier, was a favorite of Queen Elizabeth I and founder of the American colony of Virginia. Under the reign of James I he did not fare so well and was executed. To his executioner, who evidently asked Raleigh to place his head in a certain way on the block, the gallant courtier said:

> "It matters little how the head lies if the heart be right. Why dost thou not strike?"

He also said to the executioner:

> "Show me the axe, show me the axe. This gives me no fear. It is a sharp medicine to cure me of all my diseases."

HEDLEY VICARS, one of the godliest soldiers ever to serve in the British Army, was killed during the Crimean War. Dying on the field of battle, he exclaimed:

> "The Lord has kept me in perfect peace, and made me glad with the light of His countenance."

CHRISTOPHER COLUMBUS (1451-1506), the Italian navigator and sailor, made several voyages westward and is credited with the discovery of the West Indies. An ardent Roman Catholic, he established Catholic missions wherever he landed. When he died, the parting message from his lips was:

> "Lord, into Thy hands I commit my spirit."

COLONEL JAMES CAMERON, who was killed at Bull Run, 1861, rushed forward shouting:

> "Scots, follow me."

EPAMINONDAS (418-362 B.C.), Theban general and statesman, on being told that the Thebans were victorious, said:

> "Then I can die happy."

GENERAL JAMES WOLFE (1727-1759), British soldier, had a similar farewell word at Quebec:

> "What! Do they run already? Then I die happy."

GENERAL ULYSSES GRANT, American general and eighteenth

President of the United States, who received the surrender of General Lee at Appomattox Court House, said:

> "I want nobody distressed on my account."

HANNIBAL (247-183 B.C.), Carthaginian general of Roman fame, died saying:

> "Let us now relieve the Romans of their fears by the death of a feeble, old man."

SEWARD, the Dane, had a last word similar to that of Louis XVIII:

> "Lift me up that I may die standing, not lying down like a cow."

JOHN ZISKA (1360-1424), Bohemian soldier and Hussite, said:

> "Make my skin into drumheads for the Bohemian cause."

BAYARD (1473-1524), French soldier and hero who was fatally wounded defending the passage of Sesia, replied to the constable of Bourbon, who expressed his sympathy:

> "Sir, I thank you; I am not to be pitied who died a true man, serving my king; but you are to be pitied who carry arms against your prince, your country, and your oath."

FILIPPO STROGG, Italian soldier who killed himself with a sword in prison, carved with its point on the walls this line from Virgil's *Dido*:

> "Raise some avenger from these bones of mine."

DE MONTMORENCY (1493-1567), a courageous French soldier and constable of France who had served his country well, reflected soldierly courage as he died:

> "Do you not think a man who has known how to live honorably for eighty years does not know how to die for a quarter of an hour?"

SIR RICHARD GRENVILLE (1541-1591), British Admiral of renown, said:

> "Here die I, Richard Grenville, with a joyful and quiet mind, for that I have ended my life as a true soldier ought to do that hath fought for his country, queen, religion and honor."

SIMON FRASER (1667-1747), Scottish Jacobite who became Lord Lovat and whose descendent founded the Lovat Scouts of World War I, was beheaded. He died saying:

> "It is sweet and glorious to die for my country."

Louis Joseph Montcalm (1712-1759), French-Canadian soldier and Field Marshal, on being told his wound was mortal, said:

> "So much the better! I shall not live to see the surrender of Quebec."

Gasparo De Coligny, the admiral who was one of the chief supporters of the Protestant cause in France, was treacherously wounded by Popish emissaries in 1570. During the uprising, Admiral De Coligny was captured and killed at the instigation of Roman Catholic lords. Besine, one of the lords, pointed his sword to the Admiral's breast, and beholding the naked blade he said to Besine:

> "Young man thou sightest to respect my years, and my infirmity of the body; but it is not thou that canst shorten my days."

Besine thrust the Admiral through with his sword, and the brave warrior fell down wounded to death. His head was cut off and was sent by the King and the Queen to the pope at Rome. The rest of his body was dishonored by the papists among the common people.

Captain Nathan Hale (1755-1776), American Revolutionary officer hanged by the British Army in America for espionage, bravely said:

> "I only regret that I have but one life to give for my country."

Marechal De Bourmont, French soldier, died saying:

> "I wish to see Alexander, Caesar, Charlemagne, and Jesus Christ, the Saviour of men."

General Robert Lee (1807-1870), great American Confederate General, had as his last word:

> "Strike my tent; send for Hill."

XVI. Infidels and Agnostics

Infidels and agnostics are usually cowards when the death dew lies cold on their brow. Unprepared to enter eternity, they lose their braggadocio as its gates open to receive them. What fear grips their hearts and how pathetic and hopeless their last words are! The only Light that could have shone through the gloom of death and pointed them to the skies was rejected, and they die, even as they lived, without God and therefore without hope.

ALTAMONT, renowned writer and agnostic of a past century, was an ingenious and accomplished infidel whose fascinating brilliance captivated the youth of his time and destroyed any religious faith they had. At his end, his smitten conscience cried:

> "It is fit Thou shouldst thus strike this murderer to the heart . . . As for a Deity, nothing less than an Almighty could inflict what I now feel. Remorse for the past throws my thoughts on the future; worse dread of the future strikes them back on the past. I turn and turn, and find no ray. Didst Thou fell half the mountain that is on me, Thou wouldst struggle with the martyr for his stake, and bless heaven for the flame that is not an ever-lasting flame, that is not an unquenchable fire. My principles have poisoned my friends; my extravagance has beggared my boy; my unkindness has murdered my wife! And is there another hell? Thou blasphemed yet indulgent God, hell is a refuge if it hide me from Thy frown."

ANTITHEUS, another infidel whose last words were so laden with remorse and despair, gave this despairing, final cry:

> "You must not let me die! I dare not die! Oh, doctor, save me if you can! My mind is full of horror, and I am incapable of preparing for death. As I was lying sleepless in my bed this night, the apparition of my friend presented itself before me, and unfolding the curtain of my bed, stood at my feet looking earnestly upon me for a considerable space of time. My heart sank within me, for his face was ghastly, full of horror, with an expression of such anguish as I can never describe. His eyes were fixed upon me, and at length, with a mournful motion of his head, 'Alas! Alas!' he cried, 'we are in a fatal error,' and taking hold of the curtain with his hand shook them violently and disappeared. This, I protest to you, I both saw and heard. And look! Where the print of his hand is left is blood upon the curtains."

EDWARD GIBBON (1737-1794), the noted English historian whose *Decline And Fall Of The Roman Empire* remains the greatest history of all times, was unfortunately another infidel who died without the consolations of the Gospel. What a bleak end was his as he said to those at his bedside:

> "This day may be my last. I will agree that the immortality of the soul is at times a very comfortable doctrine. All this is now lost, finally, irrevocably lost. All is dark and doubtful."

THOMAS HOBBES (1588-1674), was a noted English political philosopher whose most famous work was *Leviathan*. This cul-tured, clever skeptic corrupted many of the great men of his time. But what regret was his at the end of the road! What hopelessness permeated his last word:

> "If I had the whole world, I would give it to live one day. I shall be glad to find a hole to creep out of the world at. About to take a leap in the dark!"

CAPTAIN JOHN LEE, who was executed for forgery, was another who sought to do away with God, yet in death longed for the assurance and hope of faith:

> "I leave to the world this mournful memento, that however much a man may be favored by personal qualifications or distinguished mental endowments, genius will be useless, and abilities avail little, unless accompanied by religion and attended by virtue. Oh, that I had possession of the meanest place in heaven, and could but creep into one corner of it."

OLIVER, a doctor of philosophy, lived the life of an infidel but shortly before his death repented and turned to the Saviour. His final word was one of deep regret:

> "Would that I could undo the mischief I have done! I was more ardent to poison men with infidel principles than any Christian is to spread the doctrines of Christ."

THOMAS PAINE, the renowned American author and infidel, exerted considerable influence against belief in God and in the Scriptures. He came to his last hour in 1809, a most disillusioned and unhappy man. During his final moments on earth he said:

> "I would give worlds, if I had them, that *Age of Reason* had not been published. O Lord, help me! Christ, help me! O God what have I done to suffer so much? But there is no God! But if there should be, what will become of me hereafter? Stay with me, for God's sake! Send even a child to stay with me, for it is hell to be alone. If ever the devil had an agent, I have been that one."

WILLIAM POPE, who died in 1797, is said to have been the leader of a company of infidels who ridiculed everything religious. One of their exercises was to kick the Bible about the floor or tear it up. Friends who were present in his death-chamber spoke of it as a scene of terror as he died crying:

> "I have no contrition. I cannot repent. God will damn me. I know the day of grace is past . . . You see one who is damned forever . . . Oh, Eternity! Eternity! . . . Nothing for me but hell. Come, eternal torments . . . I hate everything God has made, only I have no hatred for the devil — I wish to be with

him. I long to be in hell. Do you not see? Do you not see him? He is coming for me."

PERIGOOD-TALLEYRAND (1754-1838), the renowned French statesman, best remembered as Foreign Minister under Napoleon and later Foreign Minister to Louis XVIII, was likewise known for his infidel leanings. At his deathbed, King Louis asked Talleyrand how he felt and he replied:

"I am suffering, Sire, the pangs of the damned."

VOLTAIRE, the noted French infidel and one of the most fertile and talented writers of his time, used his pen to retard and demolish Christianity. Of Christ, Voltaire said: "Curse the wretch!" He once boasted, "In twenty years Christianity will be no more. My single hand shall destroy the edifice it took twelve apostles to rear." Shortly after his death the very house in which he printed his foul literature became the depot of the Geneva Bible Society. The nurse who attended Voltaire said: "For all the wealth in Europe I would not see another infidel die." The physician, Trochim, waiting up with Voltaire at his death said that he cried out most desperately:

"I am abandoned by God and man! I will give you half of what I am worth if you will give me six months' life. Then I shall go to hell; and you will go with me. O Christ! O Jesus Christ!"

ROBERT GREEN INGERSOLL (1833-1899), famous American lawyer and prominent agnostic, lectured on Biblical inaccuracies and contradictions. His famed lecture *The Mistakes Of Moses* led one defender of the Bible to say that he would like to hear Moses speak for five minutes on *The Mistakes Of Ingersoll*. Standing by his graveside, his brother exclaimed:

"Life is a narrow vale between the narrow peaks of two eternities. We strive in vain to look beyond the heights. We cry aloud, and the only answer is the echo of our wailings."

JOHN WILHOT, who became the second Earl of Rochester, lived a life of sin and infidelity. But God met and saved him from his sin and skepticism. When he came to die in 1680, he laid his hand upon the Bible and said with solemnity and earnestness:

"The only objection against this Book is a bad life! I shall die now, but oh what unspeakable glories do I see! What joys beyond thought or expression am I sensible of! I am assured of God's mercy to me through Jesus Christ. Oh, how I long to die!"

COLONEL CHARTERIS, another infidel who at the end was not so blatant in his denial of an after life, said as he died,
"I would gladly give L30,000 to have it proved to my satisfaction that there is no such place as hell."

KAY, the infidel was the one who cried at the end:
"Hell! Hell! Hell!"
His family could not stand his groans and oaths and fled from the room until he was dead.

CASANOVA, renowned for his self-indulgence, ended his life in self-deception. On his death bed at the age of 73, he said:
"I have lived as a philosopher and die as a Christian."

The Company of Martyrs

IV.

The Company of Martyrs

These present days of martyrdom are as brutal as any endured during the early and dark ages of the Church. Do we realize that more Christians have been tortured and slain during the past five years than died under the iron heel of Rome during the early days of the Church? In Seoul, Korea, ten thousand Christians were slaughtered in one day by the Reds. The recent massacres in the Congo remind us of the price some missionaries have to pay in their effort to win the heathen for Christ.

In Colombia several thousand native believers were murdered by fanatical Roman Catholics. The toll of martyrs is high in a half-dozen other South American countries. We also learn that in one case, 450 Korean Christians were wired together, the wires being pierced through their hands, and forced to march until, one by one, they dropped dead.

Well, how do martyrs die? Burrell and Lucas remind us, "Reformation and Counter-Reformation, the futile horrors of fire and sword at Smithfield and St. Bartholomew, are reflected in the last utterances of Latimer and Cranmer, the ecstasies of St. Theresa and Jacob Boehme, the sterner fanaticism of Cromwell."

Two of the most graphic accounts of martyrdom endured by many brave saints are those to be found in Foxe's *Book of Martyrs* and Alexander Smellie's *Men of the Covenant*. How willingly and nobly these men and women died horrible deaths conceived for them by so-called religious leaders! Courageous utterances from the lips of those who sealed their testimony with their blood prove that the same are not an unsuitable topic for meditation.

Martyrs, whose blood is ever the seed of the Church, leave records of courage, holy defiance of hostile foes and a willingness to sacrifice their lives upon the high places for Christ. Since the days of Barnabas and Paul (Acts 15:25, 26), countless thousands have been ready to "hazard their lives for the name of the Lord Jesus Christ," and historical accounts of their persecutions and tortured deaths make absorbing reading.

It is one thing to die in a natural way after an uneventful life, and because of one's faith and confidence in God, enter the gate of heaven in peace and joy. It is a different experience altogether to suffer much for Christ's sake and then die triumphant in spite of the horrible, painful form of death imposed by brutal men. One cannot meditate upon the illustrious roll of saintly men and women who sealed their testimony with their heart's blood without being humbled. The majority of us know so little about sharing the cup of Christ's sufferings. If ours are "the flowery beds of ease," then let us pause to bless God for those "who climbed the steep ascent to heaven through peril, toil and pain" in order that we might have freedom to worship God and witness for Him without restraint. From various sources we have selected the following impressive instances of martyrdom.

AGAPE was one of three sisters belonging to Thessalonica, who answered Dalcatius the Governor, when asked whether she would obey the heathen law imposed:

"Not any laws that command the worship of idols and devils." For her defiant reply, she was burned to death in 304 A.D.

AGATHA, known as Saint Agatha, was a noble Sicilian lady who was upbraided by the authorities for stooping to relieve the poverty of fellow believers, because she was of distinguished birth. Her reply to the callous-hearted objectors was:

"Our nobility lies in this, that we are servants of Christ. 'Inasmuch as ye did it unto one of the least of these my brethren, ye did it unto Me.' "

For such a noble answer, Agatha too, suffered martyrdom by burning in 250 A.D. — a period in which multitudes of Christians were persecuted.

AGNES, a noble Roman lady, was no less heroic in her witness. Dedicated to Christ in early youth, she defied all imperial edicts to deny her faith. Declaring her allegiance to the Saviour and her readiness to die for Him, she was sentenced to be beheaded. When the day came for her to die, seeing the executioner ready with a naked sword in hand, Agnes said:

"I am now glad, I rejoice that thou art come. I will willingly receive into my bosom the length of this sword, that thus married unto Christ my spouse, I may surmount and escape all the darkness of this world. O eternal Governor, vouchsafe to open the gates of heaven, once shut up against all the inhabitants of the earth, and receive, O Christ, my soul that seeks Thee."

Kneeling down, she again prayed that her neck might be readier for the sword. One stroke and her head fell to the ground, and the gates of heaven opened to receive the martyr.

ALBAN is reckoned to be the first martyr from Great Britain who was beheaded during the Diocletian persecution in 304. As he died, he defied his foes in the words:

"The sacrifices you offer are made to devils. My name is Alban, and I worship the true and living God, 'Who made all things.'"

LEGRAND D'ALLERAY, an aged, godly Frenchman was brought before the Tribunal with his wife during the Reign of Terror on a trumped-up charge. The presiding judge, possibly moved by the old couple before him, hinted at an evasive reply to the charge, but the brave old D'Alleray replied:

"I thank you for the efforts you make to save me, but it would be necessary to purchase our lives by a lie. My wife and myself prefer rather to die. We have grown old together without ever having lied, and we will not do it now to save a remnant of life."

CHRYSOSTOM, being led out to exile and death, could triumphantly say:

"Glory to God for all events."

IGNATIUS, in the arena, before the lions had reached him, said:

"I am the wheat of Christ; I am going to be ground with the teeth of wild beasts, that I may be found pure bread."

JEROME, who was burned, said while the fire was being kindled:

"Bring hither thy torch; bring thy torch before my face. Had I feared death, I might have avoided it."

ANDRONICUS, thrown into prison because of his unwillingness to deny the Christian faith, was cruelly scourged and then had his bleeding wounds rubbed with salt. Brought out from prison he was tortured again, thrown to the wild beasts, then finally killed with a sword. This brave martyr, who perished in 303 A.D., was dauntless as he died:

> "Do your worst. I am a Christian. Christ is my help and supporter, and thus armed I will never serve your gods, nor do I fear your authority or that of your master, the Emperor. Commence your torments as soon as you please, and make use of every means that your malignity can invent, and you shall find in the end that I am not to be shaken from my resolution."

JOHN ARDLEY was one of those martyred by Bonner, the cruel Bishop of London, who was the means of sending hundreds of Protestants to the stake. Brutal in the extreme, Bonner tried to describe to Ardley the terrible pain of burning and how it must be to endure it. Ardley was not of the recanting kind and said:

> "If I had as many lives as I have hairs on my head, I would lose them all before I would lose Christ."

ANNE ASKEW, because of her adherence to the Protestant faith, was driven from her home and two children by her husband who violently opposed her faith. Imprisoned because of her witness, an apostate by the name of Shaxton advised her to recant. Anne told him that it would have been good for him had he never been born. Much torture was heaped upon her. Placed on a cruel rack, her joints and bones were pulled out of place. Recovering from a swoon, she preached for two hours to her tormentors. On the day of her execution, she was carried to the stake in a chair, her bones being dislocated so that she could not walk. At the last moment she was offered the King's pardon if she would recant, but in suffering she was silent and died praying for her murderers in the midst of the flames. Her last words were:

> "I came not thither to deny my Lord and Master."

ANN AUDEBERT, the French martyr who was burned at the stake in 1549, when the rope was fastened around her, called it the wedding girdle wherewith she would be married to Christ. As she suffered the gruesome death, she said:

> "Upon a Saturday I was first married, and upon a Saturday I am being married again."

BABYLAS, Bishop of Antioch, was another of those early martyrs whose souls are under the altar. He died in 251 A.D., rejoicing that he was counted worthy to suffer for Christ's sake. His last word was:

> "Return unto thy rest, my soul, for the Lord hath dealt bountifully with thee."

JAMES BAINHAM, the English martyr condemned to die at the stake, as the train of gunpowder came toward him said to those responsible for his death in 1582:

> "God forgive thee, and show thee more mercy than thou showest me."

ROBERT BARNES was the faithful minister of the Gospel who was burned at Smithfield, England, in 1540, and who, as he was committed to the flames, addressed the onlookers with these farewell words:

> "I trust in no good works that ever I did, but only in the death of Christ. I do not doubt but through Him to inherit the kingdom of heaven. But imagine not that I speak against good works, for they are to be done, and verily they that do them not shall never enter into the kingdom of God."

CONSTANTIA BELLONE was a martyr of Roman Catholicism. Because she refused to go to mass, a priest ordered slices of flesh to be cut from various parts of her body. Finally the priest ordered a company of musketeers to fire upon her, and as they raised their muskets, the brave Protestant said:

> "I was brought up in a religion by which I was taught to renounce the devil, but should I comply with your desire and go to mass, I should be sure to meet him there in a variety of shapes. What horrid and lasting torments will you suffer in hell for the trifling and temporary pains which I now endure."

THOMAS BENET was another who felt the fury of Rome for not obeying her dictates. When arrested in 1531, his Catholic tormentor said to him: "Pray to our Lady and all will be well!" The martyr's answer was:

> "No, no, it is God only upon whose name we must call, and we have no advocate but only Jesus Christ."

MAURICE BLANC (1530-1547), was the young martyr of Merindol who prayed as he went out to die:

> "Lord God, these men take away my life full of misery, but Thou wilt give me life everlasting."

BLANDINA, a female Christian slave, died in 107 A.D., at Bienna as a martyr for the Gospel's sake. Her idolatrous persecutors grossly tormented her in many ways. Her frail body was torn and mangled through scourgings and exposure to wild beasts. As her foes took her, enclosed her in a net and then threw her to a bull, she exclaimed:

"I am a Christian, and no evil is among us."

JOHN BRADFORD, Chaplain to Edward VI in 1552, was one of the most popular preachers of his day in England. With the accession of Queen Mary, Bradford was arrested for seditious utterances and heresy. Refusing to recant, Catholic power condemned him to be burnt at Smithfield, and he met his death tied to the same stake as a young man found guilty of the same supposed crime. As the flames covered their bodies, Bradford consoled the youth by saying:

"Strait is the gate, and narrow is the way, which leadeth unto life, and few there be that find it."

WILLIE BROWN was a boy martyr burned at the stake during the reign of Queen Mary. Asking one of the spectators to pray for him, young William received the reply, "I will no more pray for thee than I will for a dog." Then said the lad as the fire blazed:

"Son of God, shine Thou upon me."

CIPRIANA BUSTIA was another martyr who died because of his defiance of Rome. Captured, he was thrown into prison and confined there until he perished with hunger. When dead, his corpse was thrown out into the street and devoured by dogs. Why such brutal treatment by a supposedly Christian church? Because when asked to renounce his religion and turn Catholic, he replied:

"I would rather renounce life or turn dog."

CALCONIS, who died about 108 A.D., had been a pagan but witnessing the martyrdom of two Christians, was so impressed by their wonderful patience under terrible sufferings, that he shouted out with admiration:

"Great is the God of the Christians."

Immediately he, too, was struck down and died.

NICHOLAS CAREN, the English martyr put to death in 1539, testified at the end:

"I bless God for my imprisonment, for I then began to relish the life and sweetness of God's Holy Word, which was brought to me by my keeper, one Phillipi, who followed the Reformation."

GEORGE CARPENTER was the renowned martyr of Munich who, as he perished in 1527, uttered this last word:

"My wife and my children are so beloved that they cannot be bought for all the riches of the Duke of Bavaria: but for the love of my Lord I will willingly forsake them. Jesus, Jesus, Jesus!"

CHRISTOPHER CHOBER was the martyr who said as he stepped onto the scaffold:

"I come in the name of God to die for His glory. I have fought a good fight and finished my course, so, executioner, do your office."

PAUL CLEMENT was an elder in the church who, as he viewed the bodies of a number of Protestants that had been executed in the market place, said in the hearing of all the spectators:

"You may kill the body, but you cannot prejudice the soul of a true believer. With respect to the dreadful spectacles which you have here shown me, you may rest assured that God's vengeance will overtake the murderers of those poor people and punish them for the innocent blood they have spilt."

Immediately the Monks who had supervised the hangings laid hold of Clement and hanged him, the soldiers being allowed to amuse themselves by shooting at his body.

CHARLES IX, of France (1550-1574), was responsible for the massacre of St. Bartholomew when, under oath of safety, the principal Protestants of France were in Paris to celebrate the marriage of the King of Navarre with the sister of the French King. Instigated by his mother, Catherine de Medici, Charles ordered the massacre, and more than five thousand protestants were murdered in the city of Paris alone and about thirty thousand in all were killed. Rome received the news with joy, and a medal was struck, having an image of the pope on one side and on the other a rude representation of the massacre. That the King was haunted by such a gory spectacle is evident from the fact that as he died, the blood of those thousands who were brutally murdered haunted him, and he cried:

"What murder! What blood! O, I have done wrong – God, pardon me."

THASCIUS CYPRIAN was the Bishop of Carthage and famous as a teacher of rhetoric in that city. He was stedfast in his resolution to correct the abuses of the church, earning thereby the hostility of religious leaders. In 257 A.D., he was brought before the Proconsul Paternus, declared himself a Christian and refused to sacrifice to the gods of Rome. Condemned to be beheaded, he died in the presence of his sorrowing people, leaving behind this famous testimony:

> "I am a Christian and cannot sacrifice to the gods. I heartily thank Almighty God, who is pleased to set me free from the chains of this body."

EPIPODIUS was another triumphant martyr of those early centuries when so many were forced to forfeit their lives for Christ's sake. Because of his allegiance to Christianity, he was first beaten, then placed on a rack where his flesh was torn with hooks, after which he was beheaded. As he died in 179 A.D., he had grace to say:

> "The frame of man being composed of two parts, a body and soul, the first, being perishable, should be brought into subjection to the latter. Your pleasures lead to eternal death, our pain to eternal pleasures."

FLORA, who was martyred in 850, belonged to Carduba. Although her father was a Mohammedan, her mother was a devout Christian, and through her influence, Flora became a Christian and a nun. Brought before the Cadi, or Mohammedan judge, and urged to renounce her faith, refusing to recant, she was beheaded. In her defence before being led out to the place of execution, she boldly witnessed saying:

> "I am a woman of pagan extraction whom you punished with stripes some time ago because I would not deny Christ. Hitherto through weakness of the flesh I hid myself, but now, trusting in the divine grace, I fear not to declare that Christ is the true God, and to denounce your false prophet."

FYE, burned at the stake in 1549, was led by his persecutors to the ship in which his companion Eelken was beheaded and was then shown the stake at which he was to be burned. Monks urged Fye to take the Sacrament. "Will you not do such a work of mercy as to receive this bread and wine before you die?" Fye answered:

"For your bread and wine I do not hunger. Food is prepared for me in Heaven."

Taken to the stake, the executioner took the cap from Fye's head, filled it with powder and then, strangled the victim. Fye was left to burn. As he was about to be received up into heaven, the martyr prayed:

"Lord, receive Thy servant."

FRANCIA GAMBA, the martyr burned at the stake in 1554, was presented with a wooden cross by a monk but rejected it saying:

"My mind is so full of the real merits of Christ as I die that I want not a piece of senseless stick to put me in mind of Him."

THOMAS GARRETT was the English minister who was burned with Barnes and Jerome in 1527. All three godly pastors embraced, submitted to the tormentors and perished at the same stake. Said Garrett as the fire was lighted:

"To my remembrance I have never preached anything against God's Holy Word or contrary to the true faith, and thus do I now yield my soul up unto Almighty God, trusting and believing that He of His infinite mercy, according to His promise made me in the blood of His Son Jesus Christ, will take it and pardon all my sins. Pray with and for me, that I may patiently suffer this pain and die in true faith."

ELIZABETH GAUNT was the English martyr whom William Penn saw die and declared that she behaved herself in such a calm manner that all the spectators of her burning were melted to tears. She was cruelly and unjustly treated simply because she had in the kindness and charity of her heart sheltered a needy person who informed upon her, and thus earned his own freedom from prison. Elizabeth left this testimony behind before she went out to die in 1685:

"I desire to bless His holy name that He hath made me useful in my generation to the comfort and relief of many desolate ones; the blessing of many who were ready to perish hath come upon me."

GELEAZIUM, a martyr of St. Angelo, Italy, was strongly urged by his friends to save his life by denying the Christian faith. He went out to die saying:

"Death is much sweeter to me with the testimony of truth than life with the least denial."

CATELIN GIRARD was the Waldenese martyr of Revel who was burned at the stake in 1500. As he was being prepared for death, he asked the person tying him with cords to give him a stone, which request was refused fearing that Girard wanted to throw it at someone. Girard said he only wanted the stone to illustrate what he wanted to say as a last word. The stone was given him, and looking at it earnestly, Girard said:

> "When it is in the power of man to eat and digest this stone, the religion for which I am about to suffer shall have an end."

ROBERT GLOVER, who died in 1555, was dragged from a sick-bed, thrown into a dismal prison and finally burned at the stake. On his way to the stake he saw a friend and clapping his hands, cried out:

> "Austin, He comes! He comes!"

GORDIUS, the martyr of Calsaria who died at the stake in the Third Century, left the world this testimony to God's unfailing justice:

> "Weep not for me, but rather for the enemies of God; who always make war against the Christians. Weep for them who prepare for us a fire, purchasing hell-fire for themselves in the day of vengeance."

THOMAS HANK was consigned to the flames around 1555, in the days when the Romish Church dealt brutally with all those resisting her false claims. Asked by the Catholic bishop what he thought of the Roman confession, Hanks replied:

> "I say it is abominable and detestable, yea, a blasphemy against God and His Son Jesus Christ, to call upon any, to trust any, pray to any, save only Jesus."

JOHN HUSS, Bohemian martyr, eminent reformer and contemporary and friend of Jerome of Prague, died at the stake in Constance, Germany, on his 42nd birthday. His death was a judicial murder. He died for believing the Scriptures to be an infallible authority and the supreme standard of conduct. At the last moment, the Duke of Bavaria urged Huss to recant, only to receive the heroic reply:

> "What I taught with my lips, I seal with my blood."

His religious foes decked him with a paper cap of blasphemy adorned with "three devils of wonderfully ugly shape" and inscribed with the word "Heresiarcha". Falling on his knees, Huss chanted Psalm 31, and as the flames choked him, he repeated with "a merry and cheerful countenance" the words:

"Into Thy hands, I commend my spirit."

ELLERT JANSEN, whose life was taken in 1549, refused to escape with others from prison. When asked to flee, he replied:

"I am now so well satisfied to be offered up, and feel myself at present so happy, that I do not expect to be hereafter better prepared."

As Jansen was led out to the scene of execution he said:

"This is the most joyful day of my life."

JEROME OF PRAGUE (1365-1416), the Bohemian reformer of noble birth, came under the influence of Wyclif's writings and cooperated with John Huss in the Reformation. When Huss perished, the council succeeded in getting Jerome to retract, but the next day he withdrew his retraction. He was tried again, condemned as a heretic and burned at the stake in Constance. As the flames enveloped his body, Jerome died triumphantly singing a hymn:

"This soul in flames, I offer, Christ, to Thee."

GASPAR KAPLITZ was 86 years old when he was condemned to die. Told that a pardon would be granted him because of his age if he would only ask for it, he replied:

"I will ask pardon of God, whom I have frequently offended, but not the Emperor. No, no, as I die innocent and with a clear conscience, I would not be separated from this noble army of martyrs."

HUGH LAVEROCK was aged, somewhat lame and forced to use crutches. During the Puritan persecutions of the Fifteenth Century, Laverock and a blind man named Apprice arrived together at the stake, and as the flames commenced to ascend, Laverock said to his companion:

"Be of good comfort, brother, for my Lord of London is our good Physician. He will cure us both shortly: thee of thy blindness and me of my lameness."

AYMOND DE LAVRY was one of the French Protestant ministers martyred in 1555. First strangled, he was then burned to ashes. At the stake, his last words to his friends were:

"Lord, make haste to help me! Tarry not, despise not the work of Thy hands. My friends, study the Gospel, for the Word of God abideth for ever. Labour to know the will of

God; fear not them that kill the body, but have no power over the soul."

JEAN MECLERC, the wool-comber of Meaux, was to be tortured and then burned alive at Metz in 1524. On the way to the stake his persecutors beat him, and reaching the place of burning, irons were heated in the fire that was to consume his body, and Meclerc was branded. Strange though it may seem, at the last moment he was set at liberty, and going to Metz, Meclerc was so stirred in spirit at the idolatry of the people that he broke down the images in a Catholic church and scattered the fragments on the altar. He was arrested, and his fate was a dreadful one. His right hand was cut off, red-hot pincers tore away his nose and his body was mangled beyond recognition. But his constancy never wavered, and as he died a horrible death, he was heard to say:

> "Their idols are silver and gold, even the work of men's hands. . . . They that make them are like unto them; so is every one that trusteth in them. Oh! Israel, trust thou in the Lord; He is their help and shield."

GALEYN DE MULER, suspected of Bible reading, was brought before the dreaded Titelmann, who delighted in torturing and killing Christians. When Muler refused to recant, Titelmann asked him if he loved his wife and children, and if so, was he not prepared to deny the faith and live for them. Muler, who still adhered to his decision, replied to Titelmann's question as he was taken out to die:

> "God knows that were the heavens a pearl, and earth a globe of gold, and were I the owner of all, most cheerfully would I give them all to live with my family, even though our fare be only bread and water."

JULIUS PALMER was martyred during the reign of Queen Mary in 1556. As he was young with life before him, he was urged to recant. "Take pity on thy golden years and pleasant flowers of youth before it is too late." But such an eloquent plea failed to move young Palmer, who replied:

> "Sir, I long for those springing flowers which shall never fade away. We shall not end our lives in the fire, but make a change for a better life."

JOHN PEARY was a Welsh martyr who died for his Lord in 1593. His ministry had been greatly blessed, and as he faced his final hours he said:

"Howsoever it goeth with me, I labor that you may have the Gospel preached among you. Though it cost my life, I think it well bestowed."

PETER was the youthful martyr of Lampsacus. Accused of being a Christian, he was brought before Optimus who commanded him to sacrifice to Venus. Peter bravely protested saying:

"I am astonished that you should command me to worship a woman, who according to your own history was a vile and licentious character, and guilty of such crimes as your own laws now punish with death. No, I shall offer to the only living and true God the sacrifice of prayer and praise."

The response to such holy defiance was a most revolting end. Peter's bones were torn upon a rack, his head cut off, and his body thrown to the dogs.

PROBUS was another of those early Christians who sealed his witness with his blood. Scourged until the blood flowed, he was loaded with chains and cast into prison. A few days later he was brought out and commanded to sacrifice to the heathen gods. Knowing that further torture would be his if he refused, he courageously answered his tormentors:

"I come better prepared than before, for what I have suffered has only strengthened me in my resolution. Employ your whole power upon me, and you shall find that neither you, nor the Emperor, nor the gods you serve, nor even the devil, who is your father, shall compel me to worship idols."

Back Probus went to further suffering and death by the sword. He was only one among great numbers martyred in that dreadful Third Century.

RAFARAVAVZ, the female martyr of Malagasy, suffered death by spearing in 1837 by the command of the Queen of Madagascar. Firm and composed to the end, she was forbidden by the Queen to pray. But pray she did, although in irons, and preached Christ to the crowd that followed her to the place of execution where she was speared to death. In a last note to a friend she said:

"Do not fear on my account. I am ready to die for Jesus, if such be the will of God."

JOHN ROGERS (1500-1555), was the Protestant martyr who was friendly with Tyndale and Coverdale and became active in the Reformed Church. During the reign of Queen Mary, Rogers strongly denounced Romanism, was seized, endured many month's imprisonment and then burned. On the way to the stake he was asked to recant and replied that what he had preached he would seal with his blood. The officer in charge of the burning then denounced him as a heretic, to which Rogers replied:

> "That will be known when we meet at the Judgment Seat of Christ."

FRANCIS ROMANES was a native of Spain who, as he was led to the place of execution dressed in a garment painted over with devils, was commanded by one of the priests to kneel before a wooden cross near to the pile where he was to be burned. Fearlessly, Romanes refused, saying:

> "It is not for Christians to worship wood."

DEPUTY BAILIFF WIRTH AND JOHN WIRTH, father and son, were brave Covenanters who were martyred. The father, aged though he was, was subjected to terrible torture and executed. About to die, he turned to his younger son and said:

> "My son, we die an undeserved death; but never do thou think of avenging it."

John, the elder son who was beheaded with his father, was fearfully abused, and as he called upon God for grace and comfort, his torturer said, "Alas! where is your Christ now?" John answered not a word. But upon the scaffold he turned and said to his father:

> "My beloved father, henceforth thou art my father no longer, and I am no longer thy son: but we are brothers still in the Lord, for whose name's sake we are doomed to suffer death. So now if such is God's will, my beloved brother, let us depart to be with Him, who is the Father of all. Fear nothing."

GIROLAMO SAVONAROLA (1452-1498), was "the great Dominican preacher, who for five years held within the hollow of his hand the destinies of Florence." To escape the stifling atmosphere of sin surrounding him, Savonarola fled to the silence of the cloister. After seven years in the Dominican convent of Bologna, he was transferred to that of San Marco at Florence and there began his great career as preacher, reformer and prophet. Loyal to the Roman Catholic Church, he strove to purify its vices, but a powerful hostile party was formed against him in Florence.

He was excommunicated by the pope, handed over to the Inquisition and he was publicly burned after being severely tortured. Among the last words of Savonarola were:

> "My Lord was pleased to die for my sins; why should I not be glad to give up my poor life out of love to Him."

While Savonarola was in no sense of the word a *Protestant,* he yet lived and acted as one, and in silence and with unflinching courage, died as many brave Protestants had done at the hands of Rome.

John Bradford, who, while studying Law in London, heard Latimer preach a powerful message which directed him to the ministry, became Chaplain to Edward VI. With the accession of Queen Mary, he was arrested for seditious utterances and heresy and sentenced to be burned at the stake. On the day of his death he displayed great courage. Kneeling and praying, he took a faggot in his hand and kissed it, and as the flames arose he looked up to heaven and prayed:

> "O, England, England! repent thee of thy sins, repent thee of thy sins. Beware of idolatry, beware of false antichrists; take heed they do not deceive you."

Then Bradford turned to a young man who had also been condemned to die for his faith, and as the flames crackled, Bradford said to his suffering companion:

> "Be of good comfort, brother, for we shall have a merry supper with the Lord this night."

John Hooper, the martyred Bishop of Gloucester, was one of the lesser lights among the Reformers martyred for Christ's sake during the reign of Queen Mary. He had a high reputation for personal holiness and Spirit-inspired preaching. Refusing to recant the Protestant faith, Hooper spent lingering months in prison and was finally sentenced to die as a heretic in his own diocese of Gloucester. On the day of his martyrdom some seven thousand gathered around the stake. Ere the fire was lit, a free pardon was offered him if he would but recant. Scorning it, he said:

> "Away with it; if you love my soul, away with it."

Beating his breast with one hand till it was burned to a stump he died praying:

> "Lord Jesus, have mercy on me; Lord Jesus, receive my spirit."

BAILLEY, on his way to the guillotine, was told: "Why, how you shake!"

"Yes," he replied, "It is very cold."

LAMBERT, as he was pitched into the flames, was firm in his witness to the last:

"None but Christ! None but Christ!"

SAINT LAWRENCE, said to have been boiled alive on a gridiron around 258 A.D., humorously said:

"This side enough is toasted, so turn me, try and eat; and see whether raw or roasted I make the better meat."

SERVETUS (1511-1553), Spanish theologian, was another who died at the stake. Calvin insisted on his saying, "The eternal Son of God," but he refused and was burned to death, and as he died, he said:

"Christ, Son of the Eternal God, have mercy upon me."

POLYCARP suffered much for Christ's sake as Eusebius, the church historian, tells us. The Roman Proconsul commanded him to swear allegiance to Caesar, saying, "Swear, and I will set thee at liberty; reproach Christ." How courageous and magnificent was Polycarp's reply!

"Eighty and six years have I now served Christ, and he has never done me the least wrong; how, then, can I blaspheme my King and my Saviour?"

Further efforts to make him deny his Lord failed, and Polycarp was condemned to be burned at the stake. When the day came for him to be burned alive, those responsible for the burning wanted to nail him to the stake, but Polycarp protested saying:

"Let me alone as I am: for He who has given me strength to endure the fire, will also enable me, without your securing me by nails to stand without moving in the pile."

Whereupon he was not nailed to the stake but only tied to it with his hands behind his back. Polycarp, looking up to heaven, prayed:

"Oh Lord God Almighty, the Father of Thy well-beloved and blessed Son, Jesus Christ, by whom we have received the knowledge of Thee; the God of angels and powers, and of every creature, and especially of the whole race of just men who live in Thy presence: I give Thee hearty thanks that Thou hast vouchsafed to bring me to this day and to this hour; that I should have a part in the number of Thy martyrs, in the cup of Thy Christ, to the resurrection of eternal life, both of soul and body, in the incorruption of the Holy Ghost, among which may I be accepted this day before Thee, as a fit and acceptable sacrifice, as Thou the true God, with whom is no falsehood, hast both before ordained and manifested unto me, and also hast now fulfilled it. For this and for all things else, I praise Thee, I bless Thee, I glorify Thee, by the eternal and heavenly High Priest, Jesus Christ, Thy beloved Son, with whom, to Thee and the Holy Spirit, be glory both now and to all succeeding ages. Amen!"

VICENTIUS, whose sufferings for Christ Augustine refers to in one of his *Sermons,* was one of the early Spanish martyrs during the dreadful persecution under Diocletian when so many were martyred. Describing the terrible suffering Vicentius had to endure, Augustine said of him when utterly destitute of any worldly comfort:

"Hast thou prepared a terrible rack, O cruel tyrant, O devouring lion, for the martyr's bed? The Lord shall make that bed soft and sweet unto him. Rackest thou his bones and joints all asunder? His bones, his joints, his hairs are all numbered. Tormentest thou his flesh with mortal wounds? The Lord shall pour abundantly into all his sores the oil of gladness. Thy scraping-combs, thy searing irons, thy parched salt, thy stinking prison, thy cutting shells, thy pinching stocks shall turn for this patient martyr to the best; altogether shall work contrary to thy expectation. Great plenty of joy shall he reap into the barn of his soul, out of this mighty harvest of pains that thou hast brought him unto. Yea, thou shalt prove him *Vicentius* indeed: that is, a vanquisher, a triumpher, a conqueror: subduing thy madness by his meekness, thy tyranny by his patience, thy manifold means of torture by the manifold grace of God, wherewith he is plentifully enriched."

EULALIA, the other Spanish martyr, was a Christian maiden of noble parentage who lived in the city of Emerita. Scorning a life of ease and luxury, she was most courageous in her witness for the Master. Brought before the judge and given the opportunity to recant and thereby escape a terrible death, Eulalia spurned such an appeal. She was handed over to the executioners, who with their cruel instruments tore her joint from joint until her mangled body with its white and fair skin was a bloody mass. During her dreadful torture, she sang with a bold spirit and exclaimed before she rested in peace:

> "Behold, O Lord, I will not forget Thee; what a pleasure is it for them, O Christ, that remember Thy triumphant victories to attain unto these high dignities."

It is impossible for anyone to peruse the histories and testimonies of the multitude of martyrs of the Christian era without coming to the conclusion that Rome has been the implacable enemy of New Testament Christianity. In apostolic times and through the first two centuries of Church history, Imperial Rome through its successive Emperors – particularly Nero – poured out its contempt upon the followers of "another King, one Jesus" and mercilessly destroyed them. The blood of martyrs flowed freely, but although the bush of the Church burned, it was not consumed. Proud Rome was made to bow before the conquering Christ. But when Imperial Rome became Papal Rome, with popes exercising supereme power, a worse blood bath awaited the true children of God. "Drunk with the blood of saints," is an apt description of that supposedly Christian church.

Modern-day missionaries have faced death bravely. In his thrilling account of the advance into Dutch New Guinea of intrepid Christian missionaries who daily risked their lives to bring the Gospel to Stone Age Dani tribesmen, Russell T. Hitt describes the closing moments of Dr. Robert A. Jaffray, one of the great missionary pioneers of all time. During World War II, Dr. Jaffray was made to suffer indescribable indignity and anguish at the hands of the Japanese. Before he died on his filthy prison cot at Parc-Parc two weeks before the war ended and prisoners were freed, Dr. Jaffray in his last report exhorted his fellow workers to be faithful unto death:

> "Let us keep our eyes steadily upon the goal. . . . For when we hear the shout from the skies, all else will fade into utter nothingness. For the Lord shall descend – from heaven with a shout. Even so, come, Lord Jesus."

In this same moving story, *Cannibal Valley*, Hitt describes a fierce attack by a tribe of Dani warriors upon a group of missionaries and native Christians. As the warriors plunged forward, they speared anyone in their pathway. Daniel, a Papuan from the New Guinea Coast, a devout believer and helper, became the first Dani Christian martyr. Seeking to flee from the oncoming demon-possessed murderers, a spear stopped him as it passed through his body. As he fell, he cried:

"Jesus, Jesus."

Another remarkable missionary biography from the gifted pen of Russell T. Hitt is *Jungle Pilot*, in which he graphically narrates the life and witness of Nate Saint, the inventive genius of "Operation Auca". Nate Saint was one of the five young missionaries whose martyrdom shocked the World on that terrible day, January 8, 1956, when the long, black, wooden lances of the Aucas sent Nate and his companions into the presence of the Master they sacrificially served. What their last words were as they died in the Lord, we shall never know. Their bodies were later found and buried in a common grave under a tree-house. As Nate and one of the rest prepared to leave for Palm Beach, they urged those left behind to pray for them, and said:

"Today is the day things will happen. This *is* the day."

And it was their great day, for during it they passed over into heaven to see the King in all His beauty. What happened that day aroused the Church to the need of a heathen world.

One could go on indefinitely quoting the dying sayings of "others who were tortured, not accepting deliverance; that they might obtain a better resurrection," but the foregoing are sufficient to prove how valiantly saints can die. There are other *Last Sayings* we would like to have. What an inspiration it would be to have Paul's farewell word before his noble head was severed from his frail body and he died for the Lord he dearly loved. We would also like to have Peter's dying utterance as he was crucified upside down for Christ. While we have John's last recorded message, "Even so, come, Lord Jesus" (Rev. 22: 20), we would value his final word as he died a prisoner on the isle of Patmos.

A perusal of martyrdom literature convinces one of two facts. First of all, there was the new attitude towards death which Christianity brought to men. Everywhere in early Christian burial grounds there were images of hope. Saints were not afraid to die. With Paul, they knew that to die was gain. A dominant, tranquil confidence was theirs. They met and defied death with heroic cheerfulness and grateful expression of heart for the blessed life their bitter end was bringing them.

The other impression gained is this. Saints and martyrs were eager to die in harness. They remained at their sacred tasks until their voices were silenced by death. Threats never moved them. On they went in their witness, deeming any sacrifice they might be called upon to make, a privilege to be coveted.

We have endeavored to give a selection out of the numberless host of those who, because they followed Christ so completely, came to their Calvary. How different it was with one who might have had a similar victorious death! FRANCIS SPIRA was the Venetian lawyer, an Italian of wealth, learning and eloquence who, attracted by the fame of Martin Luther and the principles of the Reformation, became a preacher and for six years proclaimed the evangelical doctrines represented by the Reformation. The persecutions of the time, directed against Christians, frightened him and he became an apostate. In the presence of two thousand people he recanted and acknowledged once more the Roman Catholic doctrines. As soon as this public recantation was over, Spira took seriously ill and implored someone to kill him. Friends came to bid him farewell and were horrified at his cursing and blasphemy against God. In his last hour he confessed in a somewhat lengthy fashion:

> "I have denied Christ voluntarily and against my convictions. I feel that He hardens me, and will allow me no hope. It is a fearful thing to fall into the hands of a living God! I feel the weight of His wrath burning like the pains of hell within me. I am one of those whom God has threatened to tear asunder. Oh, the cursed day! Would I had never been at Venice. I am like the rich man, who though he was in hell was anxious that his brethren should escape torment. Judas, after betraying his Master, was compelled to own his sin and to declare the innocence of Christ, and it is neither new nor singular that I do the same. The mercy of Christ is a strong rampart against the wrath of God; but I have demolished that bulwark with my own hands. Take heed of relying on that faith which works not a holy and unblameable life, worthy of a believer. It will fail. I have tried. I presumed I had the right faith, I preached it to others. I had all places in Scripture in memory that might support it. I thought myself sure, and in the meantime lived impiously and carelessly. Now the judgment of God hath overtaken me, not to correction, but to damnation."

WILLIAM LAUD (1573-1645), the notorious Archbishop of Canterbury who became Chief Minister to Charles I, was active for many years in repressing Puritanism. The means he adopted to force Christians to deny their faith — cropping the ears, slitting noses and branding foreheads with hot irons — were not only unchristian but cruel and detestable, but Laud reaped what he had sown. At the age of 72, he was found guilty of religious intolerance, stripped of all his honors and beheaded. It is said that at the end he repented and prayed:

> "I am coming, Oh Lord! as quickly as I can. I know I must pass through death before I come to Thee, but it is only a mere shadow — a little darkness upon nature: Thou hast broken the jaws of death."

Records of Dying Words

V.

Records of Dying Words

We are greatly indebted, in our search for the last words of those who have gone before, to a number of authors who have written on the subject. The following citations are just a sampling of the many works available.

I. *More Than Notion*

More Than Notion, appears to be a strange title for the book J. H. Alexander gave us, but it is taken from the couplet by Joseph Hart —

> "True religion's more than notion,
> Something must be known and felt."

In this historical volume, the author describes a group of people in Shropshire who were influenced by a revival of religion towards the end of the Eighteenth Century.

There was *Mrs. Gilpin,* wife of the Rev. William Gilpin, onetime principal of Cheam School, to which Prince Charles went in 1958 for his 'prep' school education. Mrs. Gilpin died in 1831, her last words being:

> "I am not triumphant like that dear sister of mine, but I have peace. There was a cloud, but it has passed, it has passed. Eye hath not seen, nor ear heard the glories of that glorious change. I shall behold them soon. I shall sing Alleluia! Alleluia! I shall be washed in the blood of the Lamb. I shall be clean and white. I shall have a white robe, the fine linen which is the righteousness of the saints, and from the blessed company in that joyous song — Worthy is the Lamb that was slain."

When Elizabeth, one of the daughters of the Gilpins, reached her end at the age of forty-nine she was heard to say:

> "It's wondrous! Glorify! Mercy! Jesus! Redeemer."

Another character in *More Than Notion* is the gay and care-less Bengal officer who was brought to Christ through a serious illness. *Lieutenant Francis Jeffreys,* born in India, was the son of a minister, but on the death of his mother came back with the family to England. After his conversion, Francis became a most exemplary Christian but died in his thirtieth year. His final days were days of wonderful rejoicing in the Lord. Here is the account of his last hour and message:

> He asked to be moved, "But first let's have some reading," he said. A hymn by Joseph Hart, "Come, Ye Sinners," was read. Francis was quiet meditating on the line, "On the bloody cross behold Him," and then he said, with tears streaming:
> "We must hide ourselves in the dust and say, His atoning blood be upon us for ever!"
> Later on he looked so happy his sister said, "You remind me of the Pilgrims in the second part of *Pilgrim's Progress,* fol-lowing each other over the river, one of them stood still and sang a hymn in the middle of it, and so could you if strong enough."
> "Yes, I could," he said.
> She added, "He that has brought you down dry-shod into Jordan will lead you safely up the bank on the other side." He smiled, and said:
> "Oh yes, He will!"
> Being moved, his lungs were disturbed. He said faintly:
> "This is death!" and was gone.

Farmer Oakley, another character in the book who was caught up in the revival, likewise had a triumphant end. His wife, writing of his last hours, describes how her husband continued praying and praising God the final day of his pilgrimage. At the end, he said:

> "Shut the door while I endeavour to pray, if the Lord will teach me."

After praying for a blessing on all gathered, he cried:

> "Holy, holy, holy is the Lord God Almighty, which was, and is, and is to come."

His daughter tried to hush the loud praying and singing of her dying father to which he replied:

> "O, I shall have cause to shout in heaven, if I am in the lowest place there!"

Maurice Perkins, who died at the early age of twenty-eight, was another of the small group of which J. H. Alexander writes.

During the last week of his life, his soul longed to be fed with the Word of God, and his brother had to read to him almost incessantly. On the morning of his death he said:

"I cannot praise Him now, but I shall praise Him afterwards."

His brother said to him, "Do you feel happy?" Maurice whispered softly:

"I know He loves me! Glory! Glory!"

and he was gone.

The group at Pulverbach had had many precious fellowship meetings in the home of *Thomas Nunn* who died in the winter of 1844 and whose last words were:

"Is this death? How peaceful and quiet! How happy! Let me lean my head on your shoulder. The Lord reward you all for your troubles."

He breathed his last in his chair, none perceiving when.

One of the most fascinating characters of J. H. Alexander's book is the rough farm girl, *Sukey Harley*, who was the first to be affected by the revival and then exercised a tremendous influence over others. She once said:

"I often think about my death. The folks will be gathered together to see old Sukey Harley die; and they'll think to hear glorious words from my mouth. But they will hear nothing. No, I sha'nna have a word to say when I am dying."

She proved to be a true prophetess, for on her last day, her spectacles were found in the last chapter of Mark's Gospel, but for hours neither voice nor language was heard. Sukey's eyes were closed, and all was silent as if the Lord were in the room and it were holy ground, and so it was. She had often expressed a desire to leave the world on a Lord's Day, and the wish was granted her, for as the sun began to dawn on her last Lord's Day, she entered Glory to see the Lord Himself.

The outstanding personality of the group was *Pastor Bourne* whose remarkable ministry was so interwoven with the lives of those this book depicts. He died at the age of eighty-four about the sixtieth year of his spiritual life and the forty-first year of his ministry. In an age of erroneous and empty profession, he preached the Word of God with marvellous results. His last message was:

"The Government shall be upon Christ's shoulder. So it is! So I have found. I have nothing to say to them but I love

them all, and that the truths I have preached to them will
do to live by, aye, and to die by too! That they will!"

The day before he took to his bed, Pastor Bourne directed the
words from Joshua 21:35 to be inscribed on his grave, marking
them in his Bible:

"There failed naught of any good thing which the Lord had
spoken: all came to pass."

II. *Brief Memorials Of Departed Saints*

Brief Memorials Of Departed Saints, written and published
by the Rev. J. M. Chapman, is another of those interesting
volumes designed to exhibit the animating and supporting influence of Christianity in the labors, suffering and death of
saints. Always deeply interested in Christian biography, Chapman compiled his selection in the hope that the publication of
same would help liquidate the debt of the chapel of which he
was the Pastor.

Joseph Miller Chapman (1801-1841), was born of godly parents who early trained him in the observance of religious or-
dinances. He enjoyed a relatively long pastorate at Yeovil
where he exercised a far-reaching influence through his Bible-
centered and eloquent preaching.

Chapman was only forty years of age when death suddenly
concluded his powerful earthly service for the Master. His last
sermon was in the nature of a funeral discourse for an aged
deacon of his church. The moving message was based on the
last words of the patriarch Jacob, "I am to be gathered unto my
people, bury me with my fathers . . ." (Gen. 49:29-33). Those
who heard Chapman preach said that he preached as if he
were preaching his own funeral sermon; had he known it would
be his last, it could scarcely have been more solemn or pointed.

At the Lord's table after the sermon, in all the vigor and
bloom of health, he joined with the congregation and sang with
unusual ardor and sweetness —

"When this poor lisping, stammering tongue
Lies silent in the grave,
Then in a nobler, sweeter song,
I'll sing Thy power to save."

Chapman little knew that before the next Lord's Day, his "poor
lisping, stammering tongue" would be "silent in the grave" and
that he would be singing "a nobler, sweeter song" above.

After that memorable funeral service, being somewhat excited and heated, he caught a cold on the way home in the unusually humid and foggy air, and by the Friday morning he was dead. Two hours before his transportation to heaven, the only language escaping his lips was:

"Christ is all — all is well."

The *Brief Memorials* Chapman cited in his volume reveal how widely versed he was in biographical literature. We herewith record an abbreviation of some of the Puritans he mentions.

John Dod (1549-1645), was converted to God while studying at Jesus College, Cambridge. A preacher of great spiritual power, hundreds were saved under his ministry. Because people flocked to his independent church, Anglican ministers became jealous, and Dod was suspended from his charge and silenced by the Archbishop. With the accession of King James, Dod was restored to the ministry he loved, where he remained for the rest of his days. Subject to a good deal of physical pain, Dod used to say that:

"Sanctified afflictions are spiritual promotions."

He finished his course and received his crown of righteousness at age ninety-six. With eyes and hands lifted up to heaven, the last word uttered was:

"I desire to be dissolved, and to be with Christ."

Robert Bolton (1572-1631), was educated at Oxford and became famous for his learning and many accomplishments. Converted in his thirty-fifth year, he resolved to enter the ministry where he remained until his death. An industrious student, a devout and humble Christian and an energetic and awakening preacher, Bolton was greatly used of the Lord. A severe illness brought him low, and during his last days he was full of praise to God for His grace and goodness and sought to comfort his wife and children, as well as the church members and friends who came to see him. As tears were shed, he would say:

"Oh! how much ado there is before one can die!"

As the moment of his departure came, he shook the hands of all around the bed and exhorted them:

"Make sure of heaven; and keep in mind what I have formerly delivered unto you. The doctrine which I have preached to you for the space of 20 years is the truth of God, as I shall

> answer at the tribunal of Christ; before whom I must soon appear."

As he spoke the pangs of death were upon him, and a friend, taking his hand, asked if he felt much pain. Bolton replied:

> "Truly no, the greatest pain I feel is your cold hand."

John Bruen (1560-1625), was descended from an ancient and honorable family. At the age of thirty-two, he came under God's transforming power and thereafter used his talents and money in the extension of His cause. A man of much prayer it was true of him, as traditionally recorded of James the Apostle, that his knees were hardened with much kneeling in prayer. Seized with a sudden illness, pain of body and pangs of approaching death, Bruen proved that the consolations of the Gospel were more than enough to sustain him. The morning before he died, many friends visited him and desired his parting blessing, and lifting up hands and heart to heaven for them, he said:

> "The Lord is my portion, my help and my trust. His blessed Son, Jesus Christ, is my Saviour and Redeemer, Amen! Even so, saith the Spirit to my spirit. Therefore come, Lord Jesus, embrace me with the arms of Thy love. Into Thy hands I commend my spirit. Oh, come now, and take me to Thy own self. Oh, come, Lord Jesus, come quickly! Oh come, oh come, oh come."

Catherine Brettergh was the pious daughter of John Bruen. At twenty years of age she married but only lived some two years after her marriage. A burning fever attacked her, and at times she became delirious and would utter doubts about God and His salvation. She emerged into a calm and trustful state of mind, and before she fell asleep in Christ, she lifted up her eyes and with a sweet countenance and a quiet voice said:

> "My warfare is accomplished, and mine iniquities are pardoned. Lord, whom have I in heaven but Thee? And I have none on earth but Thee. My flesh faileth, and my heart also; but God is the strength of my heart, and my portion for ever. He preserved Jacob, and defendeth His Israel — he is my God, and will guide me unto death. Guide me, O Lord my God, and keep my soul in safety."

William Lyford (1598-1653), is the next Chapman mentions in his *Brief Memorials*. He was nominated one of the Assembly of Divines, but in all humility declined such an honor. Although he lived in a time of grievous civil wars, Lyford was an avowed advocate of peace and moderation and exercised a tremendous spiritual influence during his ministry. When his end came, with much difficulty he left this testimony:

> "My dissolution is more comfortable to me than my marriage day. Thanks be to God, which giveth us the victory, through our Lord Jesus Christ."

William Gouge (1575-1653), a renowned divine of his time was endowed with great powers of mind with which he not only mastered his studies but devoured Scripture. Exact and conscientious in all his ways he became known as the *arch-puritan.* He became minister of Blackfriars, London, where his gifts as a preacher drew large congregations. Though many invitations to other spheres came his way, he refused them all. He used to say:

> "It is my highest ambition to go from Blackfriars to heaven."

— which he did. At one time he was cast into prison for nine weeks for re-publishing a book on "The Calling Of The Jews", but in 1643 he was nominated one of the Assembly of the Divines, Westminster, and exercised a tremendous influence in his denomination.

Toward the end of his life he was much afflicted with asthma and the stone, and under these painful maladies he often groaned but never murmured. Before he died, after three days of drowsiness, he spoke much of the rich grace and mercy of God in Christ Jesus. When he revived after his period of drowsiness, he inquired what day it was, and when told exclaimed:

> "Alas! I have lost three days."

As he died, full of unspeakable comfort, having been minister of Blackfriars for nearly forty-six years, his departing testimony was:

> "Now I have not long to live. The time of my departure is at hand. I am going to my desired haven. I am most willing to die. I have, blessed be God, nothing else to do but to die. Death is my best friend, next to Jesus Christ. I am sure I shall be with Christ when I die."

Jeremiah Whitaker (1599-1654), was educated at Cambridge where, because of his scholastic attainments and Christian virtues, he was held in high esteem. He loved to preach the Gospel and had an undying passion for the souls of the people.

> "I had much rather be a minister of the Gospel than an Emperor,"

he used to say. When invited to become Master of College, he refused saying, "My heart doth more desire to be a constant preacher of the Gospel than to be master of any college in the world."

During the latter part of his life, he suffered from a most painful affliction. When asked how he endured so much pain, he replied:

> "The bush is always burning, but not consumed: and though my pains be above the strength of *nature*, they are not above the supports of grace."

Through the whole of his affliction, Whitaker exercised unshaken confidence in God and enjoyed uninterrupted assurance of His favor. When agonizing fits of pain came upon him, he usually said:

> "Now in the strength of the Lord, I will undergo these pains."

As death approached and agonizing fits became more frequent and painful, he was heard to say:

> "This is a bitter cup, but it is my Father's mixing, and shall I not drink it? Yes. Lord through Thy strength, I will. . . . Help me to be thankful! How much worse might this affliction have been! I might have been distracted, or laid roaring under anguish of spirit."

Thomas Wilson (1601-1653), was another of those godly ministers of the Sixteenth Century whom God mightily used for the ingathering of souls. Entering the ministry, his faithful Gospel witness was singularly blessed of God to the salvation of souls. In 1634 he was suspended from the ministry for four years because of his refusal to read the *Book of Sports* and was confined to prison. A man of deep piety and unflinching courage, he feared God and none else. After being in Wilson's company, the renowned William Fenner would say:

> "I am ashamed of myself, to see how Mr. Wilson gallops towards heaven, and I do but creep at a snail's pace."

When his Bridegroom came, Wilson was ready to go. Calling his family together he said:

> "Though we must be parted for a season, we shall meet again to part no more for ever."

And he finished his course and died in peace his last word was:

> "I bless God, who hath suffered me to live so long to do Him some service; and now I have finished the work appointed for me, that he is pleased to call me away so soon."

Samuel Bolton (1606-1654), orthodox in judgment, philan-thropic in spirit, and a celebrated interpreter of Scripture, his pre-eminent desire was to win souls for the Master. His godly life was an excellent comment on the doctrine he taught for he not only preached the Word but lived it.

When a fatal sickness overtook him, he exercised great pa-tience and was joyfully submissive to the Divine will. To a friend who visited him, Bolton said:

> "Oh, this vile body of mine! When will it give way that my soul may get out and go to God?"

When symptoms of approaching death were evident, he called them, "the little crevices through which his soul peeped." His final word was a request to be buried as a private Christian and not with the outward pomp of the Master of Cambridge:

> "I hope to rise in the day of judgment and appear before God, not as a *doctor*, but as a *humble Christian.*"

John Janeway (1633-1657), author of *Token Of Children,* a record of the dying testimonies of children, was well versed in Latin, Greek, Hebrew, mathematics and astronomy by the time he was seventeen years of age. Great learning, however, was mixed with much modesty and prudence. At the age of eighteen he became concerned about his soul's salvation, and Richard Baxter's *"Saint's Everlasting Rest"* was used for his con-version to God. Having a great love and compassion for souls, he labored for the salvation of his own kith and kin. During the closing period of his life, he became wholly employed in the contemplation of Christ, heaven and eternity. At length, suc-cumbing to rapid consumption, he knew that his end was near. To his dear mother he said:

> "I am dying, but I beseech you be not troubled. Through mercy, I am quite above the fear of death. I am going to Him whom I love above life."

A few hours before his happy exit, he called all his loved ones together and gave them one more solemn warning, saying:

> "I commend you to God, and to the world of His grace, which is able to build you up, and to give you an in-heritance among them which are sanctified."

Then came his final prayer:

> "Dear Lord, my work is done. I have fought a good fight, I have finished my course, I have kept the faith; henceforth

there is laid up for me a crown of righteousness. Come, Lord Jesus, come quickly."

Sarah Savage (1664-1752), is specially remembered as the sister of the celebrated expositor, Matthew Henry. Even as a young girl she would write out the points of sermons she heard preached — a custom she continued to her old age. Deeply taught in Scripture, she was greatly used among friends and neighbors in the exposition of the same. Her faith and patience were severely tried when "the king of terrors" left her a mourning widow. On the death of her aged husband, she wrote:

"A heavy stroke falls upon me unexpectedly, by the sudden death of my dear yokefellow, with whom I have lived in great amity and affection these forty-two years and six months. *Lord, what is man?*"

Her own end came at the ripe age of 88. To her minister who was at her deathbed she said:

"Pray for patience to bear the pains and troubles of sickness — for pardon of all sins — and the evidence of that pardon, acceptance with God in the beloved — our Lord Jesus Christ, and a welcome reception into His presence."

The diary of this saintly woman is a spiritual classic — so full of expressions of praise and gratitude to God and of confidence in His providential care and goodness. One item speaks of being in much pain, and that if it was a messenger of death, she had no fear. Then she wrote this translation of Psalm 73 which was to be her experience when death did knock:

"What if the springs of life were broke,
    And flesh and heart should faint?
God is my soul's eternal rock,
    The strength of every saint."

Ann Hulton (1668-1697), was the sister of Sarah Savage. Like her sister, Ann knew from childhood days the Holy Scriptures and read them with great delight. When about eleven years of age she commenced to write out sermons she heard and continued the exercise all her days. At 20 she was married to John Hulton, but they were not to have a very long partnership.

At 29, conscious that she had the sentence of death within her, she was not at all disturbed. Much joy was hers as she testified to all who came to see her that Christ was all-sufficient.

At the end she was delirious, yet even then it was evident her heart was set on God. Her last words were:

> "I have hope in my death, for Christ hath said, 'Because I live, ye shall live also'. I shall be gathered to my people, and I have those that are godly, both rich and poor."

Thomas Halyburton, (1674-1712) son of the manse, was son of a man who was among the three hundred Scottish ministers ejected from their parishes and homes for refusing submission to episcopal government. After the death of his father, Thomas went to Holland along with his mother and other members of the family to escape episcopal persecution. They returned to Scotland, and Thomas was licensed to preach, but impaired health made it difficult for him to undertake ministerial obligations. The last week of his life was a trying one, yet amid much conflict he had a sweet calm of soul. After a sore struggle to breathe, he said:

> "When I shall be so weakened as not to be able to speak, I will give you, if I can, a sign of triumph, when I am near to Glory."

A little later, trying unsuccessfully to relieve himself of phlegm, he managed to say:

> "I am effectually choked. Pity, pity, Lord. The Lord's way is the best way, and I am composed. Whether I do away in a fit of vomiting, or fainting, 'tis all one."

A friend said to him: "I hope you are encouraging yourself in the Lord." But being unable to speak, Thomas lifted up his hands and clapped and almost immediately entered heaven.

Lady Selina Shirley (1707-1791), better known as the Countess of Huntingdon, is a renowned name in English evangelical history. Mistaking her fancied eminence in piety for a life lived in Christ, the Countess, during the revival influence under the Wesleys, was brought under conviction and came into a deep experience of God's saving grace. The change of heart and life was manifest, and from the hour of her conversion Lady Huntingdon was zealous for the extension of the cause of Christ. She was left a widow at 39, and two years later moved to London and opened her house in Park Street for the preaching of the Gospel. George Whitefield identified himself with her Ladyship's efforts to evangelize rich and poor alike. Much grief and disappointment were hers. She followed nearly all of her children to the grave. When her own end came, she was fully prepared to depart and be with Christ. The last words of the noble Countess were:

> "I shall go to my Father tonight. My work is done; I have nothing to do but go to my Father."

Isaac Toms (1770-1861), was one of those valiant dissenters of the Seventeenth Century. The descendant of a line of ancestors eminent for their piety and sufferings in the cause of Christ, Isaac was a conspicuous linguist. After a theological course, he functioned as an itinerant preacher for sixteen years and later became pastor of a dissenting church. He labored for over forty years as a good minister of Jesus Christ. Feeling that old age prevented him from fulfilling all ministerial obligations, for two years he preached only once a week. In 1800 he said farewell to the house of God he dearly loved and remained at home to await his call to higher service above. Under the pressure of weakness he said:

> "I perceive that I am gently slipping into eternity."

To a neighboring minister who visited him and spoke to him of the great reward awaiting him, Isaac Toms replied:

> "Sir, when I arrive at the world of blessedness, I shall shout, Grace, grace!"

When he could speak no more his looks expressed the devotion of his soul and glorious expectancy.

Thomas Jones (1729-1762), was another called forth to stand firm in support of the cardinal truths of the Christian faith at a time when the church lightly esteemed them. He was not privileged, however, to live long as an able and eloquent preacher of the Gospel for the Lord took him to be with Himself when he was but 33 years of age, after a most tedious, painful and prolonged illness. Having been used to encourage many a tried saint to bear the chastenings of the Lord, grace was his to kiss the rod and be grateful. At the end he said:

> "I am so full of pain, indeed, that I can think but little; yet I know, that Jesus is carrying on the interests of my poor soul, notwithstanding."

His last saying was:

> "I am of the church of the first-born, who shall stand on Mount Zion; one chosen from among my brethren; a sinner saved, a sinner saved."

John Adams was esteemed one of the most eminent preachers of his day. This good and holy man was greatly used of God for the salvation of sinners and the sanctification of the saved. A friend present at the deathbed of John Adams wrote of his calm resignation. In a sweet composure of mind, he said to those in the room:

> "Come here, all ye that fear God, and I will tell you what He hath done for my soul."

Then he related to those present the grace and goodness of God, and expressed the most earnest longings for the full employment of the unutterable bliss awaiting him. Shortly before he passed away, apparently free from pain, he murmured:

> "Oh, when shall I see Him, as He is, in His transcendent glory? When appear before His face?"

John Ryland (1753-1825), one of the bright stars in English Baptist History, was one of the founders of The Baptist Missionary Society. Descended from a family eminent for its piety, John Ryland was a child prodigy that could read Psalm 23 in Hebrew when only five years old and read the Greek, Latin and French languages when but nine years of age. Ryland was a great friend of William Carey, and worked closely with other Baptist stalwarts, such as Reynold Hogg and Andrew Fuller. Approaching his "threescore years and ten," he caught a severe cold which developed into his fatal illness. About two months before his death, he penned the following "musings in a time of affliction":

> "In that day
> Oh! grant I may
> Find mercy, Lord, with Thee;
> Through Him who kept Thy holy law,
> Without a blemish or a flaw.
> Then he died upon the tree."

During his illness he would often repeat passages from the Psalms in the Hebrew original. A petition oft repeated was:

> "Lord, grant me an easy and gentle dismission into Thy heavenly kingdom,"

and his petition was mercifully answered; he fell asleep in Jesus with a composure and serenity that no language can adequately describe.

Alexander Waugh (1754-1827), is the last Character from Chapman's *Brief Memorials of Departed Saints* which we select. From his ordination in 1780 to his death in 1827, his preaching discourses amounted to 7,706. His favorite aphorism was:

"Work on earth — rest in Heaven."

Waugh was one of the founders of The London Missionary Society and for 28 years acted as its chairman. He was also associated with The British and Foreign Bible Society, The Religious Tract Society and many other societies. His public labors were abundant, yet amid all his multitudinous activities, he walked closely with God in secret.

A fall when the scaffolding gave way at the laying of the foundation stone of an orphan asylum hastened his end, as did the death of his dear son, 'the son of his right hand,' as he called him. Almost at the end he was seized with apoplexy and partial paralysis. He held out his hand to his dear wife and muttered:

"Wife, my face, my life; I am better now."

Mrs. Waugh said:

"When you are now in the deep Jordan, have you any doubt that Christ will be with you?"

The dying man replied:

"Certainly not! who else? who else?"

III. *Deathbed Scenes And Pastoral Conversations*

Published in 1830, the three volumes by Dr. Warton, bearing the title of *Death-bed Scenes And Pastoral Conversations*, make interesting reading for all those who have the care of souls. The different individuals Warton dealt with and how he approached them as they came to die reveal how faithful a minister should be in warning sinners to flee from the wrath to come.

Describing lengthy conversations he had with an infidel by the name of Waring, Dr. Warton relates how this man died in dreadful agony. Endeavoring to catch his last words, all Warton could hear was:

"It is very comfortable to me . . ."

The sentence was never finished. Grasping the dying man's hand, Warton asked him if he was dying in the faith of Jesus Christ, but no sign was given.

Another man whom Warton sought to win for the Saviour was a Mr. Maddox who evidently was the personification of despair. As he reached his end, concern regarding his readiness for eternity possessed him. Dr. Warton tried to lead the man into the assurance of salvation. Anguish of soul was his, and the last words he uttered before dying of a convulsion were:

> "If my life were to be spared — which cannot be — might not the same thoughts and the same desires return as my strength returned? Would not the same companions get about me, as before: and ridicule my past fears, and my present temperance; and laugh me again into my former vices? Oh! I have too long been unused to all goodness; every act of it would be strange and uneasy to me. And will God pardon and reward such a temper as mine? I cannot hope it — I am lost for ever."

IV. *History Of The Martyrs Of Lyons And Vienne, France*

Eusebius *History of the Martyrs of Lyons and Vienne, France,* makes gruesome reading. The treachery, torture and terrible deaths both men and women endured reveal how low wicked men can sink in brutality. Yet with bodies mangled and pierced until they ceased to look like human forms, those saints of a past age were faithful even unto death. As they died, they praised God that they should depart out of this life in such a way.

One of those courageous saints was *George Wisheart* who perished by fire in 1546. His executioner was so overcome by the godliness of Wisheart and his defiance of being burned alive that, falling on his knees, he said to Wisheart:

> "Sir, I pray you forgive me, for I am not the cause of your death."

Wisheart kissed his cheeks and replied:

> "Lo, here is a token that I forgive thee. My heart, do thine office."

Falling on his knees the doomed saint thrice repeated the prayer:

> "O Thou Saviour of the world, have mercy upon me. Father of Heaven, I commend my spirit into Thy holy hands."

When the captain of the castle where Wisheart had been imprisoned approached him, he bade him be of good courage and asked Wisheart to pray for him that his sin might be pardoned.

Wisheart said: "This fire torments my body, but no whit abates my spirit."

His last word was from the cruel and heartless Cardinal Beaton, who from a high window feasted his eyes upon the agonies of the sufferer. Ere his breath ceased, Wisheart said to Beaton:

> "He who in high state, from that high place, feeds his eyes with my torments, within few days shall be hanged at the same window, to be seen with as much ignominy as he now leans there with pride."

Needless to say, Wisheart's prophecy of the Cardinal's doom was fulfilled to the very letter.

Condemned to die along with Latimer and Ridley, *Archbishop Cranmer* recanted, yet in the end died bravely for the Faith. Tied to the stake, he stretched forth his right arm and said:

> "This is the hand that wrote the recantation, and therefore it shall suffer punishment first."

True to his purpose, as the flames arose, Cranmer thrust his hand into them saying:

> "This hand hath offended! this unworthy right hand!"

He was unmoveable and with countenance raised to heaven, he prayed with the Church's first martyr, Stephen:

> "Lord Jesus, receive my spirit."

V. *Token For Children*

While the bulk of the last words we have gathered are associated with adults, there is a small book by J. Janeway, *Token For Children*, published over a hundred years ago. This pocket book of some one hundred pages is made up of the conversion, witness and joyful deaths of several young children. Some of the accounts, if actually true, reveal a remarkable spiritual experience for children to have had. For instance:

Sarah Howley was between eight and nine years old when she came under conviction of sin. Later she became more affected and wondered how she could be saved. When about fourteen years of age, she broke a vein in her lungs. Her end was not far distant, and her last days were marked by an awareness of eternity. She dearly loved her godly parents with whom she meditated constantly upon spiritual matters. The day before Sarah died she prayed:

> "How long, sweet Jesus? finish Thy work: come, Lord Jesus; come quickly; good Lord, give me patience to wait the appointed time: Lord Jesus, help me!"

The next day found her calm and confident, and the last words she was heard to utter were:

> "Lord, help! Lord Jesus, help! dear Jesus! blessed Jesus."

The next account is of a boy who, through the religious influence of his home, accepted Jesus when he was about three years old and developed great eagerness for the Bible and prayer. Taken sick, he was asked if he was willing and prepared to die. The boy replied:

> "I am willing, for I shall go to Christ."

As he died at about six years of age, he cheerfully committed his spirit to God, saying:

> "Lord Jesus! Lord Jesus!"

— in whose bosom he sweetly slept.

Mary, a little girl who became a Christian when she was between four and five years old, is the next Janeway tells of in his *Token*. When Mary's father died, she told her mother not to weep so much.

> "Dear Mother, you have no occasion to weep so much, for God is a good God still to you."

A child of great tenderness and kindness, Mary delighted in her Bible and other good books, and was greatly used to interest other children in spiritual things. When about twelve years of age she fell sick. As she lay dying, she seemed to be troubled and cried out:

> "I am none of his."

Her mother asked what was the matter, and Mary's final word was:

> "Satan did trouble me, but now, I thank God, all is well. I know I am not his, but Christ's."

The next child to receive mention is a girl who, when about four years old, had a conscientious sense of duty towards her parents and an understanding of God's mercy and goodness.

Stricken with a fatal sickness, she was asked whether she was ready to die and replied:

> "Yes, because God has pardoned my sins through the blood of Christ."

Charles Bridgman, who died at twelve years of age, is another child Janeway refers to as one who early in life loved to read his Bible and desired spiritual knowledge. Ever grateful to God for all things, young Charles would rebuke his brothers if they forgot to thank God at meal times. Smitten with a lingering disease, he became much occupied with thoughts of heaven. Being asked whether he had rather live or die, he answered:

> "I desire to die, that I am go to my Saviour."

As Charles came to yield his spirit unto the Lord, his last words were:

> "Pray, pray, pray; nay, yet pray; and the more prayers, the better all prospers. God is the best Physician: into Thy hands I commend my soul! Now close mine eyes; forgive me, father, mother, brother, sister and all the world! Now I am well; my pain is almost gone, my joy is at hand. Lord have mercy upon me: O Lord, receive my soul unto Thee!"

John Sudlow was introduced to the things of Christ as soon as he was capable of understanding and at the age of four was serious-minded and would ask his maid religious questions. During the time of the plague, he was smitten soon after his twelfth birthday. An hour before his death the visiting minister asked John if he was afraid to die.

> "No," he answered, "if the Lord will but comfort me in that hour."

The minister further asked: "Do you expect comfort and salvation, seeing you are a sinner?" John replied:

> "Yes, in Christ alone."

Tabitha Alden, the daughter of a local minister, was almost nine when she died a triumphant death. She was familiar with the Scriptures and loved to read and hear about the Saviour. Stricken with illness, her devoted parents sensed that Tabitha's end was near, and she herself sensed death was at hand. When asked what the Glory was like that she said her eyes were fixed upon, she replied:

"I cannot say what, but I am going to it, will you go with me? I am going to glory. Oh that all of you were going with me to that glory."

Susannah Bicks had a relish for spiritual things from her earliest years of understanding. During the pestilence that raged through Holland in 1664, this sweet child was smitten. During her illness she could be heard saying:

"If thy law were not my delight, I should perish in my affliction."

Days of extreme feebleness followed, and Susannah's admirable behavior as death approached impressed all who visited her. The end came in her fourteenth year of age, and her last testimony was:

"Here, father, you see that my body is this tabernacle which now shall be broken down; my soul shall now part from it, and shall be taken up to heaven. There I shall dwell and go no more out, but sit and sing, Holy, holy, holy is the Lord God of Hosts, the Lord of Sabaoth!"

Often she asked of the Lord a quiet and easy departure, and her desire was granted. As she fell asleep in Jesus, she was heard to say:

"O Lord God, into Thy hands I commit my spirit! O Lord, be gracious, be merciful to me, a poor sinner."

Jacob Bicks, brother of Susannah, was only seven years old when he died. Like his dear sister, he was very heavenly minded for his tender years. Visited with a sore sickness, his parents wanted to send for the doctor, but little Jacob said:

"No, the Lord will help me. I know He will take me to Himself, and then He will be all my help."

His father said: "Oh, my dear child, thou hast such strong faith." Before the boy quietly breathed out his soul he replied:

"Yes, God hath given me a strong faith upon Himself, through Jesus Christ, that the devil himself shall flee from me."

Then came the last short word of prayer —

"Lord, be merciful to me, a poor sinner."

John Harvey is the last child of whom Janeway speaks. The death of one of her brothers greatly distressed Mrs. Harvey. Seeing her crying, John said:

"Pray mother, do not weep so much. Though Uncle is dead, does not the Bible say that he will rise again?"

The family was in London during the Great Plague of 1665. John's eldest sister was the first to be stricken and died. Fourteen days later, young John became a victim and suffered much pain. Speech began to fail him, but his heart was taken up with the prospect of Glory. Asked by his mother if he was ready to go to the heavenly Father, the dying lad replied:

"Yes, I am ready and willing to leave you, and go to my heavenly Father."

Asked if he would like a little to eat, he answered in a kind of divine rapture:

"Oh, what a supper is prepared for me in Glory."

Bowing his head, John spoke no more but went cheerfully and triumphantly into the presence of the Saviour a few weeks away from his twelfth year.

The Scottish Covenanters

VI.

The Scottish Covenanters

Two of the most remarkable books associated with the last testimonies of faithful saints are *A Cloud Of Witnesses*, or "The Last Speeches And Testimonies Of Those Who Have Suffered for the Truth in Scotland Since the Year 1680," and *The Dying Testimonies Of The Scots Worthies*, which contains not only a few records mentioned in *The Cloud of Witnesses* but others collated from *Naphtali* and several ancient accounts. These are priceless volumes for students as they tell of the slaughter of unoffending, peaceable believers whose horrible suffering was accompanied by cold-blooded deceitful mockery.

William McGavin, in his *Preface to Dying Testimonies*, reminds us:

> "Scotland was one of the last of the kingdoms that submitted to the Roman yoke, and she was one of the first to throw it off. As a political measure the Reformation of England preceded that of Scotland by a number of years; but in a religious view it gained ground more extensively among the Scots while the court was against it, than it did in England with the court in its favour. In England it originated with the court which gave it the character of secularity and worldly splendor. In Scotland, it originated with the people, including some of the nobles, and found its way upward to the court, which after a hard struggle was compelled to give way and to establish the Protestant Faith and Order in that simple and unostentatious form which was most agreeable to the people. This was not effected without much bloodshed. Deceit and violence in their cruelest forms were employed by the image of the beast, whose seat was in St. Andrew's, to extinguish the light of the Reformation."

How dearly ministers and laymen alike suffered for Christ's sake! Thousands endured imprisonment and exile. Thousands more were hanged on the gibbet or slaughtered in cold blood by armed savages, who were hunting them as if they had been wild beasts, fit only to be taken and destroyed. Think of the unspeakable persecution of the Covenanters during the reigns of Charles II and of his brother James VII! How happy a deliverance they experienced with the arrival of King William and the Revolution of 1688!

The majority of the last messages we are to consider are related to the twenty-eight years before the Revolution. Here we have some of the first martyrs of the Reformation. What precious documents were those National Covenants which were the means God used from the outset of the Reformation to cement and strengthen His people in Scotland in their adherence to His Truth.

The main cause of contention was:

> "Whether Christ alone or King Charles should be owned as head and lawgiver to the Church; and whether the Divine form of government and discipline which Christ had instituted should continue in her, or if a usurper should have leave to mould it, as he pleased, and conform it to the pompous dress of the Romish whore."

It was because so many of the noble Scots chose Christ alone that they endured such horrible torture and death for His dear sake.

Down through the ages, the last words of Christ's noble heroes and martyrs have proved His prophecy to be true, "It shall be given them in that hour what they shall speak." Granted, many of these dying words were not embellished with oratory and fine language, seeing they came from the lips of people of meager education. But they were full of the language of heaven, and they remain as an instruction and example to saints.

As space forbids any long extracts from the lengthy and courageous speeches many of the martyrs made in their own defense before they were unjustly condemned and murdered, we must content ourselves with a few brief facts about each warrior-saint along with his last testimony. Before the year 1660 A.D., we have the final words and dying messages of Scots worthies like these —

PATRICK HAMILTON, who was among the first to suffer and die in Scotland for Christ, was artfully seduced into a confession of his faith, condemned as a heretic by the Archbishop of St.

Andrew's and condemned to die. The same day he was sentenced, he was hurried to the stake, and while the fire was being prepared, he divested himself of his outer garments and handing them to his servant said:

> "These will not profit me in the fire, yet they will do thee some good."

As he commended himself to God, one of his persecutors called to Patrick, "Convert, heretic, pray to our Lady, and say 'Salve Regina.'" Patrick replied:

> "Wicked man! thou knowest I am not an heretic, and that it is the truth of God for which I now suffer. So much thou didst confess to me private: and whereupon I appeal to thee to answer before the Judgment Seat of Christ."

As the fire burned, the noble martyr only twenty-four years of age exclaimed:

> "How long, O Lord, shall darkness overwhelm this realm? How long wilt Thou suffer this tyranny of men?"

He then ended by praying with Stephen —

> "Lord Jesus, receive my spirit."

RUSSELL and KENNEDY were companions in suffering as Ridley and Latimer were at a later date. Both were young men, not more than twenty years of age, of liberal education and promising talents. Kennedy, while before the Archbishop, was enabled to make a remarkable speech as, falling on his knees, he said:

> "O, Eternal God! How wonderful is that love and mercy Thou bearest to mankind, and unto me the most caitiff (mean or despicable) and miserable wretch above all others! Even now when I would have denied Thee and Thy Son, our Lord Jesus Christ, my only Saviour, and so have cast myself into everlasting damnation, Thou by Thine own hand hast pulled me from the bottom of hell, and hast made me to feel that heavenly comfort which hath taken me from the ungodly fear by which I was oppressed. Now I defy death."

Turning to his persecutors, young Kennedy said:

> "Do what you please — I praise God I am ready."

Russell manifested great composure of mind while before his accusers and ingeniously rebutted the charges made against him. But found guilty and condemned, he was hurried to the place of execution to die along with his friend, Kennedy, to whom he said:

> "Brother! fear not — more mighty is He that is in us than he that is in the world; the pain that we shall suffer is short and shall be light, but our joy and consolation shall never have an end; and therefore let us strive to enter in, unto our Master and Saviour, by the same strait way which He hath taken us before. Death cannot destroy us, for it is destroyed already by Him for whose sake we suffer."

WALTER MILL, whose death as a martyr is said to have contributed most effectually to the downfall of popery in Scotland, took orders in the Church of Rome and became a priest. But Mill came under the power of God, was converted, and forsook Mass. In 1538 he was arrested and condemned. He escaped and fled for his life to Germany where he remained for twenty years. He then returned to Scotland with a desire to instruct in the Protestant faith those he had previously cared for as a priest. Again Mill was arrested, tried and condemned as a heretic. During his trial he powerfully defended himself from Scripture and made a deep impression over those who were present. Led forth by a guard of armed men to execution, he was called upon by some hard-hearted Catholics to recant, to whom he replied:

> "I marvel at your rage, ye hypocrites, who do so cruelly pursue the servants of God; as for me, I am now eighty-two years old and cannot live long by course of nature; but an hundred shall rise out of my ashes, who shall scatter you, ye hypocrites, and persecutors of God's people, and such of you as now think yourselves the best shall not die such an honest death as I now do. I trust in God, I shall be the last who shall suffer death in this fashion, and for this cause, in this land."

It is generally understood that Walter Mills was the last person to die in this way in the cause of Reformation from popery. Standing upon the sticks before he perished Mill said:

> "Many faithful martyrs have offered their lives most gladly, so this day I praise God that He hath called me, among the rest of His servants, to seal His truth with my life; which as I have received it of Him, so I willingly offer it up for His glory. Therefore, as ye would escape eternal death, be no longer seduced by the lies of bishops, abbots, friars, monks, and the rest of that sect of antichrist, but depend only upon Jesus Christ and His mercy, that so ye may be delivered from condemnation."

Drawn up and bound to the stake, as the fire kindled, Walter Mill cried:

> "Lord, have mercy on me: Pray, pray, good people, while there is time."

ROBERT BRUCE, one of the most distinguished men of his time, entered the ministry and became prominent in Edinburgh. Scrupulously maintaining the established forms of the church, he exposed himself to much persecution for the truth's sake, which he endured with unshrinking constancy. Before he died he called for the family Bible and said to his daughter:

> "Cast up to me the eighth chapter of Romans, and set my finger on these words, *I am persuaded that neither death nor life . . . shall be able to separate me from the love of God which is in Christ Jesus my Lord.*"

Then Bruce said: "Is my finger on them?"
"Yes," said his daughter. Then he replied:

> "Now God be with you my children; I have just breakfasted with you, and shall sup with my Lord Jesus this night."

SAMUEL RUTHERFORD, whose "Letters" have endeared him to all who love the Lord, was educated at Edinburgh University, and while still a young man, elected professor of philosophy there. Later on, he became a minister and renowned for his devotional exposition of Scripture. He suffered much, however, on account of his ardent nonconformity. In 1661 it was proposed to indict him, but happily he was removed from threatened evils to the presence of the Master he deeply loved. His last words, along with his testimony to the work of the Reformation since 1638, were signed by him only twelve days before he died. The concluding paragraph of this lengthy document reads:

> "Yet we are to believe Christ will not so depart from the land, but a remnant shall be saved; and He shall reign as victorious conquering king to the ends of the earth. O that there were nations, kindreds, tongues and all the people of Christ's habitable world, compassing His throne with cries and tears for the spirit of supplication to be poured down upon the inhabitants of Judah for that effect."

ARCHIBALD CAMPBELL had a great zeal for the Presbyterian cause in Scotland. He not only promoted the cause by his talents and influence but defended it by his sword. In 1649 he assisted in reinstating Charles II to his father's throne and received tokens of favor from the monarch. The tide of fortune turned, however, and in 1660 he was arrested for alleged high treason and brought from Scotland to the Tower of London to be tried. He was tried and found guilty and suffered the death of a supposed traitor. The essence of his alleged crime was his rigid adherence to Presbyterianism. Dressed in gentlemanly fashion, he mounted the scaffold with great serenity, like one going to his Father's house, and saluted all who were around it. His Lordship then addressed the spectators from the scaffold, his last words being, before he laid his head on the block:

> "I desire you, gentlemen, all that hear me this day, to take notice, and I wish that all who see me might hear me, that now I am entering into eternity, and am to appear before my Judge; and as I desire salvation, and to expect eternal salvation and happiness from Him— from my birth to my scaffold, I am free from any accession to my knowledge, concerning counsel, or any other way, in his late Majesty's death; and I pray the Lord to preserve his Majesty, and to pour His best person and government, and the Lord give him good and faithful counsellors."

Then turning to his friends he said:

> "Many Christians may stumble at this, and my friends may be discontented, but when things are rightly considered, my friends have no discredit of me, nor Christians no stumbling block, but rather an encouragement."

As he kneeled down most cheerfully upon the block his final word was:

> "I am not afraid to be surprised with fear."

James Guthrie suffered a similar fate three days after Argyle's death. While at St. Andrew's University he came under the godly influence of Samuel Rutherford and in 1638 became a minister of the Presbyterian Church. In spite of love for his country and loyalty to his king, he was hated by some for his staunch witness for the truth, and on account of certain statements he had made, he was charged with high treason, found guilty and executed. His speech on the scaffold was a long and moving one. Before he died he lifted the napkin from his face and cried:

> "The covenants, the covenants, shall yet be Scotland's reviving. Now let Thy servant depart in peace, since my eyes have seen Thy salvation."

WILLIAM GOWAN, who suffered along with James Guthrie and who was executed just after him, was charged with deserting the king's standard at Hamilton. It was also alleged against him that he was present on the scaffold when Charles I was beheaded. Practically all we know of him is found in his last speech. At the scaffold he took a ring from his finger and requested it to be given to his wife with the message:

> "I died in humble confidence, and found the Cross of Christ sweet."

As the cord was fastened around his neck he said:

> "I am near my last, and I desire to reflect on no man: I would only acquaint you of one thing: the commissioner and I went out to the fields together for one cause. I have now the cord about my neck, and he is promoted to be his Majesty's Commissioner; yet for a thousand worlds I would not change lots with him! Praise and glory be to Christ for ever."

THOMAS PATERSON, a Glasgow merchant, was one of the eighty prisoners brought to Edinburgh after the defeat of the Covenanters at Pentland in 1666. Shortly after, he was condemned to be executed and would have shared the fate of others had he not died of his wounds before the date of execution. The day he was condemned, Paterson wrote on behalf of all in prison awaiting death:

> "We therefore, the unworthiest of all the faithful, do in the Spirit of God and glory, testify and seal with our blood and lives, that both the national covenant and solemn league and covenant, are in themselves holy, just, and true and perpetually binding . . . This is our faith, so it is our hope to all that wait for the salvation of God, that our God will surely appear for His own glory, and vindicate His cause and persecuted people, and render vengeance to His adversaries, even the vengeance of His holy temple and broken covenant . . . Be not moved with our sufferings, which are but light and momentary, for they 'work for us a far more exceeding and eternal weight of glory', and for you also a strong confirmation, and abounding consolation against the like trial that possibly may befall you."

JOHN McCULLOCH was another of the ten covenanters who suffered for conscientious adherence to the faith. He was regarded as the most distinguished among the prisoners at Pentland. He affixed his name along with the rest of the condemned to a testimony subscribed to in the Edinburgh prison on the day of their death. The conclusion of this historic document reads:

"The Lord will judge His people, and repent Himself for His servants when their power is gone, and there is none shut up or left. Therefore, rejoice, O ye nations, with His people, for He will avenge the blood of His servants, and will render vengeance to His land and people. So let Thy enemies perish, O Lord, but let them that love Thee, be as the sun when he goeth forth in his might."

HUGH MCKAIL was one of the youthful martyrs who was executed for conscience sake. When only twenty years of age, he was licensed as a preacher. Preaching in one of the large Edinburgh churches, he made the remark, "The people of God have been persecuted by a Pharaoh on the throne, a Haman in the state and a Judas in the church." Enemies who heard him said that he alluded to the then rulers, and the next day he was apprehended. He escaped, however, and managed to conceal himself for four years. People, both in the south and west, combined in defense of their rights and young Hugh joined them. At last he was taken and, along with another prisoner, Neilson of Corsack, was subjected to the torture of the boots — a contraption gradually crushing the feet. Later on, with five others, he was executed. Because of his tortured feet he could not walk to the scaffold, and guards carried him. Kneeling he said that as his years in the world had been but few, so his words at that time should not be many. Toward the end of his moving testimony he said:

"Farewell father and mother, friends and relations; farewell the world and its delights; farewell meat and drink; farewell sun, moon and stars. Welcome God and Father; welcome sweet Lord Jesus, the Mediator of the new covenant; welcome Spirit of grace, and God of all consolation; welcome glory; welcome eternal life; welcome death."

HENRY COLQUHOUN, who was condemned along with McKail, was a plain, unlettered man who loved the Lord. Because of his adherence to the Covenant, he was falsely charged and condemned. On the scaffold he called for his Bible, and when it was brought, he read aloud apt passages. Then he addressed his friends and the spectators, concluding with the words:

"I commend all you, the lovers of our Lord Jesus Christ, to God Himself, and to the good word of His grace, which is able to build you up until the day of His appearance, and to give you all an inheritance with them which are sanctified through faith in our Lord Jesus Christ: and subscribe myself an expectant and apparent heir of the grace of Christ."

JAMES LEARMOUTH, a tradesman of East Lothian, was another who was beheaded as a traitor. There are few cases of more lawless oppression and more wanton cruelty than that exhibited in the death of this godly man. He was present at a preaching convention, and nearby a soldier was killed in an affray. Learmouth was seized and, along with another who was present at the convention, charged with the murder of the soldier. The other was condemned to perpetual banishment, and Learmouth was ordered to be beheaded as a traitor and to have his property confiscated for his Majesty's use. Before the sentence was carried out, he made a long statement as to his innocency and faith in God and left behind this last word:

> "As for the Archbishop, I charge my blood upon him, with all the blood of the innocent suffers in the cause, which by their means and their associates has been shed, and all the other sufferings the covenanted people of the Lord have been put to, all which cry for just revenge from the righteous Lord and Judge of all. I have my mind more fully expressed in another paper, that is more large, all which I subscribe as a dying man, who am to appear immediately before the righteous Judge, and I hope to receive the sentence, 'Well done faithful servant, enter into your Master's joy,' — though not by my merit, but through the merit and purchase of Christ. So farewell all enjoyments in time — farewell all ordinances, and welcome precious Christ."

JOHN KING was seized along with seventeen others. Taken to Edinburgh for trial, they were condemned and executed and their heads and right hands were nailed to the Netherbow Port, further manifestation of the injustice and cruelty of that period. After his lengthy testimony, with its firm and faithful denial of any rebellion and its clear witness to the faith, King's last words before he died were:

> "Now I bid farewell to all my friends and dear relations; farewell my poor wife and child, whom I leave on the good hand of Him who is better than seven husbands, and will be 'a father to the fatherless'. Farewell all creature comforts, and welcome everlasting life, everlasting glory, everlasting love, and everlasting praise. 'Bless the Lord, O my soul, and all that is within me.'"

DAVID HACKSTON was a noble covenanter who was charged with participation in the murder of the Archbishop of St. Andrew's in 1679. Taken prisoner and carried to Edinburgh, he was ordered to receive the most terrible torture possible and die in a most barbarous and revolting fashion. Nailed to a cross, his right hand was cut off, and after some time his left hand. Taken down still alive, his bowels were removed, and his heart taken out by the hangman and shown to the crowd. Heart and bowels were thrown into a fire, and then his head was cut off and the rest of his body divided into four quarters. In his last letter to his sister this brave martyr wrote:

> "If the free grace of God be glorified in me, ought not all to praise Him? Christ came not to call the righteous, but sinners. Many of this generation think they have so much grace that they cannot sin: but I must tell them, grace doth not warrant from sin, and they may so think of it."

ARCIHBALD ALISON, David Hackston's companion in suffering, was tried and sentenced to be executed in the Grassmarket, Edinburgh.

One would like to reproduce the lengthy, dying testimony of Alison as he outlined the events leading up to his arrest, his reasons for being a Covenanter and his stirring appeal to the godly, to the seekers after God and to the ungodly in view of his near martyrdom. The concluding paragraph reads:

> "I take my farewell of all the serious seekers of God, for a short time. And you that are calm, prudent professors, I leave you under process, till you repent for casting off Christ and His Cross, and bringing up an evil report over the land, and for your wronging of the cause. And ye rulers, farewell for ever more, without repentance and deep humiliation, for wronging of Christ and His people. Return, my soul, unto thy quiet rest. Farewell all created comforts in time, and welcome Father, Son and Holy Ghost, into Thy hands I commit my spirit."

JOHN MALCOLM, a weaver by trade, was charged along with David Hackston. Tried and sentenced accordingly, Malcolm, died in great assurance. The striking feature in the experience of all these brave worthies is that they were allowed to write their testimonies as to why they were Christ's and willing to suffer in His Cause. All of these long, detailed testimonies form a most inspiring, spiritual treasury of heartwarming literature. The last word of Malcolm, as he laid down his life as a sufferer for Christ, reads:

> "I shall say no more, but wish that ye would all seek repentance in time, before it be hid from your eyes. I recommend my soul and spirit to Him, 'that is able to save to the

uttermost all that come to Him through Christ;' and desire to take leave of all created comforts. Farewell all relations, farewell world, farewell sin. Welcome Christ, Welcome Heaven, and glory for ever more."

JAMES SKENE was a convert of Donald Cargill's mighty preaching. Although he had no idea that he was attached to the persecuted cause of the Covenanters, he was apprehended and charged with having been connected with the insurrections of Bothwell Bridge and Airmoss. The authorities could bring no crime against James; yet he was found guilty and sentenced to be hanged. Skene's last words consist of several letters to his friends. The close of his speech on the scaffold is in this form:

> "Now, farewell dear friends! I hope the Lord will have a glorious Church in Scotland, and that He will raise His glory out of the ashes of the burnt Covenant. Now, farewell sun, moon and stars! Farewell, Holy Scriptures! Oh! I am going to a life where I shall be no more troubled with a body of sin or death. Oh! I am going to a mansion of glory that my Lord has prepared for me. I shall have a crown of life; because I have been, by my blessed Lord's assistance — though I stepped aside — made faithful to death. Now, welcome Father, Son and Holy Spirit, Thou hast redeemed me by Thy price, and by Thy power. Oh! Lord God of Hosts, into Thy hands I commit my spirit."

ARCHIBALD STEWART, converted to God while in Holland, became a friend of Donald Cargill and suffered accordingly. Arrested, he appeared several times before the Privy Council, and a confession was extorted from him by means of the terrible boot. After suffering much torture, Stewart was executed. His last testimony ended:

> "'I bless God for all that He hath done for my soul, and for this way He hath taken me, in carrying me to the land of praise, where I shall sing that sweet song throughout the ages of Eternity, which shall never have an end. Oh! I long to be with Him; for if ye knew what I have got of His love and presence, ye would sometimes be giving a look to time, and bidding it be gone. Now, even let it be gone, that I may enjoy my Best Beloved."

Upon the scaffold Stewart sang the Second Psalm and read Malachi 3. He was not permitted to pray publicly, however, for as he started, "Oh! Lord, what wilt Thou do with this generation, what wilt Thou do with bloody Charles Stuart?"

immediately the drums were beaten loudly and the dying man's mouth stopped.

Isabel Alison, whose trial and death was a flaming proof of the iniquity of the period in which she lived, was a young unmarried woman of sober and religious habits. Seized because of her condemnation of the way religious people were persecuted, she was taken to Edinburgh where the council forced her to acknowledge her acquaintance with others of like faith as herself. She was found guilty of treason and condemned to die on the scaffold. At the scaffold she sang Psalm 84 and read Chapter 16 of Mark, and then uttered loudly:

"Rejoice in the Lord, ye righteous, and again, I say, rejoice."

As she ascended the ladder she cried out:

"Oh! be zealous, sirs, be zealous, be zealous! Oh! love the Lord, all ye His servants. Oh! love Him, Sirs! for in His favor there is life. Oh! ye His enemies, what will ye do, whither will ye fly in that day? For now there is a dreadful day coming on all the enemies of Christ. Come out from among them, all ye that are the Lord's people. Farewell, sweet Bible in which I delighted most, and which has been sweet to me since I came to prison. Farewell, Christian acquaintances."

Marion Harvie was a servant girl of twenty years of age, but from her godly covenanting father she had received a religious training. She took every opportunity of hearing the persecuted preachers like Donald Cargill, John Welch, Richard Cameron and others. On her way to hear one of these preachers, she was apprehended and brought before the council. Simply and clearly she confessed her love for the Bible but protested her innocence of any complicity in the crime with which the magistrates condemned her. As usual, she was found guilty of treason and sentenced to be executed. Her answers before the council and the justiciary court, and her dying testimony make impressive reading. When she came to the scaffold she joined Isabel Alison in singing Psalm 84 to the fine old tune, "Martyrs." When Marion came to the ladder, she said:

"Oh! my fair one, my lovely one, come away; I am not come here for murder, for they have no matter of fact to charge me with, but only my judgment. I am about twenty years of age. At fourteen or fifteen I was a hearer of the curates and indulged; and while I was a hearer of these I was a blasphemer and Sabbath-breaker; and a chapter of the

Bible was a burden to me; but since I heard this persecuted Gospel I durst not blaspheme, nor break the Sabbath, and the Bible became my delight."

Such a strong testimony was too much for her executioner, and the major called the hangman to draw the rope and choke her. No executions of those cruel times excited more sympathy or a deeper interest throughout the land than when these two Cameronian women were hanged at Edinburgh.

MARGARET McLAUCHLIN gained a fame neither she nor her persecutors ever dreamed of.

She was a widow about sixty-three years of age and a woman of piety and virtue. While devoutly worshipping God with her family, she was taken by the soldiers and indicted for attending covenanting conventicles. She had a long and sore imprisonment, kept without necessary fire, bed and diet. She was ordered to be tied to a stake within the seamarks in the water of Blednoch, Wigtown. Sometimes she would be thrust under the water and then pulled out again to see if she would repent, but with undaunted courage she affirmed her innocence and yielded up her spirit to God.

MARGARET WILSON was a young woman about twenty years of age, who, with her younger brother and sister, set out to visit their friend Margaret McLauchlin. Betrayed by a false friend, Margaret Wilson was brought before the magistrate and forced to take the objuration oath and own the king as the head of the church. Refusing, she endured the same cruel imprisonment as her friend, Margaret McLauchlin, and died the same death as she at Wigtown. When asked what she thought of her fellow sufferer wrestling in the water, Margaret Wilson said:

"What do I see but Christ mystical wrestling there?"

When taken out of the water and given the opportunity of recanting and saying, "God Save the King," she replied with Christian meekness:

"I wish the salvation of all men, but the damnation of none. I am Christ's, let me go."

We now group a trio of martyrs together for they issued a joint testimony at their trial. WILLIAM GOUGER, CHRISTOPHER MILLER, and ROBERT SANGSTER died together. Their confessions were similar. Gouger was evidently the spokesman for the three when they reached the scaffold. The soldiers showed great cruelty as he attempted to speak. He started to leave a dying testimony by saying:

> "I am come here for owning Christ to be Head and King in Zion."

The drummers were ordered to beat loudly to drown Gouger's speech. When offered his life upon one condition; namely, that he would own the king, he replied:

> "I will own none but Christ to be King in Zion."

Then he was asked: "Will ye not retract anything, sir?" Immediately Gouger replied:

> "No, no, I own all; I adhere to all."

DONALD CARGILL, shines as one of the brightest stars in the history of Scottish religious persecutions. Because of his fearless witness to the truth and his condemnation of the dominant party in the country, he was in continual jeopardy and peril. In 1662 he was banished to another part of the country. He was at the battle of Bothwell Bridge, where he was severely wounded. Later on, he surprised his enemies by escaping from them. The government became more hostile toward Cargill, whom they labeled as "one of the most seditious preachers and a villainous and fanatical conspirator." Wherever he preached, principally in fields, the Lord wonderfully blessed his labors in the salvation of lost souls and in the edification of the persecuted saints. He was seized while in bed and hurried off to trial. The sentence passed was, "Let him go to the gallows and die like a traitor."

When he came to the scaffold, Cargill sang a part of Psalm 118, then looked up to the windows on both sides of the scaffold with a smiling countenance beseeching the people to compose themselves as he addressed himself to three sorts of folk — to those persistent in their persecution of the works and people of God; to the ministers of the Church of Scotland; to the poor remnant who feared sinning more than suffering. Occasionally the drums were beaten to drown his voice. Among his last words before the axe fell were these moving ones:

> "Now I am near to getting to my crown, which shall be sure; for I bless the Lord, and desire all of you to bless Him that He hath brought me here, and makes me triumph over devils, and men, and sin! they shall wound me no more. I forgive all men the wrongs they have done to me, and pray the Lord may forgive all the wrongs that any of the elect have done against Him. I pray that sufferers may be kept

from sin, and helped to know their duty . . . Farewell reading and preaching, praying and believing, wanderings, reproaches, and sufferings. Welcome joy unspeakable and full of glory."

THE DUKE OF ROTHES, president of the Supreme Council of Scotland and one of the chief persecutors of Christians under Charles II, had a remorseful end. As he was dying, his bed shook under him and his cries could be heard over the immediate neighborhood. To some who stood around his deathbed he said, concerning Donald Cargill, the courageous Covenanter whose execution he had ordered:

"We all thought little of that man, his preaching and his sentence. But, oh sirs, I find it binding on my conscience now, and it will bind me to all eternity."

JAMES BOIG was another of Cargill's intimate friends and followers who paid the price of allegiance to Christ. Little is known of Boig apart from the fact that he was the son of an Edinburgh merchant and that as a student of divinity he was a young man of piety and talent. Arrested for his association in the Bothwell uprising and the Sanquhar Declaration, which disowned the king's authority, Boig was examined, tried, found guilty and put to death. His final word was:

"I am fairly on the way, and within the view of Immanuel's land, and in hopes to be received as an inhabitant there within the space of a few hours. Farewell all earthly comforts, farewell all worldly vanities, farewell all carnal desires, welcome cross, welcome gallows, welcome Christ, welcome heaven and everlasting happiness. Grace, mercy and peace be with you. Amen!"

ROBERT GARNOCK was greatly inspired by the preaching of the Covenanters at their conventicles. Garnock was esteemed as an outstanding Christian and a man of high attainments, great knowledge and experience in the things of God. Returning from a coventicle one night he was arrested and taken to prison where he was kept for a year and one-half. While in prison, he wrote an autobiography from which we can learn all there is to know about him. He appeared before the council and was convicted of disowning the council's authority and that of the king and his government. His dying word was of a touching character:

"As a dying martyr for Christ, I would leave it on all of you to make haste and prepare for the strokes, for they are at hand; and do not think that they will not come because they are delayed . . . Time is precious. Oh! make use of it, and act for God against all enemies. Fear not the wrath of men . . . Farewell, holy and sweet Scriptures, wherewith I have been refreshed many a day . . . Farewell sweet reproaches for my lovely Lord Jesus . . . Farewell sweet prison for my royal Lord Jesus Christ; it is now at an end. Farewell, all crosses of one sort or another — welcome eternal life, and the spirits of just men made perfect."

JAMES STEWART was a man whose case was remarkable, even in this period, for the degree of cruelty displayed under the cloak of religion. He had come to visit his brother who was in prison at Edinburgh. Somehow the brother escaped, and when the keeper returned, James was found alone. Immediately he was brought before the council and ensnared by questions. Stewart remained silent, whereupon the chairman threatened to take out his tongue with a pair of pincers if he failed to answer. He was found guilty on a trumped-up charge and died with four others. From his dying testimony we take the following paragraph:

"I was a brand plucked out of the fire; and He hath brought me through many difficulties, temptations and snares, and made my soul escape as a bird out of the cunning fowler's net, and brought me to a prison at length, to suffer bonds for Him. He made all things sweet to me, the company sweet to me, even bad company. He made reproaches sweet . . . Now He is faithful, into whose hands I commit my spirit and soul, and He will keep it against that day."

ROBERT GRAY was an Englishman whose indictment reveals for what little reason life was taken away in the time when tyrants ruled. In his own town Gray had been warmly attached to the persecuted cause of the Covenanters. Although a complete stranger to him, he wrote a letter to a prisoner named Anderson consoling him. In his letter, Gray expressed certain sentiments with regard to the king and his government. This letter fell into the hands of the authorities, and Gray was apprehended and kept in prison for ten months. He was then tried by the council, found guilty and sentenced to be executed. The gross injustice of his sentence is seen in the fact that Gray was not guilty of any overt act of treason, but merely of holding certain opinions which his judicial persecutors were pleased to call "treasonable." Furthermore, he was not a Scot and therefore not subject to the Scots' Law. Having received sentence of death from those who were unjustly taking away his life, Gray wrote a most heart-moving testimony in which he declared that he was about to die simply for adhering to the truth. At the scaffold he sang Psalm 84 and read John 15. After he had prayed, Robert Gray looked upon the multitude and said:

> "Sirs, you are feeding your eyes upon me; but what see you upon me? Surely you see not the wrath of God upon me. But if you would look up to the heavens ye might see the wrath of God against yourselves. I am brought out of another nation to own that Covenant which you have broken, and to seal it, and the glorious work of Reformation, with my blood . . . I die in the faith of it that He is on His way returning to the land."

Then turning to the executioner Gray said:

> "I am ready, I am ready."

JAMES ROBERTSON, a most godly man, was a travelling merchant who went up and down the country with a pack of goods. He visited his friend John Finlay, then a prisoner in the local jail, and while there, without offense or provocation, he was seized and carried to the guardhouse. After being kept in close confinement for twelve days, he was brought before Major White who ill-treated him because he refused to take the oath. The Major twisted Robertson's nose until blood gushed out. When he refused to drink the king's health, the soldiers tied his head and feet together with cords and left him in this posture out in the cold all night. The next day they tied his feet together and strapped him under the horse's belly, and in this way he suffered all the way to Edinburgh. He was found guilty by the jury, and the court sentenced Robertson to be hanged. At the scaffold, he tried to speak, but the ruffling of the drums prevented him from saying anything. When he complained of this, Major Johnston, who was in charge of the hanging, beat him in a most barbarous fashion. Amid this abominable rudeness, Robertson remained patient and cheerful, and his demeanour greatly impressed the spectators. Among the last testimonies of the martyred Covenanters, Robertson's is the longest. Here is its last paean of praise:

> "I rejoice in my lot, for it hath fallen to me in pleasant places, and I have a godly inheritance. I will not exchange it with the greatest monarch upon the earth. Oh! let heaven and earth praise Him; sun and moon praise Him. Oh! all the creation praise Him; angels and glorified saints praise Him through all

the ages of eternity. Now farewell all things in time. Welcome heaven. Welcome praises for evermore."

JOHN FINLAY, who died at the same time as James Robertson, was the friend he visited in the Kilmarnock prison. Finlay was tried for matters of opinion as the following section from the court proceedings reveal:

"Being interrogated, whether it be lawful to rise in arms against the king, refuses to answer. Refuses to say *God Save The King*, but says he loves the king as well as any person — confesses he was preset at Drumslog, but without arms. Asked if he conversed with Donald Cargill, refused to answer; otherwise than that, a man is neither by law of God nor man bound to have a hand in shedding his own blood. He also declares he cannot write."

For these reasons he was condemned to die. Among his last words we have this witness:

"I have peace in my lovely Lord; He has made my prison become a palace unto me, and He has made me many a time to bless Him for my lot, for which my soul shall praise Him through all eternity. Therefore, my dear friends, let none of you think it strange, concerning the fiery trial, as though some strange thing had happened unto me, for it is in His holy wisdom He hath made my lot sweet; for He has made out His sweet promises unto me, one of which is of more worth than all the world, giving me the witness of the Spirit, bearing witness with my spirit that I have a right to them all. Farewell all Christian friends! Welcome heaven."

WILLIAM COCHRAN, who died with Finlay and Robertson, in his testimony brought out with clarity the reason why he and others were unwilling to say *God Save The King*, because it would be regarded as an approval of all he had done against the church and the people of God and the true subjects of the kingdom. Cochran, who was executed, left a bright testimony which concluded with this exhortation:

"Let none offend at such a work as helping the needy who look upon themselves as members of His body; what may follow leave in the Lord's hand, Who doeth all things well; and nothing can harm His people, being found rightly in the way of their duty. Now, as to those who count the pure way of truth a wild principle. I count it a greater mercy to be wild from the way of sinning, than to be tame thereunto; as alas! most of the generation are. Farewell, all true friends in Christ, farewell holy and sweet Scriptures; farewell sinning and suffering. Welcome heaven and the full enjoyment of God through all eternity."

JOHN WILSON was a Captain in the Presbyterian Army at the battle of Bothwell Bridge. In a "Proclamation Against Rebels," Wilson is mentioned along with eighty-eight others condemned to forfeit their life, lands and goods for being implicated in the Bothwell uprising. Wilson, in spite of his acute and able reasoning, was found guilty and executed.

He concluded his long and well-reasoned testimony by saying:

"Now I die, commending to all the people of God that duty of unity, conform to 2 Timothy 2:22. 'Follow righteousness, faith, charity, peace, with them that call on the Lord out of a pure heart.' And that, 'if we walk in the light, as He is in the light, we have fellowship one with another and the blood of Jesus Christ His Son cleanseth us from all sin' (1 John 1:7). I do not say this to make up an union or joining with those I testify against."

DAVID MCMILLAN, who perished in company with John Wilson, left few particulars of his personal history. It is known that he was examined by the justiciary and found guilty of bearing arms at Bothwell and of judicially owning the lawfulness of joining with the other Covenanters present. McMillan maintained his innocency to the last but without avail. His last word had a ringing challenge about it:

"I die in the faith that He will return, for the Lord is most wise in His dealings; He can bring things about for His own glory and the good of His people; however difficult it may seem now. But I think the Lord, for innocent blood and other acts, shall sweep away the most part of the generation. I adhere to the Confession of Faith, to the Larger and Shorter Catechism, to the National and Solemn League and Covenant; and I leave my testimony against hearing of Curates, paying cess, and against the Indulgence. And now I bless Him who made me see the odiousness of sin, and nakedness, and a white raiment from Himelf for a covering, and made me accept and close with Him on His own terms. My soul shall bless him through all the ages of eternity."

JOHN WHARRY is another evidence of the injustice of this period. An Alexander Smith was being taken to Edinburgh, charged with being at Bothwell with the Covenanters. He escaped out of prison disguised in woman's clothing. Wharry and a friend sat down to rest themselves and were found by the soldiers seeking a company of country people who had assisted in Smith's escape. He and his friend were apprehended and found guilty of being involved in the escape. They protested their innocence in the matter without avail and were condemned to death. At the end, John Wharry left the world a gallant witness:

> "Oh! praise Him, all ye people, but it may be nearer to the breaking of the day of our King Royal, than ye are aware. God has long been silent, and conscience has been dumb amongst His people. Oh! be ye aware that ye have not these two, when He arises to make war for all the wrongs He has sustained. We beseech you in His name, try whose ye are, what ye are, and in whose list ye are. Know ye not, that true faith is the substance of things not seen, but hoped for, in Him, and will be made forthcoming to the sensible feeling of His own elect."

ANDREW GUILLAN was arrested as a nonconformist and for refusing to drink to the king's health. Although the council had nothing whatever against Guillan, they found him guilty of being present at the Archbishop's death, and he was sentenced to die. The cruel manner in which Guillan was treated is almost unbelievable. At the foot of the gallows, both his hands were cut off; then after he was hanged, his head was cut off and fixed to a pole. The rest of his body was taken and hung up in chains.

The executioner, who performed the grim task of cutting off the sufferer's hand, was drunk. When the right hand was cut off, Guillan held out the stump in view of the onlookers and said:

> "As my blessed Lord sealed my salvation with His blood, so I am honored this day to seal His truths with my blood!

GEORGE MARTIN suffered in prison for over four years. Day and night he was in irons without fire and other necessities during the winter. He bore his privations with much patience, and the marvel is that he lived to be tried. Like all other innocent covenanters, Martin was found guilty of refusing to pray for the king, to renounce the Covenant. He died praising God for His free grace, adhering to the Christian faith and firmly trusting Him for salvation. Listen to this echo of Calvary's forgiving spirit:

> "Being honored to die for adhering to the faith, and to die

this same day, being the 22nd of February, 1684, I do hereby forgive all persons all wrongs done to me, and wish them forgiveness, as I desire to be forgiven of God. And now I leave all friends and Christian relations to the guiding of Almighty God and bid all of you farewell in the Lord. Farewell all worldly enjoyment and created comforts, and welcome Father, Son and Holy Ghost, into whose hands I commit my spirit."

JAMES NISBET, came to Glasgow to attend the funeral of a martyr. He was recognized by his own cousin and taken prisoner. (One can see how the bitter persecuting spirit broke all the bonds of nature itself and had no respect for the nearest blood relations.) Refusing to renounce the Covenant and thus recognize the king's authority, he was found guilty of treason. He was offered his life upon the condition that he acknowledge the king's supremacy over the Church. As might be expected of a brave Covenanter, he refused. Harshly treated in prison, he died at the gallows. His remarkable last testimony reveals how utterly regardless he was of his doom. Before the usual "Farewells" the martyrs gave, we have this final gem of Nisbet before he died:

"I can freely and heartily forgive all men what they have done to me as I desire to be forgiven of my Father which is in Heaven; but what they had done against a holy God and His image in me, that is not mine to forgive them, but I leave that to Him to dispose on as He sees fit, and as He may most glorify Himself."

ARTHUR TACKET, a young tailor, joined the Covenanters in their struggle at Bothwell Bridge although only eighteen years of age. He was seized and taken to Edinburgh, but released. Two years later he was again apprehended when coming from hearing a sermon preached by the famous Renwick at a conventicle. Brought before the Committee for Torture, Tacket was ordered to suffer the horrible boot. As the hangman was about to apply the screws, a surgeon who was present told the advocate that because of Tacket's youth and slenderness of his legs, a few screws would crush them in pieces, and he would die before the gallows were reached. So the boot was stopped and the thumbkins were brought. Tacket endured this torture most heroically. He died courageously by hanging. The closing sentence of his last witness speaks of the glad submission of the slender young man to the Divine will:

"I have found by experience, that the Lord my God has sweetly and gently led me through the greatest difficulties that I have been trysted with since He made choice of me to suffer for His noble cause. Oh! if ye knew what of His love I have met with, and what sweet ingredients of the Lord's matchless love have been intermixed and put in my cup, ye would not be afraid to venture upon the sweet cross of Christ, which has been made sweet and easy unto me."

JAMES RENWICK comes in for special mention as the last who suffered publicly at this tribulation period in the history of the Scottish Church. It is recorded that the death of this most godly man was the means of ending the barbarous deeds of those times and checking the bloodthirsty dispositions of those who swayed the sceptre of power. From the very outset of his public career as a preacher he was persecuted and hunted from place to place with all the vigor and hellish fury that malice could suggest. A reward of 100 pounds sterling was offered to any who brought in James Renwick dead or alive, but such was the influence of this persecuted preacher that no one came forward to betray him.

After four years of privations and persecutions, Renwick was captured in Edinburgh. A waiter overheard the godly man at his devotions and suspecting he was James Renwick, gave the alarm. He was seized, hurried to prison, hastily tried and executed. When upon the scaffold, Renwick sang Psalm 103 and read Revelation 19. Then praying he said:

"Lord, I die in the faith that Thou wilt not leave Scotland, but that Thou wilt make the blood of Thy witnesses the seed of Thy Church and return again, and be glorious in our land. And now, Lord, I am ready — 'the bride, the Lamb's wife hath made herself ready.'"

As the napkin was being tied about his face, Renwick said to the friend attending him:

"Farewell. Be diligent in duty. Make your peace with God through Christ. There is a great trial coming. As to the remnant I leave, I have committed them to God. Tell them from me not to weary, nor be discouraged in maintaining the testimony. Let them not quit nor forego one of these despised truths. Keep your ground and the Lord will provide you teachers and ministers, and when He comes, He will make these despised truths glorious upon the earth."

As he finished his course, having served his generation and witnessed a good confession for his Lord and Master, Renwick was heard to say:

"Lord, into Thy hands I commit my spirit, for Thou hast redeemed me, Lord God of truth."

JOHN BROWN was another godly Covenanter, who sealed his testimony with his life's blood. While in his fields one day, he was suddenly surrounded by Claverhouse and three groups of dragoons. When Brown was asked if he prayed for King James and recognized him as head of the church, he answered "No!" Claverhouse said, "Go to your prayers, for you shall immediately die." His wife, a young child in her arms, stood by as her fearless husband prayed.

"Lord, may every covenanted blessing be poured upon my wife and her children, born and unborn. Refresh by the influence of the Holy Spirit."

John Brown prayed on, but Claverhouse could stand it no longer. He dragged the intercessor from his knees, and Brown's last words were:

"Blessed be Thou, O Holy Spirit! that speaketh more comfort to my heart than the voice of my oppressors can speak terror to my ears!"

Immediately Claverhouse ordered six of his dragoons to shoot Brown, but they stood motionless, afraid to kill such a courageous man. Whereupon Claverhouse took his own pistol and shot John Brown through the head. As Janet, his tenderhearted wife, went to cover the bullet-riddled body, Claverhouse with jaunty jeers said to her: "What thinkest thou of thy husband now woman?" The bereaved, noble wife replied:

"I ever thought much good of him, and now more than ever."

Claverhouse, seeing her courage, said:

"It were but justice to lay thee beside him."

Fearlessly she answered:

"If ye were permitted, I doubt not your cruelty could go that length — how will you answer for this morning's work?"

With an indifferent countenance that belied his words, Claverhourse said:

"To men I *can* be answerable, and as for God, I will take *Him* in my own hands."

As the student of religious history in Scotland will observe, we have only given a selection of the 150 or more who suffered under the pretext of law and judicial trial. All of these persecuted Presbyterians, nicknamed "Cameronians", were faithful unto death. But there were hundreds of others who perished before they reached the scaffold, who either died or contracted their deaths in prison because of the severities of cold, hunger, thirst, foul air, fetters and tortures such as whipping and branding with a hot iron. Although these died before they were able to write their memoirs and last words, we can be certain that in death they were valiant and triumphant and gave a dying witness to the sufficiency of Divine grace. The same applies to the uncounted number of Covenanters who were slaughtered in the open fields without trial, conviction or any process of the law by the executioners of the murderous Edict of the Council during the unlawful and tyrannical administration of the governments of Charles II and James VII. Then, of course, there were those who were forced into voluntary exile or banished to be sold as slaves, among whom were ministers and thousands of godly men and women. They were sent to Holland, The Barbados, America and other places. Of this we can be certain that wherever these noble-hearted Covenanters were exiled to, that there they were as faithful to God as they had been in their native country from which they had been torn.

WILLIAM JENKYN died a martyr in Newgate in the seventy-second year of his life. White at prayer with friends, he was taken prisoner and thrown into prison. When physicians certified that his life was in danger by reason of his close imprisonment and begged for his release, King James II replied: "Jenkyn shall be a prisoner as long as he lives." Shortly after he died, and a nobleman said to the King: "May it please your Majesty, Jenkyn has got his liberty."

James said: "Ay, and who gave it to him?"

The nobleman replied: "A greater than your Majesty, the King of Kings."

The Fear of Death

VII.

The Fear of Death

Not all of mankind can sing with happy confidence:
   "The fear of death hath gone forever."

For some the sentiment is that of William Alexander Stirling in *Doomsday*, "Of all things that are feared, the last is death."

Suso, poet of the early mystic movement who was inspired by the romanticism of his age of chivalry, wrote *Orologium Sapientlae*. This Fourteenth Century work contains a dialogue on, "The most profitable sentence to deadly men in which they may learn to know to die," and the "Image of Death" is answered, "Lo, I am so greatly feared with the dread and horror of death, and so bounden with the bonds of death, that I may not see nor know what I shall do."

Then in his quaint style Suso goes on to describe the feeling of death. "But right as the partridge constrained under the claws and nails of the hawk is half dead for dread, right so all vice (wit, or sense) is gone from me; thinking not else but how I might in any wise escape this peril of death, and which nevertheless I may not escape."

FRANCIS BACON in his Essay, *Of Death*, remarks:
   "Men fear death as children fear the dark."

SHAKESPEARE in *Othello* wrote:
   "The weariest and most loathed worldly life
   That age, ache, penury, and imprisonment
   Can lay on nature, is a paradise
   To what we fear of death."

DR. EDWARD YOUNG in his *The Complaint* written some 250 years ago, expresses a similar idea:
   "Man makes a death, which Nature never made;

209

Then on the point of his own fancy fails;
And feels a thousand deaths in fearing one."

JUVENAL, the Roman poet, bids us —

"Pray for a brave mind, wanting in fear of death, which regards the last stage of life as among the gifts of Nature, which is able to bear any labors."

SENECA, the Roman statesman and philosopher, exhorts us to

"Free ourselves from fear of death."

Francis Bacon, English philosopher and author, also attributes this gem to SENECA:

"The pomp of death alarms us more than death itself."

Another Proverb said to have come from SENECA reads:

"It is folly to die of the fear of death."

Proverbs from other sources can be noted:

"The fear of death is worse than death itself."
"He that fears death, lives not."

Sir JOHN DENHAM, a sixteenth century Irish writer, asked:

"Why should we
Anticipate our sorrows? 'Tis like those
That die for fear of death."

Medical authorities would have us know, "death has no terrors". At least, this is the contention of Lester Howard Perry, Managing Editor of *The Pennsylvania Medical Journal*, in an article he wrote on such a subject for *The Reader's Digest* several years ago.

"It is not unpleasant to die. The dying person slips drowsily away much as we all, hundreds of times, have drifted into sleep. At the last there is no pain. Doctors say so. Those who come close to death say so. With their last words, those who die say so.

"While the body still fights for survival, there may be great suffering, but that familiar and sinister phrase, 'a man in his death agony,' has frightened many of us into a false belief that our very last moments, as we relinquish this life forever, must also be horrible.

"Let us hear the testimony of Sir James F. Goodhart, eminent English physician who, when a resident in Guy's Hospital, arranged to be present at the bedside of every dying patient. He reached the conclusion that 'there is nothing terrible to the dying person in death itself. The veil between the two worlds is but a cloud, and one passes through it imperceptibly' . . . One of the truly comforting facts of life is this: those experiences which we fear most as we anticipate them nearly always lose much of their terror when actually encountered. That is true of death. When it comes close, it is friendly."

IRWIN S. COBB, American journalist and humorist who came near to death during a lecture tour, is quoted as saying, "Some may look upon death with a shrinking dread in their souls. To all such, I, who have skirted the Valley of the Shadow, say that we will face it without fear and without bitterness, without reluctance and without repining, without suffering, whether physical or mental; we shall find it, at the last, but a peaceful transition, an eternal change mercifully accomplished."

Careful analysis of the recorded "last words" of 1229 distinguished individuals has been made; at the most, one statement in sixty might be interpreted as intimating some sensation of fear or pain; the experience of the other fifty-nine ranges from indifference to ecstasy. Thus one of them, GRANT ALLEN, distinguished British author, wrote:

"The knowledge that I have experienced death has had a great deal to do with my utter physical indifference to it. Dying is as painless as falling asleep. It was only the previous struggle, the sense of its approach, that was at all uncomfortable, but even that was not half so bad as breaking an arm or having a tooth drawn. There was a total absence of craven shrinking."

We relax, and in our relaxation we face life's greatest adventure with serenity:

"Like one who wraps the drapery of his coach
About him, and lies down to pleasant dreams."

Without doubt the mental attitude toward death has considerably changed through the last half century. Death, we are told, is no longer a name to dread or "the king of terrors" as Job names it. Neither is it, "the potent weapon in the armory of the evangelist for piercing false security," as it used to be.

The grass appears to be growing thick upon the old hymns in which the awful repulsion of death is dealt with. We seldom hear the Wesley hymn beginning:

"No room for mirth or trifling here,
For worldly hope or worldly fear,
If life so soon be gone."

We are being told that man has outgrown any fear of death. But can it be that in spite of all the remaking of formulas and efforts to create confidence in dying, the old fear remains? Does not observation and experience prove that death is not a phantom which the adult mind of the race would feel shamed to fear?

We can specify beliefs in Spiritism and in Evolution as having contributed, to a large degree, to the altered viewpoint regarding death. Spiritism, or Spiritualism, increasingly active these days, has given us a view of death couched in terms of pleasing confidence. Those who die do not actually die, nor do they pass *away* — they pass *over* into a happy, bright sphere where they engage in trivialities. The Spiritualists have not only "dethroned death, but rolled him in the dirt." Their description of the dead in the unseen world proves how, "they have degraded high tragedy to the level of rather flat comedy." It is regretable that poignant grief and tragic bereavements are exploited by mediums who "peep and mutter."

The pagan philosophy of Evolution has also resulted in a softened attitude toward death. Evolution has exerted a most destructive influence upon the cardinal truths of Christianity. It deals in a most unbiblical way with sin and atonement. Death, as the bitter fruit of sin, is totally rejected by evolutionists. Death is looked upon as "the remedy for all ills." What is the law of evolution but, "the recognition everywhere of a continued unfolding, a steady progress from stage to stage toward an ever-higher order. There is no death; what seems so is transition." The dissolution of the body is thus not the end, but a new beginning. Viewed in this way, death is the consummation of life. "*It is not a curse entailed by sin,* but a beneficent ordinance of the Creator."

The consistent teaching of the Bible, however, is that the curse entailed by sin is not "death simple and bare," but "the fear of death," which as we shall presently see, Christ came to destroy. With the disobedience of our first parents there came the pronouncement of death, the dissolution of the body. They must return to the dust from which they had sprung.

"If death is associated with *preceding* sin, it is also associated with *succeeding* judgment in the dread trinity of sin, death and judgment," says Dr. Miller Neatby, the renowned English physician in his *Modern View of Death*. The Bible declares, in no uncertain voice, "It is appointed unto men once to die, and after that the judgment."

The good news of the Gospel is that Christ came not to destroy death, but to strip it of its alien terrors. A close study of Hebrews 2:14, 15, will reveal that "the fear of death" was not an unreasonable fear. Christ's supreme victory over the devil secured deliverance for those, "who through fear of death were . . . subject to bondage." The divine message to man then is not, "Do not fear death; there is nothing to fear in so normal, harmless and beneficent a thing as death." The message is, "Do not fear death: I, the Lord, have vanquished Satan who had the power of death and expiated the sin that introduced death."

Christ died such a death as no man ever died or ever could die. As the sin-bearer, "He tasted death (deaths) for every man." All deaths were rolled into one, and He died that death. Now for the Christian, death is a falling asleep in the arms of Everlasting Love. It has been stripped of its terrors. By the Cross, the curse has been transmuted into blessing. Not by "any natural or evolutionary process, but by the revolutionary process of man's new life, death has become the gate of Life. To all who accept the Christian view of Death, the waters once so chill are warm and grateful to the soul on its way home to God. "Then said *Hopeful*, 'Be of good cheer, my brother: I feel the bottom, and it is good.'"

The fear of death, then, is not something we are to overcome, but something Another overcame for us. Death is a conquered foe, and the fear and sting have gone. Though the reality has to be faced, we face it not in any stoical way, but as "those who know that He Who has the 'keys of death' will be with us as we journey through the valley into eternal sunlight." "Perfect love casteth out fear, because fear hath torment. He that feareth is not made perfect in love" (1 John 4:18).

> "I fear no foe with Thee at hand to bless,
> Ills have no weight, and tears no bitterness;
> Where is death's sting? where, grave, thy victory?
> I triumph still if Thou abide with me."

The Art of Dying Well

VIII.

The Art of Dying Well

John Wesley affirmed that all his people died well. Each of us, irrespective of our profession or position, should also discover the art of dying well. We are plagued these days with books on "The Art of Growing Old," "The Art of Right Eating," "The Art of Living with Others," and a hundred other "Art" themes. Too little is said or written about the graceful art of folding up our earthly tent.

"The art of living is the least learned of all arts," says E. Stanley Jones in *Mastery*. Would it not be truer to say that the art of dying is the least learned of all the arts? Dr. Jones goes on to speak of facing the business of living with adequacy, which preparation is necessary if one is to have a life well worth living. But is it not likewise important to face the fact of death with adequacy? Does not the Bible exhort us to be prepared to meet our God when life on earth terminates?

The majority seem to be content to "get off the stage with what grace their own wits can find them." But surely there is a more excellent exit.

James Montgomery gave us a glimpse of a triumphant death in the lines:

> "So when my latest breath
> Shall rend the veil in twain,
> By death I shall escape from death,
> And life eternal gain.
> That resurrection-word
> That shout of victory;
> Once more, 'For ever with the Lord!'
> Amen, so let it be!"

Grace can be ours to "live in eternity's sunrise," and to come to the end of the road with a quiet assurance that all is well, seeing the One Who ended "Death's despotism and dominion is our Companion, and Who opens for us the door into the New Jerusalem". When we come to pass over the River, it can be with the Pilgrim's watchword on our lips, "Farewell, Night! Welcome, Day!"

Why should our hearts shudder at the thought of death? We can depart in peace, if our eyes have seen the salvation of the Lord like Simeon of old (Luke 2:29). Death may mean the snapping of precious friendship, but it also means an eternity in fellowship with Him and with the glorious citizens of His Court. Surely this is a reason why a Christian should be happy in dying as well as in living.

"I want, and this sums up my prayer,
    To glorify Thee till I die:
Then calmly yield up my soul to Thy care,
    And breathe out in Faith my last sigh."

Sir Noel Paton's picture, *Lux in Tenebris*, depicts the girl who walks through the Valley of the Shadow with her hand clasped in Christ's hand. Trust is conquering terror on her face, and she grows confident that no enemy will vanquish her. It can be so with us as we "enter the ravine and breast the chilling floods." Commenting on Mark 13:36, ". . . lest coming suddenly He should find you sleeping," Dr. James Morison, refers to Theophylact, the commentator, who said, "Blessed are you, Father Arsenus, for you always kept this hour in view." Watts Wilkinson, who ministered in London almost 150 years ago, came to his end saying:

"Christ is worth more than ten thousand worlds.
O let me catch one glimpse of Thee,
And then drop into eternity."

Here is the secret of dying well. "I die," said another of the Lord's faithful servants, "resting on oaths and covenants and blood." Yet another left this record, "I have been at the point of death. But I found that the one great mysterious death of Calvary was all I needed at the point of death." The end of all such is always peace. "Mark the perfect man and behold the upright, for the end of that man is peace" (Psalm 37:37). To all thus pardoned, death is no leap into the dark but into the loving embrace of the Saviour.

FRANCIS BACON in Essays — *Of Death* — gives us these consoling thoughts:

"It is natural to die, as to be born."

"Death hath this also: that it openeth the gate to good fame and extinguisheth envy."

EDWARD YOUNG, in *Night Thoughts on Life, Death and Immortality*, has the couplet:

"Death gives us more than was in Eden lost
This king of terrors is the price of peace."

If this is so, then why should we be afraid to die? If we live the life of the righteous, then we shall die the death of the righteous, and such "a fair death will honor the whole life," as the proverb has it.

We recall the expressive lines of JAMES W. ALEXANDER:

"Be near when I am dying,
    O show Thy cross to me!
And for my succour flying,
    Come, Lord, and set me free!
These eyes, new faith receiving
    From Jesus, shall not move,
For he who dies believing
    Dies safely — through Thy love."

If we would die as Jesus died, we cannot commence too soon to cultivate the habit of prayer and of trust in God. His last word, "Father, into Thy hands I commend my spirit," *is* the last word on holy living and dying. FABER has it:

"Trust in God is the last of all things and the whole of all things."

A great English saint on his deathbed is recorded as having said to his nephew, "Come near and see how a Christian dies." Reverently, we draw near the Cross and see how the Saviour died. Countless multitudes have had His final words on their lips as they reached the end. They have proved to be the strength of the strong and the consolation of the distressed from age to age. Columbus, and George Herbert, bold man of action and saintly priest; Luther, and Bernard, reformer and priest; Basil and Catherine of Siena, the theologian and the mystic; Tasso and John Knox, the poet and the fearless preacher, each found in Christ's last word from the Cross the truest and the most natural greeting of the soul as it returns to God. The Father's hand to them was what it was to Jesus, the synonym for safety, strength and security.

If we realize as we should the inevitableness of death, is it not well to "learn to die" and to die well? When it comes our way, how shall we greet it, as a friend – or a foe? Is death to be a beginning of life or its end? If one's heart is fully prepared for the future, then Death will come as a friend to rid us of a heavy burden. We meet it, as we do a welcome friend, with a smile, not with a mocking fist as some noble Frenchmen met the guillotine.

If life has not been a preparation for death, then death itself will come as a foe to rob us of a peaceful exit and of a more blessed life beyond the grave. May God grant that if we have to go home to heaven this way, that we may go, not only bravely as in the presence of a foe, but with hands outstretched in welcome as to a friend we have "long abided and looked after!" In death then we meet the Conqueror of death, even Christ, Who is alive for evermore. It is only thus that our death can become "precious in the sight of the Lord" (Psalm 116:15).

From that ancient work, *The Book of the Craft of Dying,* one can gather much wisdom regarding the true science of dying "well and seemly." We are reminded, "such a cunning is the most profitable of all cunnings, in which cunning religious men specially, more than other, and every day continually, should study more diligently than other men, that they might apprehend it." Then we are given advice as to, "the temptations of men that die – interrogations that should be asked of them that be in their deathbed, while they can speak and understand – certain obsecrations to them that shall die – instruction to them that shall die – prayers that should be said to them that be a-dying."

Briefly expressing the quaint English language of this old book in our modern vernacular: if we would die well, we must not dread death, seeing it is nothing else than a going out of prison, an ending of exile, the breaking of all bonds and an entrance into bliss and joy. To die well is to die gladly and willingly. If we have a heart and a soul ever ready Godward, then however death may come, it will find us ready.

The five principal temptations confronting those who die are then fully discussed by the unknown writer of this early treatise.

1. *Faith must be maintained.*: The devil with all his might is busy to avert fully a man from the faith in his last end. He endeavors to cloud the mind with doubt as the last hour approaches. That faith is of tremendous importance has been expressed in the lines of Anne Steele:

> Eternity, tremendous sound
>> To guilty soul a dreadful wound;
>
> But O, if Christ and Heaven be in mind,
>> How sweet the accents, how Divine!

2. *Desperation must be avoided:* When a person is sore tormented and vexed by a dying sickness, then the devil is most active adding sorrow to sorrow by bringing past sins to view, drawing thereby into despair. But the soul must cling to the pity and mercy of God and to the cleansing efficacy of Christ's blood. SAINT BERNARD is quoted, "What man is he that should not be ravished and drawn to hope, and have full confidence in God, and he take heed diligently of the disposition of Christ's body on the cross. Take heed and see:

> His mouth to kiss thee;
> His arms spread out to embrace thee;
> His hands thrilled to give thee;
> His side opened to love thee;
> His body along strait to give all Himself to thee."

So no dying person should despair of forgiveness but fully have hope and confidence in God.

3. *Impatience must be eschewed:* Whether we come to die by nature and course of age or by disease or accident, we must not murmur against God but suffer and await final deliverance patiently, gladly and with a free and a kind will of heart. In patience we must possess our soul.

4. *Complacence must be renounced:* When the devil seeth that he cannot stake a man out of his faith nor induce him into despair, neither to impatience, he assails him by complacence of himself; he tempts by spiritual pride. "How stable thou art in the faith! how strong in hope! how sad in patience! O how many good deeds thou hast done!" But all self-boasting is vain in the hour of death. Our only boast must be in the Lord and in His grace.

5. *Occupation with things around must be avoided:* "He that will die well and surely, must utterly and fully put away out of his mind all temporal and outward things, and fully commit himself all to God."

Then, this unique summary is given — "God is true to His promises and giveth us grace to withstand mightily, manly, and perseverantly; giving us might that we be not overcome, grace to get us merit, stedfastness to overcome with. He giveth rich increases of virtue that we may suffer and not fail nor fall; and that is by meekness. For as SAINT AUSTIN saith: 'They break not in the furnace that have not the wind of pride.'"

To those who would master the craft of dying, instructions are also given in certain obsecrations (supplications) to them that shall die. SAINT GREGORY is quoted as saying: "Every doing of Christ is our instruction and teaching; therefore such things as Christ did, dying on the Cross, the same should every man do at his last end, after his cunning (knowledge) and power." Christ did five things on the cross:

> He prayed, for He quoted these Psalms — 24:16; 30:6;
> He cried out on the cross, as the Apostle witnesses;
> He wept on the cross;
> He committed His soul to the Father on the cross;
> He willingly gave up the ghost on the cross.

Dying, man should pray, if not with his mouth, then in his heart. He should cry with the heart, for God taketh more heed of the desire of the heart than the crying of the voice. He must weep tears of the heart, repenting of all misdeeds. He must commend the soul to God. He must die willingly, conforming fully therein his own will to God's will.

Is it not tragic that so many come to their last hour with unspeakable sorrow of heart? They learn how to live, and live well, but they neglect to learn how to die. Thus the dread and horror of dying overwhelms them. Theirs is not a joy over death as being the avenue to life everlasting. Theirs is a wretched end as they die without hope. Against their will they die, having never learned how to die. "Learn to die and thou shalt learn to live, for there shall none learn to live that hath not learned to die; and he shall be called a wretch that cannot live and dare not die."

Bishop Ken has taught us to sing:

> "Teach me to live that I may dread
> The grave as little as my bed;
> Teach me to die, that so I may
> Rise glorious at the Judgment Day."

All who live well, and can die well, out of three deaths pass — "Twain, for they be dead unto sin, and dead unto the world; and they abiden the third death, that is departing of the body and the soul . . . Death unto the good man is the end of all evils, and entry and gates of all goods. Death is the running brook that departed from life. Death is on this half, and life is on the other half."

Among the rare and ancient books on this theme that Geoffrey Williams of The Evangelical Library in London, loaned me was a most remarkable book published some 300 years ago. It bears the title, *The Christians Defense Against The Fears Of Death*, and is made up of seasonable directions on how to prepare ourselves to die well. Its author, Charles Drelincourt, was minister of the Protestant Church of Paris from 1620 to 1669.

Originally written in French, Drelincourt's work on "Consolations" went through twenty editions, and the translation into English by Marius D'Assigny of Ireland enjoyed universal approbation by Christians of all denominations. The value of this spiritual classic is the way the author develops his theme on "How To Die Well." Here is his outline of "Consolations."

1. God will not forsake us in our grievous agonies.
2. Look upon God as a merciful Father and trust upon His infinite goodness.
3. Meditate continually upon the death and sufferings of our Lord Jesus Christ and trust upon the merits of His Cross.
4. Meditate often upon the Lord Jesus Christ in His sepulchre.
5. Meditate upon the Resurrection of our Lord Jesus Christ.
6. Meditate upon the Ascension of Jesus Christ into heaven and His sitting at the right hand of God.
7. Meditate upon our strict and inseparable union with Jesus Christ by His Holy Spirit and the fruits of His blessed immortality.
8. Consider that death delivers us from all temporal evils that we daily suffer.
9. Death delivers us from sin, which we may see reigning in the world, and from the remains of our corruption.
10. Meditate upon the glory and happiness of our souls at their departure out of the body.
11. Meditate upon the resurrection of our bodies.
12. Meditate upon the destruction of death and the eternal and most blessed life, which we shall enjoy both in soul and body after our resurrection.

Believing that the soundest philosophy is the meditation of death, Drelincourt elaborates upon the contention that whatever our employment, condition or age, we should lift up our minds and hands to God and speak to Him the language of David:

"Lord, let me know my end, and the number of my days, that I may know how long I am to live."

.

In this way we can think of death more cheerfully and find ourselves ready to be delivered from a polluted world and transported to heaven adorned with holiness. Having written so much about death and labored increastly to prepare men and women to die well, we would expect Drelincourt himself to have a triumphant end — which he had. His last sermon was based on the cry of the Psalmist: "Purge me with hyssop, and I shall be clean: wash me, and I shall be whiter than snow" (Ps. 51:7-8). Shortly after, fever struck him; in his last hours he repeated several of his favorite Psalms. His son-in-law read to him the sections from his own book, *Consolation For A Dying Minister.* His final word was to an intimate friend at his bedside:

> "You are eyewitness of my groans and sufferings: but I cannot well speak to you."

When asked if he knew his son who was nearby, he answered, "Yes," and then yielded up his soul to God in the seventy-fourth year of his age, the fifty-second year of his ministry and the fiftieth year after being called to serve the Reformed Church. Living for the glory of God, Drelincourt died in a bed of honor. In the Eight Consolations we have him speaking of death in this way:

> "There are certain pictures with two faces: the one represents most ugly features, and the other beautiful and pleasant things. This is the true emblem of Death; for it may be painted with a fearful countenance, a lean body, and iron hands, that ravish us from our goods and our honors; and that divide our persons, dragging our bodies into a loathsome spulchre. If we look upon death in this manner, we cannot but tremble and fear. We may also look upon it as a powerful deliverer, that unlooseth all our fetters, breaks our chains to pieces, raiseth our souls to the highest glory and happiness. If we consider it thus, there is nothing more lovely than death, and nothing more to be desired."

If the Saviour-Shepherd has entered our lives and has had the love of our hearts and the allegiance of our days, then when we come to say "Good-bye" to earth, ours will be the song — "Yea, though I walk through the valley of the shadow of death, I will fear no evil, for Thou art with me; Thy rod and Thy staff, they comfort me." This is the hope that —

> "Makes the coward spirit brave,
> And nerves the feeble arm for fight;
> It takes its terror from the grave,
> And gilds the bed of death with light."

The Death of the Saints

IX.

The Death of the Saints

It is not easy to think of death as being "precious" when such a grim enemy has robbed us of one so dear to the heart, yet the Bible says, "Precious in the sight of the Lord is the death of His saints" (Ps. 116:15). "Blessed are the dead which die in the Lord" (Rev. 14:13). The last enemy to be destroyed, death, can be viewed from various angles. There is what we can call *the prospective view,* that is, the *looking forward* to death. This is the position from which we instinctively recoil. Death is a part of the curse upon sin, and not even the saintliest Christian is completely devoid of sorrow over the separation such an arbitrary sovereign produces. Not only are loved and cherished ties severed, but the saint's witness for God and service for Christ are terminated.

Then there is *the retrospective view,* that is, *looking back* upon death. Once the crisis is past and the cold river forded and the enemy conquered, then the believer, safe among the palm-bearing throng in heaven, joins in the triumphant song, "Death is swallowed up in victory, mortality is life forevermore."

But there is also *the Divine view* of death. *"Precious . . .* death." How can such an unwanted visitor, who leaves nothing behind save tears and broken hearts, be thought of as *precious*. As we explore the reasons of this Divine estimation of death let us mark the limitation set by the Psalmist. Not *all* deaths are precious in God's sight — only the death of His saints, His own exclusive property. While He has no pleasure in the death of the wicked, their death is the fruit of their sin, and in the same, Divine righteousness and justice is vindicated.

The death of a saint is precious to the church. There may be a general allusion in Psalm 116 to those prophets and martyrs whose blood was shed in the cause of truth and righteousness. Deaths of martyrs, Covenanters, greatest and humblest saints for

227

the truth, we:e precious in that they brought others into the light. Stephen's cruel death resulted in the conversion of Saul of Tarsus. The martyrdom of George Wishart brought John Knox into the conflict which resulted in the Scottish Reformation.

Courageous deaths for Christ's sake are always precious in that they offer a strong argument for Christianity and the reality of grace. They also illustrate the sustaining power of the gospel and prove how God fulfils His promise, "When thou passest through the waters . . . I will be with thee." When Babylas, Bishop of Antioch, was severely tortured and then beheaded, he advanced cheerfully to his bitter end singing the words of Ps. 116:15. No matter how we may die, may ours be the death of the righteous (Num. 23:10).

The death of a saint is precious to those who remain. Among early instructions for burial services, "Precious in the sight of the Lord is the death of His saints" was chanted along with other verses at the funeral of the faithful. Death is a fresh reminder to those left behind of this transient passing world, and a solemn call to sit loose to things of earth. The death of a dear one who died in Christ is also a summons to deeper consecration of life and renewed endeavour to let the lamp of witness blaze away for the Master.

The death of a saint is often precious in that it results in the conversion of unsaved relatives. Many have found eternal life at the deathbed of a Christian friend. Further, are not the last words of those who die in the Lord treasured up in the heart, and made channels of blessing? Think of John Wesley saying as he was about to enter the pearly gates, "The best of all is God is with us." What an inspiration that must have been to his followers mourning Wesley's passing!

The death of a saint is precious to God. To "the King Eternal", the king of terrors is deemed *precious* when he attacks a believer, because the persons of all saints are precious to Him. God views the triumphant death of His own with sacred delight. What they shrink from, He welcomes. What are some of the reasons of God's pleasure in the passing of His own? Why are the dead who die in Him *blessed*?

1. When saints die they offer a tribute to the efficacy of Christ's blood. Dying without a shred of human righteousness to cover them, but only the radiance emanating from the atoning sacrifice of Christ, their death is precious in His sight. In life the happy dead faced the claims of Christ and proved the power

of His shed blood to emancipate them from sin's thraldom. Accepting Him as Saviour they became saints, not through any virtue of their own, but solely because of the stupendous price paid for their redemption. And in their death, Christ saw something of the travail of His own soul and was satisfied.

2. When saints die they prove the effectual ministry of the Spirit. Here, below, they were enabled to witness a good confession by the Spirit. They loved the Book He inspired, and lived in the precious promises He led holy men to write. The verse before us has been translated, "Precious in the sight of the Lord are His *favorites*." Well, the Spirit is Lord (2 Cor. 3:17), and all those obedient to His voice are His favorites. Obeying Him throughout their life, and ever cautious lest they should grieve the Spirit, their death was precious in His sight for it meant a reaping of reward for their sowing to Him (Gal. 6:8).

3. When saints die there is emancipation from earth's sorrows. The days of our years are marked by labor and sorrow, pain and infirmity. Some saints carry a full cup of suffering, but their death is precious in that it releases them forever from the hardships and heartaches of earth. Perhaps Solomon had this in mind when he said that the day of one's death is better than the day of birth (Eccles. 7:1).

Dying, we "pay the debt of nature." Life is a loan and the debt is paid at death. "The slender debt to nature is quickly paid." Some of us may be called to pay the debt sooner than we expect. But think of all that is the portion of those who die in the Lord, as they pass out of this doomed world to heaven! The dead in Christ behold His face and all the fruits and flowers of the upper garden where He walks among the lilies. They are cheered and refreshed by the river, clear as crystal, proceeding from the throne. They are inspired and gladdened by the music of that land where there is no discord but all is harmonious. They are awed by the pearls, gems, street of gold, and all the glorious magnificence of the Father's palace. Who would not long to exchange earth with its tears for heaven?

4. When saints die they go to people heaven. It was the Saviour's wish that His own should be with Him in glory (John 17:24). Thus their death is precious seeing they help the Lord realize His holy wish and will. As each saint leaves earth there is another addition to the Father's joy, the Saviour's delight, and the angels' wonder and delight above. Psalm 116 was one

of those Jesus sang as He went out to face the death of the Cross. How sweetly He would sing, "Precious in the sight of the Lord is the death of His saints." Death was precious to Him, seeing He was going back home to His Father.

5. When saints die, eternal death is cheated. While the bodies of the redeemed rest in God's green acre, awaiting the final trump, which will give them the redemption of the body, they themselves are within the veil alive forevermore. Their physical death was precious for believing in Jesus they die no more. Having died in Christ, they were snatched from the jaws of eternal death, the full and final consequences of sin.

Index

Index

A

Abd-er Rahman III, 77
a Becket, Thomas, 33, 71
Abelard, 116
Actors, 126-127
Actresses, 126-127
Adams, President John, 97
Adams, John, 173
Adams, John Quincy, 99
Adolphus, Gustavus, 34
Addison, Joseph, 112
Aeschylus, 34
Agape, 138
Agatha, 138
Agathocles, 34
Agnes, 138
Agnostics, 130-134
Agopetus, 33
Alban, 139
Albert, Prince, 84
Alden, Tabitha, 178
Alexander I, 83
Alexander II, 83
Alexander, J. H., 161
Alexander, James W., 219
Alison, Archibold, 192
Alison, Isabel, 194
Alleine, Joseph, 53
Allen, Grant, 211
Allen, William, 122
Altamont, 131
Amelia Elizabeth Caroline, Queen, 87
Amelia, Princess, 86
Ames, Edward R., 51
Anaereon, 35
Anaxagoras, 114
Andrew, 44
Andronicus, 139
Anne of Austria, 86
Anne, Queen, 86

Anselm, 51
Ansgar, 51
Antitheus, 131
Antoinette, Marie, 86
Antoninus, 76
Archibald, Alexander, 53
Archimedes, 114
Ardley, John, 140
Arnold, Matthew, 36
Arnold, Thomas, 52
Artists, 125-126
Art of Dying, The, 42
Askew, Anne, 140
Audebert, Anne, 140
Augustine, 54
Authors, 104-114

B

Babylas, 140, 226
Bacon, Francis, 88, 209, 218
Bacon, John, 125
Bailley, 152
Bainham, James, 141
Barnes, Robert, 141
Barneveldt, Jan Van Olden, 88
Barrie, James M., 110
Bartholomew, 48
Bassus, 35
Bateman, Thomas, 122
Baxter, Richard, 63
Bayard, 129
Beaton, Cardinal, 176
Beaufort, Cardinal Henry, 71
Beaumont, 7
Beaumont, Joseph, 59
Beddoes, Thomas L., 113
Bede, Venerable, 60
Bedell, William, 60
Beecher, Henry Ward, 52
Bellamy, Joseph, 52
Bellone, Constantia, 141

Benet, Thomas, 141
"Beppo", 24
Berlioz, 118
Bernard of Clairvaux, 119
Beveridge, William, 52
Beza, Theodore, 53
Bickersteth, Edward, 119
Bicks, Jacob, 179
Bicks, Susannah, 179
Blanc, Maurice, 141
Blandina, 142
Boehaave, Herman, 123
Boileau, 112
Blair, William, 123
Blake, William, 113
Boehme, Jacob, 116
Boig, James, 197
Boleyn, Anne, 84
Bolton, Robert, 165
Bolton, Samuel, 169
Bond, T. E., 123
Book of the Craft of Dying, The, 220
Book of Martyrs, 137
Boot, 32, 190, 203
Booth, Catherine, 53
Booth, General William, 72
Bouhours, Pere, 116
Bourne, Pastor, 163
Bradford, John, 142, 151
Brainerd, David, 63
Brewster, Sir David, 122
Bridgman, Charles, 178
Brief Memorials of Departed Saints, 164-174
Bright, John, 22
Brittergh, Catherine, 166
Bronte, Charlotte, 104
Brooks, John, 96
Broughton, Bishop, 71
Brown, Janet, 205
Brown, John, 72, 205
Brown, Willie, 142
Browning, Elizabeth, 104
Bruce, Robert, 187
Bruen, John, 166
Buchanan, James, 101
Bunyan, John, 63
Burns, Robert, 21, 104
Bustia, Cipriana, 142
Byron, George Gordon Lord, 24, 104

C

Caesar, Augustus, 75
Caesar, Julius, 75
Calconis, 142
Calvin, John, 74
Cameron, Colonel James, 128
Campbell, Archibald, 187
Cannibal Valley, 154
Caren, Nicholas, 142
Carey, William, 62
Cargill, Donald, 193
Carlyle, Thomas, 105
Caroline, Queen, 86
Carpenter, George, 143
Casanova, 134
Casaubon, Isaac, 71
Catesby, 96
Catherine of Aragon, 85
Cato, Marcus Porcius, 34
Cavell, Edith Louisa, 124
Cavier, George, 122
Cecil, Robert, 94
Ceiller, William, 123
Chalchas, 35
Chapman, Joseph Miller, 164
Charlemagne, 83
Charles of Bela, 79
Charles I, 78
Charles II (Scotland), 78, 184, 187, 193, 206
Charles II (Spain), 79
Charles V, 78
Charles VIII, 35, 79
Charles IX, 143
Charlotte, Princess, 87
Charteris, Colonel, 134
Chober, Christopher, 143
Chopin, Frederic, 118
Christian's Defense Against The Fear of Death, The, 223
Chrysostom, 139
Churchill, Charles, 105
Cicero, 29, 115
Clare, John, 105
Claremont, 24
Clarke, Adam, 54
Claude, Jean, 61
Claverhouse, 205
Clement, Paul, 143
Cloud of Witnesses, A, 183
Cobb, Irwin S., 211
Cochran, William, 200

Coke, Sir Edward, 93
Coleridge, Samuel, 21
Colquhoun, Henry, 190
Columbus, Christopher, 128
Complaints, 21
Comte, Auguste, 116
Confucius, 117
Consolation for a Dying Minister, 224
Corday, Charlotte, 94
Corot, Jean, 126
Cotton, Matthew, 58
Cowper, John, 64
Cowper, William, 106
Crabbe, George, 113
Cromwell, Oliver, 82
Cromwell, Thomas, 88
Crosby, Howard, 58
Curaens, 123
Cyprian, Thascius, 144

D

D'Albrets, Jane, 86
D'Alleray, Legrande, 139
Danton, Georges, 94
Darius II, King, 76
Darwin, Charles, 122
Dawson, James C., 72
Death, Grief and Mourning in Contemporary Britain, 41
Deathbed Scenes and Pastoral Conversations, 174-175
DeBouffles, Chevalier, 25
DeBourmont, Marechal, 130
DeColigny, Gasparo, 130
DeFontaine, Madame, 103
DeLavry, Aymond, 147
Demonax, 115
DeMontmorency, 129
DeMornay, Philip, 90
Demosthenes, 117
DeMuler, Galeyn, 148
DeMusset, Alfred, 25
Denham, Sir John, 210
DeRohan-Chabot, Cardinal, 72
Descartes, 116
DeVega, Lupe, 127
DeQuincey, Thomas, 30
D'Houdetot, Vicomtesse, 103
Dickens, Charles, 114
Dickinson, Emily, 114
Dillon, Wentworth, 106

Diogenes, 115
Disraeli, Benjamin, 95
Dod, James, 165
Doomsday, 23, 209
Drelincourt, Charles, 223, 224
Dryden, John, 21
DuDeffund, Madame, 103
Dufin, Mme. Maurice, 111
Duke of Rothes, 197
Duncan, Isadora, 127
Dunstan, 59
Durham, James, 54
Duse, Eleonora, 127
Dying Testimonies of the Scots Worthies, 183

E

Edward VI (England), 79
Edward VII, 84
Edwards, Jonathan, 54
Edwards, Jonathan, Jr., 55
"Elegy to the Memory of an Unfortunate Lad", 25
Eliot, George, 24
Elizabeth, Queen, 86
Elisabeth, 87
Elliot, John, 55
Epaminomdas, 128
Epipodius, 144
Etty, William, 125
Eulalia, 153
Eusebius, 175
"Evangeline", 22
Evans, Christmas, 55
Evolution, 212

F

Fabius, 35
Fernando I, 77
Fichte, Johann, 116
Finlay, John, 200
Fletcher, Phineas, 24
Flora, 144
Foote, Samuel, 24
Fox, George, 55
Foxe, 137
Francis of Assisi, 60
Franklin, Benjamin, 89
Fraser, Simon, 129
Frederick The Great, 79
Frederick William I, 79

Frederick V, 79
Frederick IV, 79
Fry, Elizabeth, 56
Fuller, Andrew, 66
Fye, 144

G

Gabrielle, LaBelle, 35
Gadsby, William, 67
Gainsborough, Thomas, 125
Galbu, 76
Gallus, Cornelius, 35
Gamba, Francia, 145
Gardiner, Stephen, 89
Gargill, Donald, 196, 197
Garnock, Robert, 197
Garrett, Thomas, 145
Garrick, David, 126
Garth, Samuel, 24
Gaunt, Elizabeth, 145
Geleazium, 145
Gellert, Christian F., 106
George IV, 79
Gerhardt, Paul, 69
Gianger, 34
Gibbon, Edward, 131
Gilpin, Elizabeth, 161
Gilipin, Mrs. William, 161
Girard, Catelin, 146
Glover, Robert, 146
Golding, 106
Goldsmith, Oliver, 114
Goodwin, Thomas, 56
Gordius, 146
Gouge, William, 167
Gouger, William, 195
Gowan, William, 189
Graham, John, 94
Grant, General U.S., 128
Gray, Robert, 198
Gregory the Great, 70
Greeley, Horace, 109
Grenville, Sir Richard, 129
Grey, Lady Jane, 85
Guillan, Andrew, 202
Guthrie, James, 188
Guyon, Madame Jeanne, 107

H

Hackston, David, 191
Hadrian, 76

Hale, Captain Nathan, 130
Haller, 125
Halyburton, Thomas, 171
Hamlet, 22
Hamilton, Patrick, 184
Hampden, John, 87
Hank, Thomas, 146
Hannibal, 129
Harley, Sukey, 163
Harris, Joel Chandler, 112
Harrison, William Henry, 100
Harvey, John, 179
Harvie, Marion, 194
Havelock, Henry, 127
Hawkins, Benny, 34
Haydn, 118
Haydon, 111
Hazlitt, William, 111
Heber, Reginald, 120
Hegel, George, 116
Heine, 111
Hemans, Felicia, 25, 36
Hendricks, Thomas, 102
Henry of Wales, Prince, 80
Henry II, 80
Henry IV, 80
Henry VII, 80
Henry VIII, 80
Henry, Matthew, 56
Henry, Patrick, 93
Henry, William, 123
Herbert, George, 107
Hill, Rowland, 69
History of the Martyrs of Lyons and Vienne, France, 175-176
History of the World, 25
Hitt, Russell, T., 154, 155
Hobbes, Thomas, 131
Homer's Odyssey, 36
Hood, Thomas, 107
Hooker, Richard, 68
Hooper, John, 151
Horace, 36
House of Death, The, 25
Howard, Catherine, 85
Howard, John, 62
Howley, Sarah, 176
Hulton, Ann, 170
Hume, David, 116
Humboldt, Frederick H. A., 96, 117
Hunt, Vincent, 112
Hunter, Dr. William, 126

Huss, John, 146
Hyde, Anne, 86
Hyde, Anne, 86

I

Ingersoll, Robert Green, 133
Ignatius, 139
"Indian Queen", 21
Infidels and Agnostics, 130-134
Inwood, Charles, 72
Itadach, 35

J

Jackson, Andrew, 100
Jaffray, Dr. Robert A., 154
James VII (Scotland), 184, 206
James the Son of Alphaeus, 50
James the Son of Zebedee, 46
Jane of Navarre, Queen, 85
Janeway, John, 169, 176
Jansen, Ellert, 147
Jefferson, Thomas, 98
Jeffreys, Lieutenant Francis, 162
Jenkyn, William, 206
Jenner, Edward, 123
Jerome, 139
Jersome of Prague, 247
John, 46
Johnson, Dr. Samuel, 111
Jones, E. Stanley, 217
Jones, Sir Henry, 127
Jones, Thomas, 172
Josephine, Empress, 29, 87
Jowett, Benjamin, 114
Judson, Adoniram, 70
Jugurtha, 75
Julian, 76
Jungle Pilot, 155
Juvenal, 210

K

Kant, Immanuel, 116
Kaplitz, 147
Kay, 134
Keats, John, 107
Ken, Bishop Thomas, 72, 222
Kennedy, 185
Kent, John, 120
Kershaw, John, 67
King, John, 191
Kings, 75-84

Kitto, John, 107
Knox, John, 74, 226

L

Lamb, Charles, 111
Lambert, 152
Lamentations of the Dying Creature, The, 23
Laud, William, 156
Laverock, Hugh, 147
Learmouth, James, 191
Lee. Captain, John, 132
Lee. General Robert E., 130
Leopold I, 82
Lepidus, Quintus, 35
LeVayer, LeMothe, 116
Lews, Frederick, 35
Lincoln, Abraham, 101
Liszt, Franz, 118
Livingston, David, 62
Locke, John, 115
Longfellow, Henry, 22, 105
Louis I, 80
Louis VI, 35
Louis IX, 80
Louis XI, 81
Louis XII, 81
Louix XII, 81
Louis XIII, 81
Louis XIV, 81
Louis XV, 81
Louis XVI, 81
Louis XVII, 81
Louis XVIII, 81
Louis, Duke of Orleans, 82
Louise, Madam, 86
Louise, Queen of Prussia, 87
Lulli, Jean Baptiste, 117
Luther, Martin, 73
Lyford, William, 166
Lyttleton, George, 90

M

Madison, James, 102
Malcolm, John, 192
"Man was Made to Mourn," 21
Manning, Cardinal, 72
Margaret of Austria, 84
Margaret of Scotland, 84
Margutte, 35
Maria Theresa, 104

Mark, 49
Martin, George, 202
Martin of Tours, 71
Martinuzzi, Cardinal, 71
Martyn, Henry, 65
Martyrs, 137-157
Marvell, Andrew, 112
Mary, 177
Mary II, 85
Mary of Orange, Queen, 85
Mary of Scots, Queen, 85
Masaniello, 83
Massinger, Philip, 29
Mastery, 217
Matthew, 49
Mazarin, Jules, 90
Mazzini, George, 95
McAuley, Jerry, 56
McCheyne, Robert Murray, 56
McCulloch, John, 189
McGavin, William, 183
McKail, Hugh, 190
McKinley, William, 102
McLauchlin, Margaret, 195
McMillan, David, 201
Meclerc, Jean, 148
Medley, Samuel, 121
Melanchthon, Philip, 73
Men of the Covenant, 137
Meyer, F. B., 72
Meynell, Alice, 112
Michaelangelo, 125
Mill, Walter, 186
Miller, Christopher, 195
Milton, John, 22, 105
Mirabeau, 90, 117
Modern View of Death, 212
Mohammed, 71
Mohammed I, 77
Moir, David, 123
Montcalm, Louis Joseph, 130
Moody, Dwight Lyman, 59
Moody, Vaughn, 126
Monica, Saint, 103
Montgomery, James, 217
Morata, Olympia Fulvia, 103
More Than Notion, 161-164
Morison, Dr. James, 218
Morrison, George H., 73
Mozart, Wolfgang, Amadeus, 118
Muller, Max, 112
Murat, 84

Musicians and Hymn Writers, 117-121

N

Napoleon, Emperor, 78
Napoleon III, 78
Napthali, 183
Narvaez, Ramon, 95
National Covenants, 183, 184
Neatby, Dr. Miller, 212
Nelson, Horatio, 127
Nero, 75
New Testament Personalities, 43-51
Newton, Sir Isaac, 122
Newton, John, 64
Night Thoughts on Life, Death and Immortality, 219
Nisbit, James, 203
Nunn, Thomas, 163

O

Oakley, Farmer, 162
Of Death, 218
Oliver, 132
Otterbein, Philip W., 57
Otway, 35
Owen, John, 57
Owen, Robert, 95
Oxenstiern, Axel, 91

P

Paine, Thomas, 132
Palmer, 126
Palmer, Julius, 148
Pamphilius, 35
Paradise Lost, 22
Paradise Regained, 22
Parnell, Charles, 95
Pascall, Blaise, 111
Paterson, Thomas, 189
Paton, Sir. Noel, 218
Patriots, 87-96
Paulus, 115
Payson, Edward, 61
Peary, John, 148
Pericles, 115
Perigood-Talleyrand, 133
Perkins, Maurice, 162
Perry, Lester Howard, 210
Perugino, 126
Peter, 45

Peter, 149
Peter I, 78
Peter III, 78
Philip, 47
Phillip III (France), 77
Phillip III (Spain), 77
Philomenes, 35
Philosophers, 114-117
Pierce, Franklin, 101
Pitman, Sir Isaac, 114
Pitt, William, 91
Pitt, William, Jr., 95
Placut, Phillipot, 36
Plato, 115
Poe, Edgar Allen, 36, 108
"Poets Pilgrimage to Waterloo", 25
Politicians, 87-96
Polycarp, 152
Pope, Alexander, 25, 36, 112
Pope, William, 132
Preachers, 51-73
Presidents, American, 96-102
Probus, 149

Q

Quarles, Frances, 108
Queens, 84-87

R

Rabelias, Francois, 111
Rafaravavz, 149
Raleigh, Sir Walter, 25, 128
Rameau, 118
Randolph, John, 91
"The Reaper and the Flowers", 22
Reede, Charles, 109
Reformers, 72-75
Religious Leaders and Preachers, 51-73
Renwick, James, 204
Reynolds, Joshua, 125
Rhodes, Cecil, 95
Richard I, 82
Richard III, 82
Richelieu, 94
Richmond, Leigh, 69
Robertson, James, 199
Robespierre, 95
Rogers, John, 149
Rolland, Madame, 111
Roman Actor, The, 29
Romanes, Francis, 150

Rossetti, Dante, 113
Rulers, 75-84
Russell, 185
Rutherford, Samuel, 68, 187, 188
Ryland, John, 173

S

Saint Austin, 222
Saint Bernard, 221
Saint Francis, 71
Saint Gregory, 222
Saint Lawrence, 152
Saint, Nate, 155
Saladin, Yusuf, 76
Salmasius, Claudius, 108
Salvini, Tommaso, 127
Sand, George, 111
Sanfeius, Appius, 36
Sangster, Robert, 195
Saul of Tarsus, 50
Savage, Sarah, 170
Savonarola, Girolamo, 150
"Scenes of Clerical Life", 24
Schiller, Johann, 113
Schubert, Franz, 118
Scientists, 122-125
Scott, Sir Walter, 109
Scottish Covenanters, 32, 183-206
Sculptors, 125-126
Seneca, 29, 115, 210
Servetus, 152
Severus, 76
Seward, 129
Seymour, Edward, 91
Seymour, Jane, 87
Shakespeare, William, 22, 36, 80, 110, 209
Sharp, Archbishop, 71
Skene, James, 193
Shepperd, John, 69
Shirley, Lady Selina, 171
Shurman, Anna M., 126
Sidney, Philip, 91
Simeon, Charles, 65
Smith, Sir Thomas, 92
Socrates, 115
Soldiers and Sailors, 127-130
Southey, Robert, 25
Spira, Francis, 156
Spiritism, 212
Spurgeon, James, 57
Stam, Betty, 70

Stam, John, 70
Stanley, Dean Arthur, 72
Statesmen, 87-96
Steele, Anne, 220
Stephen, 43
Stevenson, Robert Louis, 110
Stewart, Archibald, 193
Stewart, James, 198
Stirling, William Alexander, 209
Strogg, Filippo, 129
Sudlow, John, 178
Suleyman, 77
Suso, 209

T

Tackett, Arthur, 203
Tait, Archbishop, 72
Talleyrand, Charles, 95
Tasso, Torquato, 108
Taylor, Zachary, 101
Tchekhov, 127
Thomas, 48
Thousand Nights, 23
Thumbkin, 32, 33, 203
Tiptaft, William, 67
Todd, Major D'Arcy, 34
Token For Children, 169, 176-180
Tolstoy, Count, 112
Toms, Isaac, 172
Toplady, Augustus Montague, 121
Triggs, Arthur, 68
Troup, Jock, 59
Turner, Edward, 124
Turner, William J., 126

U

Usher, James, 108

V

Valla, Lucius, 36
Vane, Henry, 41, 92
Vespasian, 76
Vicars, Hedley, 128
Vicentius, 153
Virgil, 29
Voltaire, 133
Von Beethoven, Ludwig, 117
Von Goethe, Johann W., 106

W

Wallace, Lew, 109

Warburton, John, 66
Warton, Dr., 174
Washington, George, 97
Watts, Isaac, 119
Waugh, Alexander, 174
Webster, Daniel, 92
Wentworth, Thomas, 92
Wesley, Charles, 119
Wesley, John, 21, 64, 226
Wharry, John, 201
Whitaker, Jeremiah, 167
White, Major, 199
Whitefield, George, 57
Whitelocke, Bustrode, 93
Whittier, John, G., 25, 114
Wilberforce, William, 89
Wilde, Oscar, 112
Wilhot, John, 133
Wilkes, John, 94
Wilkinson, Watts, 218
William I (England), 82
William II, 83
William III, 83
William of Nassau, 83
William of Normandy, 76
William of Orange, Prince, 77
Wilson, John, 210
Wilson, Margaret, 195
Wilson, Thomas, 168
Wirth, Deputy Baliff, 150
Wirth, John, 150
Wiseheart, George, 175
Wishart, George, 226
Wolfe, General James, 128
Wolsey, Thomas, 93
Women, Famous, 103-104
The Woman Hater, 24
Woolton, John, 59
Wordsworth, William, 108
Wycherley, William, 127

Y

Young, Dr. Edward, 23, 209, 219

Z

Zahir-Din, Emperor, 78
Zeuxis, 35
Ziska, John, 129
Zuniger, 124
Zuingle, 74
Zwingli, Ulrich, 74